THE WORLD ACCORDING TO
TOM HANKS

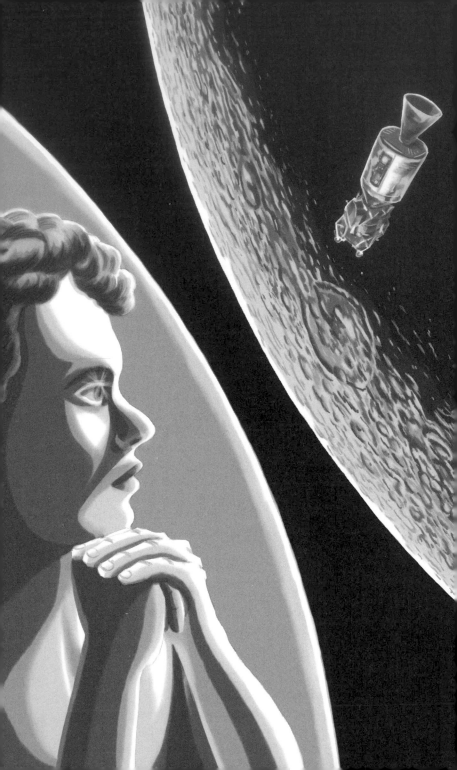

THE WORLD ACCORDING TO
TOM HANKS

THE LIFE, THE OBSESSIONS, THE GOOD DEEDS
OF AMERICA'S MOST DECENT GUY

GAVIN EDWARDS

ILLUSTRATIONS BY
R. SIKORYAK

GRAND CENTRAL
PUBLISHING

NEW YORK   BOSTON

Grand Central Publishing
Hachette Book Group
1290 Avenue of the Americas, New York, NY 10104
grandcentralpublishing.com
twitter.com/grandcentralpub

First Paper-over-board Edition: October 2018

Grand Central Publishing is a division of Hachette Book Group, Inc. The
Grand Central Publishing name and logo is a trademark of Hachette Book
Group, Inc.

The publisher is not responsible for websites (or their content) that are not
owned by the publisher.

The Hachette Speakers Bureau provides a wide range of authors for speaking
events. To find out more, go to www.hachettespeakersbureau.com or call
(866) 376-6591.

Library of Congress Control Number: 2018946512

ISBNs: 978-1-5387-1220-7 (paper-over-board),
978-1-5387-1221-4 (ebook)

Printed in the United States of America

LSC-C

10 9 8 7 6 5 4 3 2 1

For Bill Tipper:
scholar, gentleman, wombat.

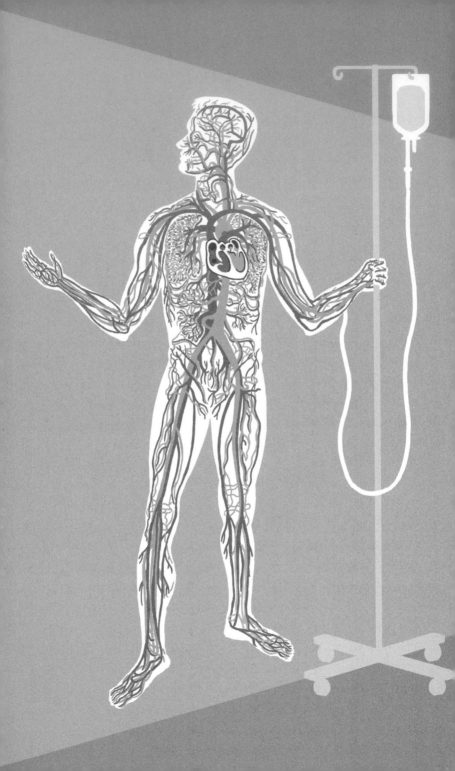

Contents

Preface

The Nice Manifesto

TOM HANKS IS A REALLY NICE GUY. Hey, wait! Where are you going?

Since "Tom Hanks is a really nice guy" is the sum total of the knowledge many people have about the actor, let's go deeper—and let's start with "nice." It's hardly ever a compliment, except in the hands of grandmothers who put a high value on politeness. It's almost a term of contempt—"nice" is what you say about an edible but forgettable meal, or about a blind date whom you won't be seeing again. Modern society, however, values feuds, celebrities who subtweet sassy insults at their exes, and reality show contestants who declare "I didn't come here to make friends."

I get it—bad behavior can be incredibly entertaining. The mass media has thrived for decades on the hypocritical game of "I am going to express my disapproval of something immoral and sexy, and I will do it in great detail so we can all get a vicarious thrill." But in recent years, all that invective migrated from the TV dating shows, gossip magazines, and the free throw line into the center of our culture, so now everything from the pop charts to the

American presidency feels like a perpetual mashup of a rose ceremony, basketball trash talk, and "Who Wore It Best?"

Nice means dull. Nice means bland. Nice means vanilla. But if everyone wants to be the rebel who embodies the counterculture, then there's no central culture left for bad girls and boys to flip off—life just becomes a race to the bottom in a counterclockwise spiral of petty bickering.

I'm not here to tell you that you should be nice because it'll make the world a better place. But I am here to tell you that a more virtuous worldview—one where you consider other people and place basic human decency in higher regard than petty bickering and side-eye sniping—is a richer and more rewarding mental landscape to pitch your tent in. Vanilla isn't the absence of flavor—it has a delicious taste of its own. (When Thomas Jefferson first encountered vanilla ice cream in Paris, in the 1780s, he was so delighted by the new culinary sensation, he wrote down a copy of the recipe, now preserved in the Library of Congress.)

Niceness—let's define it broadly as "deferring immediate self-gratification in favor of the common good"—is a road to building happy families, to making great works of art, to sending human beings to the moon. Niceness can be tough and bloody— the good guys don't win World War II if not for the sacrifices of millions of people. It doesn't matter whether you get your ethical code from religious texts, your grandparents, or *Parks and Recreation* reruns; you're going to find a way forward into your own version of niceness. Maybe you'll call it something else, like "self-sacrifice" or "human decency."

Which is where Tom Hanks and this book come in. When you interview Tom Hanks' friends, here's something that almost all of them say: "How are you going to write about *this* guy?" They understand the difficulty of selling "nice" as well as anybody. But when they're assured that you'll figure something out, they're happy to tell you how much knowing the man has affected them. Consider a few testimonials:

"I suppose it's the sheer bloody Tom Hankness of Tom Hanks that takes the breath away. He is the national treasure of America that you expect him to be, but he is not bland or smooth-edged and round-cornered, he's witty, funny, feisty, and fully human... not a mannequin of overniceness."

—Stephen Fry (national treasure of England)

"He is the most accomplished actor ever. He has this enormous box office, but he also has enormous critical accomplishments. He knows what the truth is, both in work and life, and has the confidence as an actor to believe that the truth will have dramatic power. More often than not, movies have moments that are jacked up or have a heightened sense of drama; he will not allow that, and that's what really distinguishes him. I always view him as a role model in terms of character, ethics and morality, and I will often try to project how he would handle a given situation. He is a moral compass."

—Brian Grazer (producer of *Splash, Apollo 13,* and
The Da Vinci Code)

*   *   *

"The guy could be, should have been, a professional soldier. He has the mind, the motivation, the spirit and the body to make a good officer. He's inquisitive and highly intelligent. Strip away the Hollywood crap and he's like Captain Miller: a common man in uncommon circumstances who rises to uncommon levels."

—Captain Dale Dye (USMC [retired],
senior military advisor on *Saving Private Ryan*)

"Sometimes the mind-set of actors is fueled by neuroses or intense need. He is different—the way he lives his life, it's touching to me. He's a tender soul. I don't mean to make him sound like a saint, but he is good. His goodness, it could make me start to cry. He is possibly the nicest human being, and the kindest, and the most soulful. Everything you read is all true, and I would double it."

—Holly Fulger (friend for four decades)

The point is not that Tom Hanks is an angel who walks among us in human form. Hanks will be the first to tell you that he's a regular guy with human foibles—although, when pressed to name a bad habit, he sometimes has difficulty coming up with anything worse than being slack about returning phone calls. Nevertheless, Tom Hanks has become the modern avatar of "nice guy," taking over the mantle from Mr. Fred Rogers, which is why people got so excited when it was announced that Hanks would be starring as Rogers in the movie *You Are My Friend*. It wasn't that Hanks is the spitting image of Rogers, but that it felt like he belonged in his neighborhood.

When the horrendous cascade of sexual-harassment scan-dals rolled over 2017, people clung to Hanks' reputation like it was a pop-culture life preserver. "Another Actress Steps Forward Accusing Tom Hanks of Being Nice," read one widely circulated parody news headline. The darkly ironic version of that headline was also popular: "World Doesn't Even Know Who to Admire Anymore After Tom Hanks Murders 5."

Hang on, let's allow the man to speak for himself.

"Here's the deal. I'm much more complex than this, okay? And I try to communicate this if we're having an honest-to-god, one-on-one type of conversation. I'll answer, really, anything—unless it's stuff that's nobody's business. How I do my job. What I think my place in the zeitgeist is. I'll talk about this ad infinitum. And I think it's much more compelling than 'Well, he's just the nicest guy' and 'You know what? Nice guys do finish first sometimes.' It doesn't make me mad. It's just boring."

—Tom Hanks (nice guy)

Contemplating the life, the achievements, and the obsessions of Mr. Tom Hanks may or may not give you the road map you need to find your way forward. But at the very least, I hope it'll confirm that "niceness" is a worthy destination, not a land bleached of color with child-protective plugs in all the electrical sockets. You don't have to live there if you don't want to, but I encourage you to get your passport stamped and visit whenever you can.

When we mock niceness, that disdain comes out of fear—the apprehension that being nice is volunteering to be a sucker, to be the patsy in life's cosmic joke. But the existence of Tom Hanks puts the lie to that fear. He's an amazingly successful actor, whether you're measuring by box office, Q rating, or Oscar nominations (he's got five, for movies that sum up his career reasonably well: *Big, Philadelphia, Forrest Gump, Saving Private Ryan, Cast Away*). He's insanely wealthy and ridiculously content in his family life. And he gets the joke.

His movies skewed more dramatic than comedic over the years, but Hanks remains a reliably entertaining presence on late-night talk shows, on *Saturday Night Live,* even on public radio's *Wait Wait…Don't Tell Me!* Sure, he has excellent comic timing and can do impressions, but fundamentally, he seems like good company. Hanks has the smile of a man who's lived long enough to understand how the world is put together. For Hanks, virtue has been not just its own reward but the foundation of a better life. He can't explain his philosophy to everyone who approaches him for a selfie, but he can lead by example. He can reach out to the people around him and make the world a better place.

Tom Hanks came here to make friends.

Section One

A Brief History of Tom

TOM HANKS SEEMS LIKE ONE OF THE MOST CAPABLE ADULTS in the United States: a movie star with two Academy Awards, a happily married man with four children, an actor who's earned hundreds of millions of dollars, a guy who's so reasonable and well-balanced that he's been nicknamed "America's Dad."

Like everybody else, he's the product of his upbringing, and so he peppers his speech with the vocabulary of his childhood—an argot that blends California dude-speak, Bible-study wholesomeness, and many, many hours soaking up the cathode-ray wisdom of 1960s television. In conversation, Hanks routinely uses words like "bodacious," "chucklehead," "cockamamie," and "high-falutin'." They aren't affectations—they're just the split-second exposures when you can see the child behind the man.

Memories and beliefs and words spin around inside Tom Hanks' skull, like electrons orbiting the radioactive nucleus of his Atomic Age U-238 brain, and periodically another isotopic phrase achieves escape velocity. That's why Tom Hanks punctuates his conversations with old-fashioned interjections: "For crying out loud!" "Son of a gun!" "Holy smoke!" "Jeepers creepers!" "Oh landy!" Each one of them is a reminder: to understand Tom Hanks, you have to know where he came from.

Thomas Jeffrey Hanks was born on July 9, 1956, in Concord, California—a navy town about thirty miles east of San Francisco. Tom was the third of four children, preceded by his sister Sandra and his brother Larry, and followed five years later by his brother Jimmy. Their father, Amos "Bud" Hanks, grew up poor on a farm in Willows, California—but during World War II he was stationed in the South Pacific, working as a machinist for the U.S. Navy.

After the war, Bud dreamed of attending college, and then immigrating to Australia, where he would make a living as a writer. What actually happened was that while working in a restaurant in Berkeley, he fell for a waitress, Janet Frager. They got married in Reno in 1950; one year later, they started having kids.

Bud made his living as a chef: not the grease-stained guy working the grill at a local diner, but the man in charge of banquet halls and other large-scale catering operations. Tom said, "Basically, he ran the kitchen in union dinner houses. Places with a net-and-nautical theme, with bamboo barstools, and a dirty, disgusting kitchen."

Bud and Janet split up in early 1962, when Sandra was ten, Larry was eight, Tom was five, and little Jimmy was not yet a year old. "My parents pioneered the marriage-dissolution laws for the state of California," Tom said as an adult. "There really should be a whole wing on some justice building named after them." That line has been a go-to joke for Tom over the years, letting him deflect questions about the stigma of divorce. But in fact, it was confusing and terrifying to be a preschooler given orders to pack his bags, told that he could bring only one or two toys from his closet.

"I was only five when we first started moving around. I just felt lonely; I felt abandoned, in the dark," Tom said. "No one is telling you the why, just the what: Pack your bags, get the stuff you want, and put it in the back of the station wagon."

Bud took the three older children, leaving Jimmy behind with Janet, and headed off to Reno, Nevada, where they moved in with Winifred Finley, herself a mother of eight (although her three oldest children had already left home). Two months after the Hanks clan arrived in Nevada, Bud and Janet were officially divorced; four days later, he married Finley.

"We were total strangers, all thrust together," Tom said. "I remember in school we had to draw a picture of our house and family and I ran out of places to put people. I put them on the roof. I drew Dad in bed, sleeping, since he worked so hard in the restaurant."

When Tom was seven years old, he was stopped on his way to school by three teenage girls. He didn't know them, but they accused him of having mistreated their little sister, and beat him up to teach him a lesson. "I don't know if they actually drew blood," Tom said. "But I remember, like, being hit in the face with a feminine knuckle sandwich." It was apparently a case of mistaken identity—Tom was wearing a fuzzy gray coat, like the actual male-factor. After the violent encounter, he walked to school, crying all the way—not so much because of the pain, but more because of the sheer unfairness of it all. It was one more morning when Tom wasn't in control of his own fate.

Bud was a restless man who was skeptical of his new wife's conversion to the Mormon faith. His second marriage lasted less than two years before he packed up and left town. "When he and she split up, I never saw those people again," Tom said of his former stepsiblings. "I've heard news of a few of them, but for the most part, I have no idea where they are." By Tom's count, the family moved seven times in eight years, to a variety of towns in Northern California—Redding, Sacramento, Pleasant Hill, San Mateo, Alameda, Oakland—or as Tom put it, "not much farther than half a tank of gas can get you, with a U-Haul trailer with a few things behind you."

Tom is careful to say that he wasn't traumatized by his itinerant childhood, and mostly regarded it as a way to experience different living situations. He joked, "If the house didn't have something we wanted, like a closet, we'd move to another house that had the closet."

He and his siblings visited their mom periodically, taking a Greyhound bus to her home in Red Bluff, California. "Here's what never happened," he said of those journeys. "We never sat down next to someone who was happy and who engaged us as children. We were either ignored or, a couple of times, sitting next to drunks." Sometimes the bus rides were frightening, but sometimes they were magical.

"After a while, I'd read not just the comic books I'd brought but every ad in the comic books as well. Eventually, I'd just be looking out the window and dreaming. By and large, it was like a road trip, in the great way road trips can be, but without your mom and dad in the front seat. I had a certain amount of money in my pocket and a certain distance I had to go. It was like traveling along in a peaceful cocoon. It fueled the imagination."

Tom's younger brother, Jimmy, had stayed behind with their mother when their parents split: she couldn't afford to keep more than one kid. Jimmy keenly felt the division from his older siblings—and trips where they came to visit Red Bluff and Tom tormented him didn't help bring them together.

Back home, Tom took judo classes and played Little League baseball, but he liked being alone, and said he was never bored. He could imagine a can opener was a helicopter; a leather belt would transform into a high-speed train, and either object could occupy him for hours. "I could entertain myself for days on end without any need of distraction. I pondered Woody Allen–ish kind of stuff. 'When is the sun going to burn out?' 'How come the world is so *neat*?' 'Why is James Bond cool?'" His youthful exuberance had not yet smacked into the limits that come with maturity. "Maybe at ten or eleven, I'd be wondering 'Why do I feel lonely? Why do I feel disconnected?'" he said. "But I wasn't sophisticated enough yet."

Tom's independence and self-reliance would grow even stronger: starting in 1965, the year Tom turned nine, Bud basically let the kids take care of themselves. "We never broke laws," Tom said. "Just furniture." The Hanks family was living in apartment #714 of a big complex in Alameda. Bud was working at the Castaway steakhouse in Oakland's Jack London Square, a daily shift from 8:30 a.m. to 10:30 p.m. When he was at work—i.e., all the time—the kids did what they wanted.

"We'd hang plastic models from the bunk beds, jam firecrackers into them, run out of the room while they exploded, then come back in to see them still aflame. We never got killed. I think my dad patted himself on the back for that fact: 'Well, my kids didn't get killed!'" Tom reflected, "Yeah, but, Dad, we came so close."

The kids cooked for themselves—which meant they burned lots of tomato soup and tossed the frozen peas down the garbage disposal. "We didn't know about sauces or butter or spices or things like that," Tom said. "And Brussels sprouts—you know how they look like the brains of rats? Roll 'em over on their sides and they kinda look elongated, like you can almost see the skull encasing? I can't eat that stuff, just because for about two and a half years, that was all there was."

The only discipline in Tom's life came at school—he loved it, so he never cut class. And he had a strict teacher, Mrs. Castle, whom he hugely respected. She told her students that they should be in bed by 7:30 p.m. and asleep by 8:00 p.m., so he did just that.

Tom was obsessed with baseball and the space program, but he spent most of his waking hours watching TV. "I knew what time it was by what was on television," he said. His favorite show was *Then Came Bronson* (Michael Parks rides a motorcycle around the United States, getting into adventures and changing people's lives), but he also loved *Batman* (the campy version starring Adam West), the original *Star Trek* (Jason and the Argonauts in outer space), *Leave It to Beaver* (a sunny domestic sitcom about a nuclear family), *The Brady Bunch* (an equally sunny domestic sitcom about a blended family), *Fireball X-7* (action-adventure plots as performed by marionettes), and the true-life underwater adventures of Jacques Cousteau. But one day Tom caught Kurosawa's *The Seven Samurai* on the local public television station, and the Japanese epic blew his mind—as did another subtitled movie on the same station, Fellini's mythological *La Strada*.

The unsupervised existence of the Hanks children ended abruptly when Tom was ten: his father got married for the third time. Bud's new wife was Frances Wong, a waitress at a Chinese restaurant in Jack London Square. The Hanks family moved into a house in the Oakland foothills with Wong and her youngest daughter, age five. Tom's new stepmother wanted to establish domestic order, but the three Hanks kids resisted.

Hanks said, "They tried to have rules, but the rules were unenforceable. Our first question was always 'Why bother?' You couldn't take three kids—essentially feral wolf-boys who'd been raising themselves, for good or bad—and take that freedom away. We'd gone through very formative years where we'd say, 'Oh, I can do this myself.' It was like trying to take a nomadic tribe and put them in a house in the suburbs. Quite frankly, it fell apart very quickly."

Meals transformed from pizza and burnt soup to traditional Chinese dishes. Rules and discipline were mapped onto what had once been an uncharted ocean of laissez-faire parenting. After some screaming matches, Tom's sister Sandra, now a teenager, left the home and moved in with her mother. Tom and Larry took over the bottom half of the house. "We talked to the rest of the family at mealtimes," Tom said, "and barely even then."

Larry had always been the funniest member of the Hanks family—sometimes Tom had gotten laughs at school just by repeating Larry's dinnertime quips the next day—but now Tom was finding his own voice. By the time he reached high school, he had his public persona figured out: he was the joker making wisecracks while the class was watching an educational slide show, with an excellent sense of just how far he could go to tweak authority without getting into trouble.

The school was Skyline High, in Oakland, California. "It was a big urban public school," Tom said. "Two thousand kids. A big drug culture. Very well integrated. The rules were being completely redefined. As a matter of fact, I think everybody had given up by then. By the time I got there, the attitude was 'Do whatever you want, just don't burn the place down'—which, actually, some people still tried to do."

Tom was skinny, all knees and elbows. He wasn't a good baseball player, so he joined the track team: he could run 440 yards in 61 seconds. It was a sport where diligence and enthusiasm counted for more than physical grace. Tom was now paying attention to the opposite sex, but discovered that his interest wasn't reciprocated. "I was death with women in high school," he said. "Absolutely the strike-out king. I was a little too geeky, a little too gangly, and much too manic."

Oakland was only a few miles and a few years past the San Francisco hippie revolution, but it might as well have been a different planet. "I'm not a child of the '60s, I'm a child of the '70s," Tom said. "The establishment was already in shambles by the time I could have fought against it. I was already running around in the cracks. And the counterculture had already blossomed and rotted before my very eyes. I grew up in Oakland, between the time of the violent aspects of the Black Panthers versus the good societal aspects of the Black Panthers. You could see people enjoying drugs and stuff like that. But there was no Summer of Love left, man, it was fistfights and people ripping off your car by then. That's what it was. It was a guy who would beat you up and steal your money more than it was 'Hey, there's a free concert at Golden Gate Park.' By the time I became a conscious human being, it was already gone."

So with flower power having been depleted, young Tom had to find his own epiphanies. Three discoveries rewired his mind when he was a kid: One was J. D. Salinger's 1951 novel *The Catcher in the Rye,* a traditional coming-of-age book for young literary souls that reads like a secret message from Salinger, peeling away a cynical façade to reveal a confused but tender heart. Tom felt just as alone as the narrator Holden Caulfield did—like many teenagers, he couldn't believe how accurately the book described his innermost self. Also, he was amazed that it contained the forbidden word "crap."

Another catalyst was Tom learning about the Holocaust: he saw the famous 1943 photo of a Jewish boy being removed from the Warsaw ghetto by Nazi soldiers, en route to a concentration camp. Tom read everything he could about the Holocaust, trying to understand how the systematic murder of six million Jewish people could have happened in his parents' lifetimes. It's a powerful thing for a young mind to grapple with the notion that not only is evil real, sometimes it's implemented on an industrial scale.

The third and biggest discovery for Tom: Stanley Kubrick's epic 1968 science-fiction film, *2001: A Space Odyssey.* "The most influential film, movie, story, artistic package, whatever, that I ever saw," Tom said. He marveled at the opening 40 minutes of great apes battling over a waterhole without dialogue; at how the acting was so real in the latter sections as to verge on boring; at the mind-boggling scope of the story. He was so overcome by awe that he saw all 142 minutes of the movie in theaters no fewer than 22 times. Each time he watched it he succumbed to its narrative logic, always noticing something new, one more brilliant Kubrickian flourish. Who could blame him for spending his free time at the local planetarium, or forever associating the scientific discoveries of the space program with the artistic innovations of a master filmmaker?

At home, Tom and his father had reached a stalemate of mutual incomprehension. "He was the polar opposite of me," Tom said. "He was shy, not outgoing, didn't communicate very well. He was a man who was really good with his hands. And I was good with my verbs."

Having abandoned his writing dreams long ago to spend a lifetime in the restaurant business, Bud could not fathom why his son didn't want to follow in his footsteps, putting aside any artistic ambitions in favor of a steady salary. He reminded Tom that there were jobs available down the street, at a local Jack in the Box burger joint. "Any knothead could be assistant manager in six months," he told his son.

Tom's reply: "Well, number one, thanks for the praise. And number two, I have never heard you talk about what you enjoy doing for a living." But that response was just in Tom's head—he knew better than to say it out loud.

Tom found a substitute family: the youth group at the nearby First Covenant Church. Perhaps because his father had no strong religious beliefs of his own, Tom had been exposed to a wide variety of faiths—he was raised Catholic in his early years, but his first stepmother was a devout Mormon, and he had spent a lot of time with his aunt (Bud's sister Mary Brummet), who was Nazarene (or as Tom put it, "ultra-super-Methodist"), while most of his high school friends were Jewish.

"It was not a Holy Roller place," Tom insisted. "They didn't speak in tongues. The only thing that was a little odd was that they really frowned on dancing…You did have to accept Jesus Christ as your savior. You did have to pledge your life to Christ. You did need to accept Him into your heart. I was fourteen and needed something very badly: not just something to believe in, not just some sort of faith. I needed a brand of acceptance that would combat the loneliness I had felt all the way up to then. I wanted to belong to a group…I was young and I was scared, and the world was *fucked up*."

As a born-again teenager, Tom naturally overdid it a bit, burnishing himself with the glow of the newly holy. His sister, Sandra, said, "He had a self-righteousness that goes along with being fifteen, as if he had seen the light and the rest of us were in the dark."

The church was where he found some moral grounding, and where he met his first serious girlfriend, but more importantly, it was a second home when he needed one. "I mostly just wanted to get out of the house," he said. "The house wasn't a good place to be."

Around the same time, Tom discovered something he loved at Skyline High: the drama club. Tom went to a school production of

Dracula because it starred a pal in the title role; other friends of Tom's were running the lighting board and doing tech backstage. He was immediately blown away by the energy and fellowship he saw onstage. Sitting in the audience, he thought, "How come *I'm* not up there doing that?"

So Tom started auditioning for plays and taking classes with the school's drama teacher, Rawley Farnsworth; he found that he not only loved acting, he was very good at it. "The class kind of rotated around him," Farnsworth said. "Everyone would wait for him to do his performances—pantomimes, solo acting, duo acting. He did one especially good scene from *The Odd Couple,* where he played the slob."

Hanks served as stage manager for a production of *My Fair Lady,* but soon figured out that he wanted to be onstage. He got roles in Tennessee Williams' *Night of the Iguana* (as a bus driver), Shakespeare's *Twelfth Night* (filling out the ensemble as Sir Andrew Aguecheek), and the musical *South Pacific* (as comic lead Luther Billis). He had a showstopping number in *South Pacific,* "Honey Bun," where he dressed in drag with a grass skirt and a coconut-shell bra.

Tom remembered, "My dad sat there and said, 'How does this kid get up and do this?' It was the first time I felt he had an admiration for one of my qualities, because it was a quality he didn't have." The performance brokered a rapprochement, but it didn't make the two of them close: "By the time I was actually doing something that was quite astonishing to him, it was too late for us to relate to one another in a different way," Tom said. "We never shared any bona-fide heart-to-hearts."

In the finest tradition of pretentious teens seeking attention,

Tom Hanks spent a couple of years spelling his name "Thom Hanks." He considered rendering it as "Thom Hanx," but decided that was a step too far.

To earn money—and to get out of the house—Tom started working as a bellboy at the Oakland Hilton hotel. Wearing the uniform of red blazer and rainbow tie, he schlepped bags three or four days a week, in what he deemed an ideal job: "Not much is expected of you, but you have to be smart. You can't be an idiot. Usually the bellman is unseen, the invisible employee. You can observe human behavior as if you're looking through a keyhole."

He crossed paths with actor Sidney Poitier, singer Harry Belafonte, tennis player Billie Jean King, comedian Slappy White (who criticized Tom's handling of his golf clubs by shouting "You're bending the shafts!"), and Gregg Allman (who called his then-wife Cher "Toots," a nickname Tom promptly applied to his own girlfriend). Sometimes the hotel hosted Vietnamese orphans who had been airlifted out of their war-torn homeland.

The best day was when Elvis Presley played a local show: he and his entourage took one hundred rooms. Tom caught a glimpse of the King for a few seconds in a lobby crowded with gawkers, and then the singer's bodyguards shoved him out of the way. Tom said, "The curtains in Elvis's suite were closed, but we fished at least ten stark-naked women out of the swimming pool."

In the Skyline High School yearbook, Tom was named "Class Cutup" for the graduating class of 1974. He had a C average and "lousy" SAT scores, but he sent college applications to MIT and Villanova, "knowing such fine schools would never accept a student like me but hoping they'd toss some car stickers my way for taking a shot." His third and final application went to Chabot, a community college in Hayward, California, about ten miles away from home. They accepted him—because they accepted everyone.

Considering that choice decades later, Hanks reflected, "Jeez, I should have got out of high school and gone right across the bridge into San Francisco and tried to get into the American Conservatory Theater. But hey, you know what? I turned out to be a movie star! So it worked out okay."

Teenage Tom Hanks did have movie-star dreams, and he even knew how he might achieve them. In 1974, just before graduating, he wrote a letter to Hollywood director George Roy Hill, the genius behind *The Sting* and *Butch Cassidy and the Sundance Kid* (and the uncle of a classmate), proposing that Hill "discover" him. "My looks are not stunning. I am not built like a Greek God, and I can't even grow a mustache," Hanks allowed. He nevertheless spun out a few different scenarios in which Hill cast him in a movie. "But let's get one thing straight," he concluded. "Mr. Hill, I do not want to be some big-time, Hollywood superstar with girls crawling all over me, just a hometown American boy who has hit the big time, owns a Porsche, and calls Robert Redford 'Bob.'"

It's an amazing document, and not just because Hanks grew up to become the prototypical "hometown American boy who has hit the big time." (He favored VWs over Porsches as he grew older, but did eventually know Robert Redford well enough to call him "Bob.") It's remarkable because of its joking-not-joking tone: Tom knew the odds of Hill casting him were infinitesimal, but he also knew the best way of making it happen would be to write a memorable letter.

And he got a letter back. Hill facetiously proposed that while

Hanks was heading to high school on a pogo stick, he would run over him with his car. Hill claimed his next movie would require the lead actor to be immobilized in a full-body cast up to the neck, so "BANGO—you are a star!"

Hanks had no master plan at college: since it was free, he planned to rack up some credits, surrounded by "veterans back from Vietnam, women of every marital and maternal status returning to school, middle-aged men wanting to improve their employment prospects and paychecks." He loved his class on oral interpretation, loathed the required health class, and almost flunked zoology because he killed all his fruit flies, but somehow aced "The College Reading Experience" by giving a presentation on "structural dynamics" where he basically recited the dictionary definition of the term. In what he considered a self-indulgent treat, he enrolled in one theater class per quarter.

He also goofed around on campus, eating fries and checking out girls: as he observed, "such are the pleasures, too, of schools that cost thousands of bucks a semester." Hanks said, "A public speaking class was unforgettable for a couple of reasons. First, the assignments forced us to get over our self-consciousness. Second, another student was a stewardess, as flight attendants called themselves in the '70s. She was studying communications and was gorgeous. She lived not far from me, and when my VW threw a rod and was in the shop for a week, she offered me a lift to class. I rode shotgun that Monday-Wednesday-Friday totally tongue-tied. Communicating with her one on one was the antithesis of public speaking."

Hanks loved the film-studies class he took, which exposed

him to movies like Jean Renoir's *Golden Coach* and Luis Buñuel's *Simon of the Desert*—he was already watching as many films as possible with friends and then discussing them for hours afterward. According to Hanks, "It didn't matter if I had just seen *The Godfather*, Olivier's *Henry V*, or *The Texas Chainsaw Massacre*."

For the class "Drama in Performance," he was required to read plays and then see them rendered onstage in local productions. One of them was Eugene O'Neill's *The Iceman Cometh*, presented at the Berkeley Repertory Theater. The playhouse was a run-down storefront; Hanks was worried that the lighting rig might collapse on the audience. But in a night he considered the turning point of his life, he spent four and a half hours enraptured by the intense barroom drama.

Hanks walked out with the realization that theater could be much more powerful than he had imagined from his high school productions. After that night, he saw as many plays as he could: Brecht, Ibsen, Tennessee Williams. He wouldn't bring a date—he'd just drive to any theater in the Bay Area, buy a ticket, and see the play by himself.

Around this time, Hanks ran into his high school pal John Gilkerson, whom Hanks considered to be a genius for his wide-ranging talents in puppetry, costumes, and song-and-dance routines. When Gilkerson found out Hanks wasn't acting, he actually scolded him: "Shame on you! You should be doing shows!" (Which sounds overwrought, but given Hanks' later accomplishments, Gilkerson was obviously right.)

Hanks was worried that he couldn't make time for rehearsals and performances, given his bellboy gig at the Hilton, but his boss, a bell captain named Lew Rice, was sympathetic and promised to rearrange his schedule when necessary. Hanks then auditioned for a Chabot production of Thornton Wilder's *Our Town* and won the central part of George (an innocent young man in small-town New Hampshire who falls in love with a neighbor, marries her, and ultimately grieves her death). It was an utterly sincere role that he threw himself into.

Hanks finally had a direction in life: he wanted a career in the theater, onstage or backstage. He transferred to the nearest available school with a drama major, California State University in Sacramento. There, Hanks studied theater production and got a job constructing sets in the scene shop of the school's theater, for the princely sum of two hundred dollars per show.

Two important things happened in Sacramento. One was that Hanks fell hard for a fellow theater student, Susan Dillingham (usually known by her stage name of Samantha Lewes). The feelings were reciprocal and they soon moved in together; Hanks, who had been a virgin when he graduated from high school, was finally in a stable adult relationship.

The other Sacramento turning point was a failure: for the first time in his college career, Hanks auditioned for a play and wasn't cast. Dejected, Hanks rode the bus home, moping about how his friends would all be having a great time doing the play together and he wouldn't be part of it. Having learned the valuable lesson that rejection is part of an actor's life, Hanks soon went on another audition: he heard about a community theater production of Chekhov's *The Cherry Orchard* in downtown Sacramento. The director was Vincent Dowling, an Irishman who spent his summers running the Great Lakes Shakespeare Festival near Cleveland, Ohio, and his winters picking up whatever regional theater work he could find.

Dowling was immediately impressed by Hanks. He cast him as the comic servant Yasha and—as he remembered it—told his wife, "I've found another Tony Curtis, only better." He discovered that Hanks was willing to do whatever was needed for the show, including building the sets and sweeping the stage. Dowling said, "You'd always see him moving about. Even sweeping up with those big awkward brushes, everything would be something to conquer—humorously but efficiently—to work, master, twirl around."

Dowling needed interns for the Great Lakes Shakespeare Festival; he had a six-play repertory season planned, which required cheap manpower to fill out the ensembles and work behind the scenes. The director warned Hanks that it was the last form of legal slavery, but the young actor was eager.

Meanwhile, before Hanks' first year in Sacramento ended, there was a surprise: Lewes was pregnant. Hanks and Lewes were both just twenty-two years old, they were unmarried, and they had no reliable sources of income. Hanks didn't want to abandon his theatrical dreams—but he did ask Dowling for a little extra money, and ended up earning two hundred and ten dollars a week.

By his actions, Bud Hanks had taught his family a fundamental lesson: Live lightly enough that you can pack up and move away at any time. Tom Hanks believed in this ethos. "People, if they want to," he said, should be able to "throw all their belongings in the back of the car and drive somewhere else and start again. When you make that impossible, you are robbing them of their ability to adapt and change and grow."

One way of looking at American history is that "westward expansion" and "manifest destiny" were just fancy names for waves of people—farmers, businessmen, religious leaders—trying to outrun their problems. (At the expense of the Native Americans who already occupied the land, of course.) If your life wasn't working out, or if you just wanted to reinvent yourself, the American dream was that you could saddle up and go to a new town where nobody knew you.

Bud Hanks raised his family on the West Coast, at a time when the empty spaces on the North American maps had largely been filled in. He kept moving anyway—he brought along three kids, but more than once, left his wife behind. Tom Hanks, who had grown up feeling like he had nothing in common with his father, was now reinventing himself in the same way, heading to Cleveland to pursue his dream. He just wasn't splitting up with his pregnant girlfriend.

Hanks spent three summers at the Great Lakes Shakespeare Festival, from 1977 to 1979, each time as part of a small army of interns, twenty to thirty aspiring theater artists. Sometimes the interns got cast in small parts alongside the professional performers, who were already part of the Actors' Equity Association, but their primary responsibility was backstage grunt work. Hanks sweated through eighteen-hour days, handling props, doing carpentry, and even serving as a dog wrangler (he was the minder for a Pekingese that served as a socialite's pup in the comedy *Peg of My Heart*).

He made a vivid impression on the other interns. "He was a golden retriever puppy—funny and goofy and gallumphy," said Mary Beidler Gearen, then an intern, now a theatrical producer. "And he was keenly intelligent. It was very evident that he was on a trajectory of some sort."

Ksenia Roshchakovsky, who was the festival's director of communications, remembered taking a picture of Hanks in her kitchen, eating toast and grape jam. "I really knew how to entertain," she joked. "He was refreshing, boyish with that curly hair, and he was just adorable. Women loved him."

"I had a terrible crush on him the first season," confirmed fellow intern Lucy Bredeson-Smith. "He had a mojo going all the time, always making everybody feel the best they could possibly feel. There was never anything physical between us—not that I wouldn't have liked there to be. He had a girlfriend in California and he was a good boy."

The work was exhausting. "Some nights we would get into the theater and not know which costume to put on," Bredeson-Smith said. The most grueling part of the job were the "changeovers"—because the festival was doing multiple plays in repertory, all the scenery had to be switched out between shows, often late at night. It was hot, sweaty labor, so most of the men took off their shirts—which revealed, to the amusement of his fellow interns, that Hanks had perpetually erect nipples. "Razor-tipped," testified Gearen. "It was not uncommon for those to get twizzled. Lots of laughs about that."

Sometimes the work wouldn't be done until 2:00 a.m., at which point the exhausted interns would collapse in the front row of seats and put on an impromptu variety show, taking turns running up onto the stage to do a gag or a bit. Usually, those late nights would end with Hanks and a friend doing Steve Martin routines.

The other interns remembered Hanks as a ringleader: the guy who would show up with a celebratory bottle of champagne late at night, the guy who encouraged people to slide down a fireman's pole headfirst, the guy who convinced a dozen people to make a late-night pilgrimage to the Silver Fox disco in sweaty, paint-spattered clothes.

Hanks played a variety of small roles in productions of *Hamlet, King John,* and *Juno and the Paycock.* His best work, everyone agreed, was his performance as the two-faced villain Proteus in the comedy *The Two Gentlemen of Verona*—the Cleveland Theater Critic's Circle gave him their award for best actor. Bredeson-Smith played opposite him in that play as Silvia. She remembered how he was early for every rehearsal and had his lines memorized before anyone else in the cast. "And he was able to cut through the obtuseness of Shakespeare with no problem," she said. "Working onstage with Tom, there was something there every second—he looks you in the eyes and you've got the connection."

Her favorite scene was the one where Proteus attempts to rape Silvia, a sexual assault that Hanks referred to as the "jump Lucy's bones scene." Bredeson-Smith said, "He would be bouncing up and down on top of me, laughing his head off where nobody could see him. It sounds miserable, but it wasn't—it was so much fun."

The role that changed Hanks' life was actually a smaller one: Grumio, the manservant of the lead Petruchio in *The Taming of the Shrew*. It didn't have many lines, but Hanks did get a lot of stage time, and executed a memorable comic bit where he rode a sawhorse like it was a living steed. And most importantly, going on the festival's regional tour as Grumio qualified him to join Actors' Equity. As Hanks put it, "Boom, I had a card in my wallet that said I *am* a professional actor."

Hanks always claimed that he wasn't big on long-term plans, but sometimes he would surprise his fellow interns by revealing the extent to which he had his eyes on the prize. For example, he once casually mentioned that he practiced what he would say when he was sitting next to Johnny Carson as a guest on *The Tonight Show*. "I remember thinking: *what?*" fellow intern Holly Fulger said. "The rest of us weren't at that level of focus."

After his first season at the festival, Hanks returned to Sacramento. He came back too late for the fall semester, so he dropped out of school. To earn money, he worked backstage at the Civic Theater in Sacramento—and on November 24, 1977, Lewes gave birth to their son, Colin.

At the end of his second summer in Ohio, with that Equity card burning a hole in his pocket, Hanks wanted to take the next step in his professional career. As a Northern Californian, he felt allergic to the very idea of Los Angeles—"I tell people who are coming to Los Angeles not to, because you'll just disappear in a mist and you'll be found floating in a kelp bed by the Channel Islands"—so he and Lewes decided to try their luck in New York City.

To pad his meager bank account for the move east, Hanks sold his battered 1970 beige Volkswagen Beetle to the parents of his friend Ksenia Roshchakovsky. The deal was that they would pay eight hundred dollars, but Hanks had to come over for dinner (which would be more substantial than toast and jelly). Over a home-cooked meal, Roshchakovsky's mother tried to convince Hanks that he should pursue a career other than acting, maybe carpentry—she didn't think his voice was suitable for the stage. She wasn't a vocal coach; she just had strong opinions. Hanks was undeterred. (Roshchakovsky noted that over twenty years later, she told a journalist friend who was interviewing Hanks to say hello, although she wasn't sure he would remember her. The report back: "He remembers you, your parents' names, and the license plate number of the car.")

When Hanks was ready to quit the Shakespeare Festival, he asked them to fire him instead. They did—and that favor made him eligible to collect unemployment, which gave him a small financial cushion. In 1978, he found a cockroach-infested walkup apartment renting for $285/month on Forty-Fifth Street in Manhattan, in the rough-and-ready neighborhood of Hell's Kitchen. Wielding his Equity card, Hanks made the rounds of New York auditions, with no success. "As far as TV, commercials, or soaps, I couldn't get arrested," he said. Hanks got odd gigs here and there; he once did a play at the CitiCorp building for which he was paid twenty-five dollars after four weekends of rehearsals and one weekend of performances.

Hanks vividly remembers standing at a Chemical Bank branch, waiting to deposit an out-of-state check (his unemployment benefits from the state of Ohio), frantically calculating which bills he would be able to pay if they would disburse even ten dollars, and then arguing desperately with the teller when she wouldn't release any of the funds. Somehow the young family scraped by—Hanks knew he was lucky that Colin was a healthy baby who never needed serious medical attention, because even a trip to the clinic might have broken them. "We were young and impetuous," Hanks said. "It was a fervent time. It was also real hairy."

Hanks has said that he privately dabbled with marijuana and cocaine, but feeling that drug use made him stupid, quickly gave it up. (As with Barack Obama, who made a similar confession in *Dreams from My Father,* nobody else seems to remember Hanks ever snorting coke, and his pals don't appear to be covering for him. "He had no bad habits other than an addiction to peanut M&M's," his pal Holmes Osborne said.)

Hanks and Lewes got married on January 4, 1980, at the Church of the Holy Apostles on Twenty-Eighth Street in New York, with toddler Colin running around underfoot. That summer, Hanks went back to the Great Lakes Shakespeare Festival one last time, but even there, he couldn't get any plum roles. The world of professional theater was sending him an emphatic message—*stop knocking on this door, nobody's interested*—that Hanks doggedly chose to ignore.

Hanks had a "secret formula" for keeping his enthusiasm up in the face of rejection: "I entered the auditions believing that I was just as good as 50 percent of the competition. And I believed that I was better than 45 percent of the competition. So that meant if the remaining 5 percent who are gifted geniuses that I cannot touch in a million years, if they just don't happen to show up for an audition, I've got a shot! I might just get lucky."

Then, finally, the door cracked open. Hanks auditioned for the Off-Off-Broadway Riverside Shakespeare Company, which was doing a commedia dell'arte production of *The Mandrake,* a 1518 play by the notorious political philosopher Niccolò Machiavelli.

Hanks had prepared a monologue from *Henry V,* but he embellished it on the spot by taking some large air canisters in the rehearsal space and addressing them as if they were his soldiers.

He got the lead, and although the role paid only transportation expenses—which meant subway tokens—it led to him getting a manager and then an agent. Not that everyone thought he had star quality. One agent at William Morris who didn't sign Hanks remembered their first meeting: "He had long hair like an Afro and his skin wasn't in great shape. His teeth were not good. I was not impressed."

Nevertheless, Hanks soon got cast in a low-rent horror movie, *He Knows You're Alone.* As he described it, "Everybody then was making, essentially, slasher movies. Knife-rack movies, where the girl is washing the dishes and she hears a noise. Right next to her on the counter is a knife rack and it's got eight knives in it, and she goes off and looks around and says, Gee, there's nobody outside. And then she comes back and keeps washing the dishes and then you realize *there are only seven knives in the knife rack.* That's how I started. Those movies were made for like $800,000."

The film was undistinguished, but three days of shooting earned Hanks eight hundred dollars and membership in the Screen Actors Guild. Improbably, Hollywood was interested. ABC, at the time the top American TV network with hits like *Three's Company, Eight Is Enough,* and *Charlie's Angels,* had started a talent-development program, scouting for young actors who might be fresh meat for new shows. Tens of thousands of headshots got narrowed down to hundreds of five-minute auditions, which yielded a dozen performers who were recorded on videotape.

Hanks kept surviving the cuts and was flown out to L.A. in

early 1980 to meet with the network, although he treated the prospect of a TV job casually—he arrived in Hollywood wearing a sweat suit. His agent took him shopping and spent a couple of hundred dollars on appropriate clothes.

At his network meeting, Hanks entered the room and did a pratfall, flipping his body over a couch. When he proved equally nimble with a dramatic reading, ABC signed him up for a one-year holding deal, paying him a life-altering fifty thousand dollars so he would be available to be cast in a TV series (which one was to be determined).

Hanks now had some fierce advocates at ABC. When he tested for a show that was produced by Warner Bros., the word that came back from the Warners development executive was: "We showed it to our secretaries and they say this guy, Tom Hanks, doesn't have a funny bone in his body."

Undeterred, Joyce Selznick, one of the two women in charge of the ABC talent development program, snapped, "Get new secretaries."

Hanks ultimately was cast in the last pilot commissioned by ABC that year: *Bosom Buddies,* about two advertising men who disguise themselves as women to get a good deal on an apartment in a women's-only residence hotel. It was basically a sitcom version of *Some Like It Hot,* the classic Billy Wilder film where Jack Lemmon and Tony Curtis dress in drag to go on the lam with an all-girl band that includes Marilyn Monroe. Peter Scolari played Henry (in drag, Hildegarde), while Hanks played Kip (in drag, Buffy). Scolari said, "Tom worked the Tony Curtis side of the street with the character. You know, he was sassy, he was in your face, he was non-sentimental."

Hanks moved his family to the dreaded city of Los Angeles, but he was so broke when he arrived that he had to borrow ten thousand dollars from the show's producers. (He paid them back—soon enough, he was making that much per episode.) They settled into a house in the San Fernando Valley but didn't live extravagantly. The family had just one car, a VW Bug with the stuffing poking out of the cushions—"Everybody who's ever owned a Volkswagen had the stuffing sticking through the seat in the same place," Hanks said. He would often get rides to the studio from fellow cast members, and when Scolari was out of town, he would borrow his costar's car.

Before it aired, the show weathered a three-month actors' strike. "What? They can't strike now!" Hanks complained to a show-biz reporter. "Don't they know I'm finally on a TV show?" He spent his free time taking two-year-old Colin out for a lot of Taco Bell. When *Bosom Buddies* debuted on Thanksgiving Day 1980, in the slot right after *Mork & Mindy* (which starred a young Robin Williams), it wasn't a smash hit, but its middling ratings proved good enough for it to stay on the air for two seasons.

Before *Bosom Buddies* went into weekly production, Hanks had taken a guest role on *The Love Boat* (as a college buddy of the purser Gopher—"the one guy on *The Love Boat* who didn't get lucky," Hanks said); a year later, he was doing well enough that he turned down an offer to appear on the *other* hit anthology cheesefest produced by Aaron Spelling, *Fantasy Island*.

Hanks was enjoying a taste of stardom: he received sacks of fan mail and got recognized at sandwich shops. He learned to scale down his acting for TV, reining in theatrical flourishes (although his performance was still pretty broad), letting the camera do more of the work. And he hunkered down with Scolari to make the best show they could, given the limitations of the 1980s sitcom format.

"It was like going to an airplane factory day in and day out," Hanks said. "You go into this big hangar and build a plane, and every Friday it has to fly. Sometimes the wings fall off, but other times it breaks the sound barrier. And that's what it was like for 39 shows [actually 37, but who's counting?]—the better part of two years."

Consider the seventh episode from the second season, titled "All You Need Is Love." The big comedic set piece is when the two leads, in drag in the hotel lobby, discuss their sex lives in front of a very confused clergyman. Hanks' character laments that he hasn't been getting physical with his girlfriend, played by Donna Dixon: "Oh, if I could only join the gang in that pool of cess." Meanwhile, Scolari's character meets a girl at a video dating service who seems to be the perfect match—until she casually mentions, "I belong to a choral group and I worship the devil." Hanks was smitten with the guest actress playing the bride of Satan, a young woman named Rita Wilson—but he was also a married man. On May 17, 1982, Hanks and Lewes had a second child, a girl named Elizabeth. At almost exactly the same time, ABC pulled the plug on *Bosom Buddies*. "They cancelled us because of some political machinations at the network with Paramount Studios," Scolari claimed. "We were fifteenth or seventeenth in the country when we were cancelled."

When the show went off the air, Hanks had achieved a level of fame roughly on par with Anson Williams (Potsie on *Happy*

Days). He assumed that now he knew how to be a TV star, more series would inevitably follow. Instead, he joined Hollywood's legions of the unemployed. He had some money in the bank, so at least he no longer had to wait for unemployment checks from the state of Ohio. Hanks fell back on his old auditioning habits from New York City, dressing casually and giving the impression of being unconcerned as to whether he got the part or not.

He did book one memorable TV role, as Uncle Ned, the miscreant brother of Meredith Baxter-Birney on *Family Ties,* the sitcom that made Michael J. Fox a star. Michael Weithorn, a young producer on *Family Ties,* used to spend his lunch breaks on the Paramount lot slipping into the bleachers of Studio 25 and watching Hanks rehearse with Scolari, so when he wrote an episode about a character who went on the lam after sabotaging a corporate merger, he wanted to cast Hanks.

He asked the show's creator, Gary David Goldberg, if he was familiar with Hanks. "In the fall of 1982, unless you were a *Bosom Buddies* fan, you didn't know who Tom Hanks was," Weithorn said. "In my naïve mind, I thought I was lucky to get Tom. I found out later he was struggling, he had young kids—the offer of the part on *Family Ties* was valuable to him, both financially and keeping him in the game."

It was also important for *Family Ties* in ways that were probably not obvious to a casual viewer. "At that time, halfway through our first season, we were still finding our voice," Weithorn said. "Tom came in, and he had that explosive comedic energy. His mind was constantly churning out ideas and lines. It changed the whole show, because everyone saw the show could be funny in a new way."

Hanks returned to *Family Ties* the following season in a

memorable episode where Uncle Ned was revealed as an alcoholic, but in the meantime, he auditioned for director Ron Howard and producer Brian Grazer, who were trying to cast the male lead in *Splash,* a romantic comedy about a man who falls in love with a mermaid. Hanks impressed Howard and Grazer, who agreed that if they could pick an actor based purely on talent, with no regard for box-office appeal, he would be an excellent choice. After every A-list actor turned them down, and then every B-list actor followed suit, they offered the part to Hanks.

During the *Splash* shoot, Howard taught Hanks a couple of important lessons. One was that he needed to get rid of some of his bad sitcom habits, like wringing every potential laugh out of the material. After the first read-through, Howard explained to Hanks that he had John Candy and Eugene Levy to provide full-tilt comedy, but that the movie wouldn't work without Hanks as the emotional center. "Your job is not to get laughs," Howard instructed him. "Your job is to love that girl." Hanks dutifully dialed down the mugging.

The second lesson came at the end of a day of shooting that had not gone well—a complicated shot had been twice as difficult because Hanks hadn't known his lines in advance. It was a moment when Hanks had begun to backslide from his usual Boy Scout level of preparedness—and Howard quickly cut off his drift in the direction of entitled Hollywood slackness. The director took his star aside and told him, "It would have been nice if you were a little more prepared today." Which seems comically understated, but Hanks got the message just as emphatically as if Howard had gone on an epic rant and drop-kicked a camera into the Hudson River. Hanks said, "He probably knew that if he had

yelled, I'd be paste for the rest of the day. He just let me know in no uncertain terms that I was starring in this movie and with that comes huge responsibilities, and one of them is to be ready to go. I've never forgotten that."

In the long months after *Splash* wrapped but before it was released, Hanks felt uncertain and antsy. "If I have to wait another couple of years for a job—forget it! I'll sell the house!" he threatened. "And if the wife doesn't want to come with me, I'll leave her and take the kids myself and go off to Seattle or Spokane. If the work is not here, go where you're wanted. It's a scary proposition but that's the way my life has always been. If I don't move every six months I think something is wrong." In times of uncertainty, the old Hanks family strategy of leaving town always had appeal.

In fact, *Splash* was the sleeper hit of the summer of 1984, and established Tom Hanks as a successful comic actor on par with Steve Guttenberg (also popular that year for his starring role in *Police Academy*). Hanks seized his newfound bankability with both hands and said yes to just about every movie he was offered through the 1980s. Too many movies, probably, especially since in most of them Hanks was playing variations on a hapless hero he would later call "The Guy in a Hole" (the literal dilemma of his character in *The Money Pit,* who gets trapped in his house's floorboards).

Critics said Hanks reminded them of classic film actors, including Jack Lemmon, Cary Grant, and most frequently, Jimmy Stewart. Hanks knew that the Stewart comparison was flattering—one of the biggest Hollywood stars ever, Stewart was equally adept with drama and comedy, and always believable on-screen—but Hanks heard it so often, it started to chafe. Hanks wanted to be his own man. The problem was that he had no plan on how to achieve that.

Hanks was chasing the fame that would sustain his career, chasing paychecks, chasing good times. Making a sitcom had meant commuting to Studio 25 on the Paramount lot; now he went on location in Washington, DC, the Caribbean, or even Jerusalem. "I didn't really know what I was doing," he confessed. "It was just, 'Ooooh, this is fun! I'm in a movie again.' You can do it that way."

Flawed as a lot of his 1980s movies were, many of them were watersheds for Hanks—each new challenge meant he learned something as an actor. *Nothing in Common*: he had to balance comedy and drama. *Punchline*: for the first time, Hanks vanished into his character so completely that when he saw the movie, there were scenes he didn't remember filming. *Turner & Hooch*: working with a canine costar, he had to live in the moment and respond to what was happening, because there was no guarantee the dog would follow the script. Hanks claimed, "You'd be surprised at how often I can trace work I did in other films back to *Hooch*."

Another aspect of Hanks' life that wasn't following the script was his marriage. Making a slew of movies was a leading indicator that things were not going well on the domestic front—and also a leading cause, since being away from home for months at a time hardly helped him be a better husband or a better father. "I did not have a clue as to how to be a father or a parent," Hanks admitted much later. "I was at that point in my career where it was all about getting work."

The Hanks-Lewes marriage staggered along, like so many, full of inertia and antipathy. Then in 1984 Hanks went to Mexico to make *Volunteers* and his costar was the woman who had turned his head on *Bosom Buddies:* Rita Wilson.

Rita Wilson was born Margarita Ibrahimoff in Los Angeles on October 26, 1956—just a couple of months younger than Hanks. Her ethnically Greek parents were first-generation immigrants from a region on the border of Albania and Bulgaria. When Rita was a young child, her parents Americanized their surname, inspired by a street name, Woodrow Wilson Drive in L.A. Her father had been tortured by the Communists but now happily earned a paycheck as a bartender at a racetrack.

On Wilson's first day of high school, at Hollywood High, she got spotted by a talent agent, which led to modeling work (including a bathing-suit portfolio in *Harper's Bazaar*). She also worked in retail, at the upscale clothing store Fred Segal, but, she said, "I got fired because I talked too much."

Wilson's first acting role was on *The Brady Bunch,* auditioning for head cheerleader in an episode where both Marcia and Greg's girlfriend, Jennifer, were angling for the position: when it aired in 1972, sixteen-year-old Tom Hanks was watching in Oakland. As he tells it, he noticed her and thought "that girl's cute." Wilson got her first TV commercial on her eighteenth birthday, for Peter Pan peanut butter. After high school, she booked supporting roles on shows like *Happy Days* and *Bosom Buddies.*

"I've forgotten how many times I've played the girl," she said of her TV work. "Sometimes the girl is a bimbo, a dingbat, or bitch, whose purpose is to make the hero look heroic and the heroine look good. The girl is thrown into a script when there's not much going on with the permanent cast. But she's never a threat to the cast members or the formula of the show."

Chafing at the limitations of Hollywood, Wilson moved to England for a rigorous course of study at the London Academy of Music and Dramatic Art: elocution, singing, dancing, dialects, and even fencing, plus roles in *A Midsummer Night's Dream* and the *Oresteia*. By the time she returned to the States and got her first lead role—in *Volunteers*—she was ready.

Volunteers, a comedy about Peace Corps volunteers in 1962, was set in Thailand but shot in Tuxtepec, a remote corner of Mexico. "You'd see farmers walking their horses down the middle of the street," Hanks said. On location, three-week-old copies of *The New York Times* counted as breaking news; for lunch, Hanks would sometimes drive half an hour, ride across a river on a battered ferry, and then hike up a hill. Alone in the jungle, Hanks and Wilson spent a lot of off-screen time together. He was married, but unhappily, while she was engaged, but uncertainly. They became friends, sharing their doubts and hopes, and then they became more than friends.

Hanks wasn't a player—he's said that he's slept with seven women in his life—but he was swept up in the great passion of his life. "Rita and I looked at each other and—*ka-boing*—that was that," he said.

Every evening had a gorgeous sunset and an after-hours gathering that was twice as festive as expected because of another costar: "It was a beautiful thing to fall in love around John Candy. Life is always a party—more *papas fritas!*"

When *Volunteers* wrapped, Hanks returned to the States and moved into his family's new house on Addison Street in the San Fernando Valley. Within two weeks, it was obvious that his marriage was over, and he moved out again, taking up residence at a Sheraton hotel in Studio City. He and Lewes tried to reconcile a couple of times that summer, efforts that ended in bitter arguments.

Meanwhile, Hanks had another movie on the docket: *Nothing in Common,* directed by Garry Marshall. With his life in turmoil, Hanks wanted to pull out of the movie—but the studio, TriStar Pictures, told him that if he did, they would make sure he didn't work in Hollywood for the next two years. Worried that he was going to be making a movie with a disgruntled star, Marshall preemptively called Hanks in for a private meeting: "I told him that I was sincerely sorry about his marital problems and I was sad he wasn't rushing to do this movie. But I said the cast and crew and I had nothing to do with his divorce or his contract issue. We were all innocent bystanders, so he shouldn't take it out on us."

Hanks acquiesced and headed to Chicago to play a hotshot adman who unexpectedly has to look after his aging, irascible father (Jackie Gleason). For the first time in a movie, Hanks drew deeply from his own life: like his character, Hanks was a successful guy in his thirties who had a complicated relationship with a dying father. (Bud Hanks had lost the use of both of his kidneys and stayed alive by virtue of dialysis.)

"I didn't talk to my dad while we were actually doing the film," Hanks said. "But he ended up going to see it, and I said, 'Dad, you're all over this. I went back and thought a lot about you and about being your son.'"

That opened a period of rapprochement between Tom and Bud. Hanks even came to terms with Frances, Bud's third wife: "My stepmother kept my dad alive an extra ten years because of the passion and love they had for one another," he said. Father and son spent more time together, and Hanks had his movie contracts stipulate that dialysis would be made available near any location shoot so that Bud could visit him. Bud ended up living until 1992; he spent his final years working as an advocate for kidney patients, even appearing on the cover of the magazine of the Trans-Pacific Renal Network.

(Hanks had a less fraught but more distant relationship with his mother; in his twenties, he used to remind her periodically that she hadn't actually raised him. But as he grew older, he became more sympathetic to the decisions she had made as a young woman. She remarried three times and lived until 2016, dying at age eighty-four.)

For a long time, Hanks had dealt with his personal problems by escaping into his work. The result: a successful, bankable actor who felt that he was "dead from the feet up." Hanks said, "I was sad, confused, and emotionally crippled. I guess the house of cards has to fall in before you start to figure things out." For several months, Hanks saw a therapist three times a week. The therapist told him, "You have a lot to be sad about, but you're going to be alright."

"I didn't believe him for the longest time," Hanks admitted. But after some time passed, he "felt like a world of good had been done."

In public, Hanks affected a breezy indifference when discussing his parents' many marriages, but the façade dropped when his young children came into the equation: when he moved out of the house, Colin was seven and Elizabeth was three. He couldn't shake the feeling that "somehow, no matter what I'd do to combat it, my offspring were going to feel abandoned. That's a bad thing. Because I remember feeling that same thing." He was consumed by guilt: "Food didn't taste good, life wasn't nice, I didn't sleep."

In October 1985, soon after Hanks returned to California from the *Nothing in Common* shoot, Lewes formally filed for divorce. The legal proceedings were nasty and contentious, because divorces generally don't bring out the best in people. Although the process dragged on for two years, Hanks and Lewes eventually reached a settlement. Lewes relocated to Sacramento with their two children; Hanks got partial custody. Eventually, like many divorced parents, Hanks and Lewes reached a détente for the good of the children.

Six months after *Volunteers* wrapped, Wilson had split with her fiancé and Hanks' divorce was in motion. So they went on their first "official date": a screening of *Stop Making Sense,* the brilliant Talking Heads concert film, directed by Jonathan Demme. Not long after, Wilson introduced Hanks to her parents. He made a good impression, despite wearing two shirts (à la Steve Bannon), which they thought was "the strangest thing they'd ever seen."

Soon Hanks and Wilson were living together, in what he called their "trial marriage love nest," in the Westwood district of Los Angeles, near UCLA, which he discovered was very different from the suburban sprawl of the San Fernando Valley: now he was in a trendy neighborhood with joggers and convertibles, more like the stereotypical L.A. featured on TV. "It's like Starsky and Hutch will drive by at any time," he marveled.

Hanks turned thirty in 1986, a milestone he marked with relief. "When I hit my thirtieth birthday, I thought 'At last!'" he said. "I'd been through so much to that point. I like myself more and more as I've gotten older. I feel more relaxed, happier. I don't kiss my youth a sad goodbye. I'd rather kick it out the door because I was such an idiot for so many years."

He had, for the most part, adjusted to the surreal status of being famous. Like many celebrities before him, he had to rely on his internal barometer of right and wrong as he made his way through a new world with unfamiliar rewards and hazards. Hanks said, "I was an asshole for six months and nobody would tell me I was an asshole."

Hanks reflected on his growing maturity, and how adulthood wasn't what he expected when he was a teenager. "There was a while there where me and my funny friends were always complaining because funny never got us laid. But then something happened, and I was funny and I got laid, and that was quite a moment of power, I suppose." He added, "I think I have a degree of sexual confidence that is kept in its proper perspective and that is not flaunted. I know what that comes out of because for years I had no sexual confidence, for years I was lonely. I don't feel like a dope because of that. I don't feel like I missed out on anything."

Hanks and Wilson soon realized that they weren't just in a rebound relationship: the two of them were meant for each other. One night, on a visit to New York City, they were waiting on a street corner—Wilson remembers that it was the intersection of Fifth Avenue and Fifty-Seventh Street—and Hanks told her, "You never have to change anything about who you are or what you do to be with me." She burst into tears of joy.

At the end of 1987, they flew to the Caribbean island of St. Bart's with their pal, actor Peter Weller. On New Year's Eve, they went out to a fancy restaurant, where they were seated next to Mike Nichols and Diane Sawyer (whom they would soon befriend). As the clock ticked toward midnight and 1988 loomed, Hanks had some important business to take care of: he asked Wilson if she would marry him.

"You bet!" she replied.

A few months later, Hanks and Wilson had a big fat Greek wedding. They got married under the aegis of the Greek Orthodox Church—one more denomination for Hanks—and took over a two-story restaurant for the reception. "We had a Greek band and a rock band, and whenever the Greek band was on, we danced around the room in a chain," Wilson said. "Tom actually took a square table in his teeth, balanced it in his mouth, and danced while holding this table. He transformed into a Greek. Everyone was smashing plates and throwing money at him."

Hanks discovered that since Wilson had a large, loud extended family, he now had a large, loud extended family too. For somebody who had learned as a child to place the highest value on the ability to hit the reset button and leave behind houses, hometowns, and entire family units, the permanence of this situation was new, disorienting, and comforting. Hanks said, "I've grown to really love more people than I ever thought I'd be capable of loving."

At last, Hanks had found peace. "Rita saved me," he said. He and Wilson were successful, famous millionaires, but their preferred leisure activity was having friends over to play charades. Roughly once a week, they'd go out for a nice meal and a movie—knowing that this was the most conventional night out possible didn't diminish their pleasure in it. They called it "Date Night U.S.A."

Hanks said, "Because of the love that Rita and I have, I feel I've been freed up to do a whole different kind of work than I had prior to experiencing that."

Hanks wasn't getting his own movies off the ground yet, although he had a production company (called Clavius Base, named after the lunar settlement in *2001: A Space Odyssey*). He wryly summed up his company's development deal with Columbia: "The best-case scenario is that I get to do stories and characters that are very interesting to me and Columbia gets to make and distribute movies that make phenomenal amounts of money and go down in the annals of motion picture history. The worst-case scenario is that everyone sits around and nothing gets done at all, and I go off into the apricot business or something like that. Somewhere in between there is where my deal falls."

Even if Hanks hadn't yet mastered the business of Hollywood, he was visibly becoming a better actor, pouring more of his soul into his characters. The great leap forward: *Big*, where he played a thirteen-year-old who magically wakes up in a thirty-year-old's body. "I don't want you to play *cute*. We don't need *cute*," director Penny Marshall warned him, and Hanks heeded her. With an adolescent's floppy gait and unfettered imagination, he was emotionally open, heartbreakingly vulnerable, and extremely funny. His performance earned him an Academy Award nomination for Best Actor, alongside Gene Hackman, Edward James Olmos, and Max von Sydow, losing out to Dustin Hoffman for *Rain Man*.

When Hanks was asked if he had a ten-year plan for his career, he scoffed, "No, those are for Eastern-bloc governments that eventually get overthrown." Going with the flow had brought Hanks to a new pinnacle of success—he had surpassed peers like Michael Keaton and Jeff Daniels, and was competing with rising superstars like Tom Cruise.

The next few years showed the limits of that spontaneous approach to picking roles, as Hanks starred in one misfire after another: the suburban satire *The 'Burbs,* the romance *Joe Versus the Volcano,* the cop dog buddy movie *Turner & Hooch.* He gave them his all, and learned that wasn't always sufficient. Costarring with a canine was good training as an actor, but it made for an extremely arduous shoot. Hanks said, "We just worked ourselves into the grave, and in the end, I thought, 'Did I really work this hard and invest all this care for a movie called *Turner & Hooch?'*"

Then he was wooed for the lead in a movie that looked like a guaranteed blockbuster: Brian De Palma cast him in the movie version of Tom Wolfe's hit novel *The Bonfire of the Vanities,* in the central role of bond trader Sherman McCoy. Everyone else in the world, including Hanks himself, envisioned somebody older and WASPier. "The idea of me playing Sherman McCoy is a huge, massive crapshoot," he said. "Maybe I'm perfect, maybe I'm absolutely wrong."

As it turned out, the choice was much closer to "absolutely wrong." But the miscasting of Hanks turned out to be the least of *Bonfire*'s problems: artistically and commercially, the movie flailed around like a dolphin trying to do calculus. It wasn't a big enough flop that Hanks had to enter the witness protection program—but just barely.

De Palma granted reporter Julie Salamon full access to the movie's production while it was being made: the book that resulted, *The Devil's Candy,* was a front-row seat to a cinematic Hindenburg. Hanks mostly came off well in its pages, a friendly presence who got into card games on the set while he was waiting to shoot his scenes. The most interesting part of Hanks' portrayal was how he exercised his clout in the casting sessions for Sherman's mistress: after reading dialogue with both Melanie Griffith and Uma Thurman, Hanks thought that Griffith had an indefinable spark and that Thurman, while beautiful, was acting on a level more appropriate for a high school play. He didn't throw a tantrum, but at the appropriate moment he quietly informed the studio "I just can't act with Uma," and got his way.

Hanks noted after the book was published, "Some people will assume that all that madness and indecision and overspending is how an unsuccessful movie gets made. But that's how *every* movie gets made. If *Bonfire* had been a stellar success, people would have looked at the book as some sort of blueprint of how chaotic making a great movie can be. The odds are *always* that you'll make an atrocious movie. The fact that you often don't is what makes you a Hall of Famer."

After *Bonfire,* Hanks took some time off. He had released fourteen movies in the space of seven years, and he knew that was too many. "There was a chance the American public was going to get sick of looking at me," he said. "You can easily overstay your welcome." He and Wilson had a son, Chester, born on August 4, 1990. Hanks changed his representation, signing up with the powerful Creative Artists Agency, CAA. And he thought about what had gone wrong with his career, and what he wanted to go right.

He said, "I made a particularly disappointing string of cheap comedies in which there was a goofy guy who does or does not get laid by the women of his dreams. My own rationale for taking them on wasn't what it should have been. I took whatever gig I got, whether I was tired, or whether I understood the material or not."

Hanks worried that he might turn into a well-known name that nobody cared about, like Palmolive soap. He visited the office of his pal Ron Howard and laid out his dilemma: As he put it, how did he avoid turning into Elliott Gould? (Hanks may have been thinking about Gould, whose 1970s stardom evaporated faster than one would have imagined was possible, because they crossed paths in late 1990. Gould was featured in a *Saturday Night Live* sketch where he, alongside Steve Martin and Paul Simon, welcomed Hanks to the Five-Timers Club for the show's frequent hosts.)

Hanks went in for a meeting with Richard Lovett, the president of CAA. Lovett asked Hanks, "What do you want to do?"

His answer: "Well, it's not like I know what I want to do, but I sure know what I don't want to do. And I don't want to play guys anymore going, 'Oh, I'm not in love and I wish I was and I'm just trying to get to work today but my car keeps breaking down in funny ways.' They're boring, they've got nothing to do with my life, and I don't want to have to waste time considering them."

Or put more succinctly and crudely: "I don't want to play a pussy anymore."

Instead of portraying characters caught up in events they couldn't understand or control, he wanted to play adults: men who had experienced life and endured some bitter compromises.

Easier said than done—but Hanks had enough money in the bank that he wouldn't have to take any job offer just because he needed the paycheck. "And that was that," Hanks said. "It was like a huge stack of work on my desk that just got thrown away, and what was left was, you know, much less to choose from."

Looking for an adult role, Tom Hanks campaigned for the part of a bitter, broken-down baseball slugger who washed out of both the major leagues and World War II because of a dumb drunken injury: Jimmy Dugan, manager of the all-female Rockford Peaches in *A League of Their Own.* The movie's director, Penny Marshall, had enjoyed working with Hanks on *Big;* she cast him as Dugan, on the condition that he put on enough weight that he would look sweaty and unappealing. He complied, eating his way across Indiana (lots of pork and Dairy Queen), and then had a blast chewing out the Peaches, telling them "there's no crying in baseball" and generally being irascible.

On location, Hanks discovered a forgotten side effect of not playing the lead role: you have time to kill. On long days of shooting the Peaches' baseball games, Hanks would entertain the crowds of extras in the stands by decorating baseball bats, and then using the costumed bats to improvise puppet shows from the dugout.

When *A League of Their Own* was a hit—it grossed $107 million, seven times as much as *Bonfire of the Vanities*—Hanks found that his options had dramatically expanded. His next project: *Sleepless in Seattle,* a romantic comedy with actress Meg Ryan and writer-director Nora Ephron, where he played a recently widowed father.

"It's truly great not to be playing a guy who has some kooky thing happen to him," Hanks said. "This isn't a guy who finds a suitcase full of money that the bad guys want really bad. Absolutely no magic potions are ingested. This is a guy who has lost his wife and has to deal with it. That's about as pure and clear and easily communicated a setup for a character as you're ever going to come across."

It was becoming obvious that Tom Hanks was a better actor than anyone had known. He was probably better than *he* had known. He had a core quality of likability—no matter what the role was, he came across as a nice guy.

"'Likable' can be a terrible burden to put on someone. It ends up permeating everything you try to do," Hanks said. "There have been periods in my life when I yearned to be the surly, brooding loner in the corner, but try as I may, it's just not me—I'm just innately good-natured. I used to be ambivalent about this likable thing because I felt it was causing the hard work I do to be overlooked—because I'm just so damn likable, people think my life is a total breeze, the work just rolls off me and it's as easy as getting out of bed. Despite how it may appear, this work actually isn't all that easy, and the hardest part of it is holding back the self-consciousness that goes with being in front of a camera. It takes a while to learn how to filter out everything that's unnecessary and let yourself go 100 percent full tilt."

Rather than undermine his core appeal in an obvious way—by playing a serial killer, for example—Hanks found roles where his inherent decency would be an asset. For example, *Philadelphia*. Choosing to play Andy Beckett, a gay lawyer dying of AIDS, was an artistic decision: Hanks got to work with Jonathan Demme and Denzel Washington. But it was also a political choice: Hanks used his public image and his artistry so audiences would identify with a gay man. Hanks said, "In some ways we've all been waiting for mainstream Hollywood to deal with the AIDS epidemic. But you don't get credit for being first if you don't get it right."

Hanks prepared for the role by meeting a slew of AIDS patients, asking them questions about how they found out they had the disease. "It's not just playing a disease," he emphasized, "it's playing a man." But although he thought of himself as a reasonably enlightened guy—"There were times when I got hit on by guys," he remembered casually of his life as a young actor in New York City, "and I was just as discombobulated as if I'd been hit on by a woman"—on the set, Hanks discovered that he had to overcome his own internalized homophobia.

In bed with Antonio Banderas, filming a love scene that ultimately got cut from the movie, they repeated their embrace again and again while the camera panned over their bodies. After five or six takes, Banderas quietly told Hanks, "Look, you know, I can feel you. I know you are being tentative. Just do whatever you want to do because we know who we are."

The root of acting is finding the connection you have with other people, and Hanks had more work to do in this case than he realized. "Without even knowing it," Hanks said, "I'd built up all these walls."

Hanks won the Academy Award for Best Actor in a Leading Role—an award that, like his decision to take the role, seemed to be based in both art and politics. Clutching the trophy, he delivered an emotional speech about the human toll of AIDS where he declared that "the streets of Heaven are too crowded with angels."

Steven Spielberg, who won the same night for *Schindler's List,* believed that through his speech, Hanks "communicated more about what *Philadelphia* was saying and reached more people than the movie itself will."

Hanks smartly delivered his message of tolerance clothed in the language of patriotism, underscoring that it's not a fringe Hollywood position to care for the victims of an epidemic or to treat all people as equal under the law. When he had the largest audience of his life, he tried to push the world in a better direction. Hanks said, "It's an incredibly personal moment that three billion people watch."

Part of the speech was a personal message of solidarity with a gay friend (John Gilkerson, who had spurred Hanks to return to acting by saying "Shame on you!") and a gay teacher (Rawley Farnsworth, his inspirational high school drama teacher). Gilkerson had died of AIDS in 1989, but when Hanks called up Farnsworth three days before the Oscars, the retired teacher gave his blessing to Hanks using his name. "I didn't know exactly what he was going to say, but it was just overwhelming," Farnsworth said. The retired schoolteacher found himself suddenly famous, profiled in national magazines and invited to be grand marshal of an Atlanta parade for children with HIV.

Hanks' speech was high-impact enough that it inspired an excellent comedy released two years later, *In & Out.* The plot: an actor (Matt Dillon) wins the Oscar and pays tribute to a gay teacher of his (Kevin Kline), who protests that in fact, he is straight. By the end of the movie, the teacher has come to terms with his homosexuality and pairs off with the newscaster played by Tom Selleck. Joan Cusack even got an Oscar nomination of her own for playing his jilted fiancée.

"Tom Hanks' acceptance speech was certainly the spark for *In & Out*," screenwriter Paul Rudnick said.

"That's tremendous," Hanks said of *In & Out*. "I have got some of the best reviews of my career for a movie that I wasn't even in." By the time Hanks stood on the stage of the Dorothy Chandler Pavilion, accepting his Oscar for *Philadelphia,* he had already finished his next movie: a very different project, titled *Forrest Gump*.

The movie was about the life and times of a simple-minded man traveling through twentieth-century American history, punctuating his journey with aphorisms like "Stupid is as stupid does" and "Life is like a box of chocolates"; its screenplay had been languishing in Hollywood turnaround for nine years, until Hanks and director Robert Zemeckis took it on. "They didn't want to spend the money on *Forrest Gump,*" Hanks said of studio executives. "They thought we were out of our minds. Because they said, 'What is this movie? There's no bad guy. Nothing *happens* in this movie.' They went crazy."

Hanks and Zemeckis got it made at Paramount by opting for a piece of the box office instead of their usual fees; the studio was so penurious that it didn't even want to pay for the traditional wrap party at the end of shooting, so Hanks and some of the producers paid for it out of their pockets. The movie did historically huge business—at the time, it was the fourth-highest-grossing movie ever. Reportedly, Hanks' percentage yielded him $65 million—and Paramount reimbursed everyone for the wrap party.

At the Oscars that year, Hanks handed the Best Actress trophy to Jessica Lange—and a few minutes later, won Best Actor again. He was the first man to achieve that back-to-back feat since Spencer Tracy for *Captains Courageous* in 1938 and *Boys Town* in 1939.

By the time the *Forrest Gump* phenomenon wound down, Hanks had traveled all over the world promoting it, had ascended to a white-hot level of fame, and had been given enough boxes of chocolates to last him for a lifetime. By the end, he was pleading, "Look, *Forrest Gump* was fabulous. It lasted much longer than anybody thought, and brought me a degree of attention that no human being on the planet deserves. But thank goodness, that's over."

Hanks had ascended to such a rarefied tier of stardom that even a casual side project—like doing the voice of a cowboy doll in what he assumed would be a "goofy cartoon"—ended up being a blockbuster hit. *Toy Story* brought in $191 million at the box office, making it the top movie released in 1995, and became the cornerstone of the Pixar studio.

Hanks' other 1995 movie, *Apollo 13*, told the story of a failed mission to the moon; Hanks played commander Jim Lovell. Its success ($172 million, the number three movie released that year) was a long-delayed payoff for Hanks' childhood obsession with the American space program, and confirmed that if he cared deeply about a topic, he could get the American public to care about it too.

What he had burned out on was the constant promotional grind that went along with making movies. "It seemed like it was Month 82 of talking about myself," he said. There was a screening of *Apollo 13* at the Venice Film Festival that epitomized the glamorous world he traveled in: a boat ride to the theater, a red-carpet entrance, screaming crowds. But what Hanks was thinking: "I am so friggin' tired, I'd really like to go back to my hotel and watch whatever is on Italian TV right now." The movie was important to him, he was proud of it—but he needed to do something that wasn't about the glory of Tom Hanks, if only so he could better appreciate the insanity of his life.

So, cherishing every hour of solitude where he didn't have to talk about himself, he sat down to write a screenplay about a one-hit-wonder rock band. When it was done, Hanks affected a modest pose, saying that he didn't want to receive preferential treatment from movie studios, but he knew that his status as a "big honking movie star" put him in a position unlike most first-time feature-film directors. Before he closed the deal to make the movie, he said, "Most actors I've come across have the idea that they can do it all—that they can direct. I'm not so sure I can, but I would like to find out. And I'm in this position where I can barter my way into these unearned situations."

The resulting movie, *That Thing You Do!,* wasn't a showcase for Hanks as a performer. It was a modestly scaled movie about a band that peaked with a number three single in 1964, and it was a small success. Its greatest impact on Hanks' life was probably that two of the movie's producers were Jonathan Demme, who had directed him in *Philadelphia,* and Demme's associate Gary Goetzman (who had started his career in show business as a songwriter, writing tunes for Smokey Robinson and the Staple Singers). After they made *Philadelphia* together, Hanks said, Demme pushed him and Goetzman together, telling him, "You should get together with Gary and produce some stuff and make it."

Hanks folded his old Clavius Base production imprint and opened a new one in partnership with Goetzman: Playtone, named after the fictional record label in *That Thing You Do!* The clout of Hanks and the production savvy of Goetzman proved to be a good match; their partnership led to movies ranging from *Where the Wild Things Are* to *Mamma Mia!,* plus a slew of ambitious TV shows that have collectively won fifty-two Emmys.

One of the biggest Playtone movies, however, happened because of Rita Wilson. A few years after she and Hanks had their second son—Truman Hanks, born December 26, 1995—she went to a one-woman show by Nia Vardalos, attending out of Hellenic solidarity with a fellow Greek-American performer. Wilson saw potential in Vardalos' material, and the resulting movie, *My Big Fat Greek Wedding,* a charming lightweight romantic comedy, became the most successful independent movie ever, grossing $241 million. (It was finally outpaced in 2016 by the animated *Sing.*)

Meanwhile, Hanks focused on his day job, and reeled off one success after another: *Saving Private Ryan. You've Got Mail. Toy Story 2. The Green Mile. Cast Away. Road to Perdition. Catch Me If You Can.* Some of these movies called for Hanks to do terrible things on-screen, like putting a beloved bookshop out of business or killing an innocent miracle worker; somehow, his reputation for playing nice guys was unsullied. In his golden decade spanning 1992 to 2002, Hanks starred in fourteen movies directed by other people, all of them critically well regarded and all of them box-office hits (none grossing less than $100 million in the USA, and many of them much more).

A run like that isn't an accident or good luck. In the closing months of the twentieth century, Steve Martin ran into Hanks at a party. He had a question, the same question anyone who had been paying attention to Hanks' career would want to ask. "You've become this great actor," Martin said. "What did you *do*?"

Martin admired how Hanks had complexity and depth, but still maintained a sense of the absurd. He thought of Hanks as "the complicated John Wayne—because he's iconic, but many-sided." So he pressed Hanks for an answer: "I know that acting just doesn't improve through study. There's some kind of personal growth to make that change."

It's exactly the sort of question that Hanks would usually dodge. On one movie, he had deflected the director's earnest daily inquiry into how he was doing with a two-syllable reply: "Swinging!" But he liked and admired Martin, so he tried to tell him the truth.

"I used to just show up and say 'Let's get on with it!'" Hanks informed the silver-haired comic. "But you get to that point as an actor where you realize you're examining an aspect of the human condition as opposed to just a story that starts on page one and ends on page twenty. And to do that, you have to have some other stuff that's loaded up inside you—the stuff that happened [to your character] *before* the movie began. You don't have to sit down and write it in longhand in single space on spiral notebooks. But it has to be a very tangible thing, because it has to play out in every scene."

He summed up how he embraced the technique, without complaining: "I realized it was hard work that had to be done."

The other reason for the high quality of Hanks' films: the work he put into developing them before the camera started rolling, whether they originated at Playtone or elsewhere. He would sit down with the director and systematically go through the script, punching up the dialogue and calling out lines that didn't ring true.

"One thing I find myself doing is removing the question marks from my dialogue," Hanks said. "Characters often ask bullshit questions like 'Are you saying you'll actually run for water commissioner?' I don't know how to do that—ask the expository question."

"He basically rewrites every part he plays," Nora Ephron said. "He does it in this darling way, too. He sits with the director and the writer and says, 'Wouldn't it be nice if this happened?' Or 'Why doesn't he say this?' One of the reasons Tom survived his turkeys is that he always takes good care of his own part."

Plenty of actors want to massage screenplays for their own benefit. What differentiates Hanks is that he's unusually charming about it, he brings a fierce intelligence to bear on the script, and he doesn't try to stuff all the cinematic glory into his own cheeks like an egotistical hamster.

By definition, career peaks don't last forever. And so, eventually, Hanks made a misstep. He made several at once, actually: in 2004, he released *The Terminal, The Polar Express,* and *The Ladykillers.* They were made with topnotch collaborators (Steven Spielberg, Robert Zemeckis, and the Coen brothers, respectively), but they all landed somewhere in the zone between "anemic" and "vaguely creepy."

Years before, Hanks had done a photo shoot with Jimmy Stewart, the actor to whom he was most frequently compared when he was a young actor on the rise, and then followed it up with a visit to Stewart's house to pay his respects. Hanks asked Stewart about his experiences as a bomber pilot during World War II, while Stewart gave Hanks one essential piece of advice: "Just keep those box-office grosses up."

Now, in search of a guaranteed hit to goose those grosses, Hanks made perhaps the most craven decision of his career: he starred in Ron Howard's film adaptation of *The Da Vinci Code,* squelching his intelligence and good judgment in service of a blockbuster book that had sold more than forty million copies. (At least he wasn't making a *Forrest Gump* sequel, which Paramount had long hoped for.) The *Da Vinci* gambit worked—once. Audiences turned out for *The Da Vinci Code* in droves, but stayed away from the two sequels in equally large droves.

It wasn't as if Hanks was in danger of dropping off the A-list. As Hanks noted of Hollywood, "You really have to go a *lot* of years here before you stop getting your ass kissed." Even though his professional uncertainty was relative—most actors would have committed arson to be in his shoes—that didn't take the sting away. What soothed his soul was his home life: every night, he came home to Rita Wilson.

Hanks was one of the most uxorious men in the world, and he rejoiced every time he had another opportunity to announce his love for his wife. "Rita and I have been married for seventeen years, and it seems like seventeen weeks," he said in 2005. At home, they had a normal, contented family life—their calendars got filled up with parent-teacher conferences and the kids' dental appointments. Hanks admitted that he could get moody and distracted sometimes; Wilson knew when to give him space. And Hanks had a hobby beloved by middle-aged husbands around the world: "I like to nap," he confessed. "I can just lean my head back on the couch and get bona-fide deep REM sleep. It drives Rita crazy—she can't do it."

The couple said they rarely argued, and when they did, it was usually in the car—because whoever wasn't driving disagreed with the decision-making of the person behind the wheel. Eventually, those arguments became ritualized and ended up entertaining them both. Hanks would kick off their routine by pretending to be the condescending patriarch—to make Wilson laugh, he only needed to tell her, "Don't you worry your pretty little head. All you have to do is sit there and ride and I will decide how to get there."

To the amusement of his family, Hanks could lose his temper in spectacular fashion. His son Colin said, "It's always fun to watch him yell at the computer when something's not working. He's like a caveman."

"Oh, any failure of technology can get him going," Wilson added. "One time, he smashed his cell phone."

When he wasn't confronted with system updates, balky Wi-Fi connections, and other twenty-first-century hazards, Hanks was mostly a chilled-out soul, and he knew he had Wilson to thank for it. He compared his domestic existence to Eugene O'Neill, the playwright famous for *The Iceman Cometh* and *Long Day's Journey into Night:* "I'm not as nutty a guy as Eugene O'Neill was, but his wife, Carlotta Monterey, once said that Gene's going to do his thing and I'm going to protect it so that Gene gets to do his thing. I mean, she makes sure that I don't live a life of total frivolity, but when it comes down to pursuing the things that I do, she protects me to make sure I have time and concentration."

That may be a long-winded way of saying "Rita keeps the household running and the kids on track when I'm away on location for a couple of months." (When their kids were younger, Hanks used to bring them on location—not so easy to do when you're pulling them out of school.) "Family always comes first," Wilson said. "Seeing your children become really lovely young adults and human beings is overwhelming in some ways."

Wilson had a professional life that extended beyond being the supportive spouse on the red carpet of awards shows: a stint on Broadway as Roxie Hart in *Chicago,* a recurring role as Allison Williams' mother on *Girls,* and a singing career (she's released two albums). "I'm very proud of my marriage and my kids, and I'm proud of having produced *My Big Fat Greek Wedding,*" she said. And she resisted being typecast as America's Mom. In 2011, she took on a pair of cold-blooded roles on *Law & Order: SVU* and *The Good Wife,* TV appearances that came after she told her agents, "If I play one more warm, understanding mother, sister, wife, daughter, I think I'm gonna puke. You have got to find me some crazy-ass bitches."

Something that made it easier for Tom Hanks to weather a dip in his career: he was ridiculously wealthy, able to measure his money in increments of hundreds of millions of dollars. Not that he was ostentatious about it—long after he could afford fancier cars, he drove a variety of Volkswagens and a Dodge Caravan minivan. ("I like sitting up high," he explained. "It's nice to see what's causing the traffic jam.")

Hanks never turned into a flashy or fashionable dresser—he still favored jeans and a T-shirt, even if the T-shirts later in his life cost one hundred dollars. (His closet also included Prada, Ralph Lauren, and the yoga brand Lululemon: "I asked, 'Is it appropriate for men to wear?' They said 'Yeah,' so I'm wearing Lululemon.")

Hanks conceded that he wasn't "impervious to perks"—he went on vacation with Bruce Springsteen and Barack Obama, he spent quality time on David Geffen's yacht, and he compared private planes to crack cocaine. (He hadn't flown commercial since the late 1980s.) As he joked when one particular vacation attracted attention, "Is this what's going on with social media that Oprah and I cannot go on a billionaire's boat to Tahiti with a former president of the United States and not keep it secret for godsakes?"

But in general, Hanks said being ultra-rich instead of just well-off had less impact on his life than one might imagine. As he asked, "How much better can I eat?"

He was careful to avoid debt. "If you're in debt, you can't say no," he explained. He cherished his "fuck-you money," meaning that he could afford to say "fuck you" to any offer he didn't care for, and he kept that money safely in the bank. When he bought a house, he paid cash. Barring the collapse of Western society, his family would never know want.

"I do wrestle with the amount of money I make," he said. "But at the end of the day, what am I gonna say? I took less money so Rupert Murdoch could have more?"

To set a good example for his kids, he made deliberate efforts not to be extravagant: he didn't buy a boat of his own and he lived in a "relatively modest" house. Although he acknowledged that it was lavish compared to the home of the average American, context was everything. "Relatively modest for somebody who does what I do for a living and that still takes in the same security concerns," he qualified. That was another facet of his fame: Hanks traveled with discreet but effective security.

Hanks knew that his two older children had a different range of experience than his two younger children: "They remember when life was normal. When we lived in standard houses and I sometimes had work or not. And there was not the ballyhoo that goes along with everything." The best he could do was to let the kids know that he wasn't in it for the money: "Both Rita and I have communicated to the kids that we really love what we do. We're doing it for the sheer-ass pleasure."

He felt that he was, in general, a better father with his two younger children than he had been with his two older children — largely because he made a point of not working all the time, and taking jobs closer to home. Hanks made a conscious effort to be present in the kids' lives, providing emotional stability, instead of spending all his time and emotional bandwidth on his career. "My dad is a goofy guy, so yeah, he can be embarrassing," his son Truman said. "But I realize that all parents are embarrassing, so it's fine."

Tom Hanks learned to accept that he was flying closer to earth, with some movies that overperformed, some that underperformed, and some that just vanished. (A handy rule of thumb: for some reason, audiences recently have been drawn to movies where Hanks portrayed real people. Of the eleven feature films he made between 2011 and 2017—the run immediately following *Toy Story 3*—the five where he Hanksified a real human being were the top five grossers.) He broke some of his self-imposed rules for selecting movie projects: he made cameos and he made sequels. Hanks remained an actor that A-list directors wanted to work with and so he collaborated with Clint Eastwood (*Sully*), Mike Nichols (*Charlie Wilson's War*), Ron Howard (the *Da Vinci Code* trilogy), and Steven Spielberg (*Bridge of Spies* and *The Post*). Best of all in this era may have been *Captain Phillips*, the movie he made with Paul Greengrass, where Hanks played the captain of a freighter ship boarded by Somali pirates.

Hanks made his Broadway debut in Nora Ephron's *Lucky Guy* (produced in 2013, the year after her death), he produced movies, he did charitable work, and he spent time on the Academy's board of governors. This spike in productivity came because all his kids were out of the house. His daughter, Elizabeth, and his youngest son, Truman, basically stayed out of the public eye. (Truman left home earlier than expected—for high school, he asked to go to boarding school, maybe because it's lonely being the last kid in the house. Truman enthusiastically described his experience at the Thacher School: "It's like living with thirty of your best friends and it just so happens that school is right there." Hanks and Wilson visited him every two weeks or so.) His son Colin worked steadily as an actor, with notable roles on TV shows like *Roswell, Fargo,* and *Life in Pieces.*

His son Chester tried to make a career as a rapper under the stage name Chet Haze. "You want your kids to follow their passion," Hanks said, even though he wasn't much of a hip-hop aficionado. He gave his son a backhanded compliment: "I dig his stuff. It's getting better."

Chester started his career by saying embarrassing un-Hanksian things in front of reporters like "Let's go hit on some models." As his music career failed to take off, his struggles became more obvious, because he was documenting them on social media: he sold and consumed cocaine, doing so much white powder that he couldn't physically snort it up his nose anymore. "I AM A WALKING PR DISASTER," he tweeted. But in 2015, he became the father of a baby girl and went to rehab for drugs and alcohol.

Tom Hanks, grandfather, was steadfast in his public support of Chester: "You got to applaud the bravery and the honesty when it actually comes out of your own house," he said. "As a parent, you love your kids unconditionally. You support them every step of the way."

Hanks turned sixty in the summer of 2016, an age when it's natural to think more about your legacy—through your work and your family—and your mortality. That year, Hanks revealed that he had type 2 diabetes; there was widespread speculation that he had thrashed his metabolism from gaining and losing weight for so many different movie roles, but he insisted that it was the inevitable outcome of eating junk food for decades. "I was a total idiot," he said. "I thought I could avoid it by removing the buns from my cheeseburgers."

Two years later, Wilson was diagnosed with breast cancer; she had a double mastectomy and reconstruction, which came with doctor-mandated changes in lifestyle (no more than five drinks per week), plus extra doses of anxiety and fear. To deal with the stress, she used meditation and humor. "It wasn't like I was going to be in St.-Tropez parading around topless, like I did in the '80s," she wrote in *Harper's Bazaar.* "God, I hope there are pictures."

"You just clear the decks and you circle the wagons and you join the community and you hunker down," Hanks said of how he and Wilson supported each other through medical crises. "I'm on the back nine, and I want to play more than another nine."

In a letter to this author, he laid out his busy schedule. "I have a book of my own to push," he typed, "a movie to prepare, a movie to promote, a family to care for and like, you know, exercise I gotta get."

For Tom Hanks, individual good days have added up to a mountain of well-spent days: a life that's made the world a better place.

Hanks isn't done yet. When most of Hollywood's top-echelon stars turned out to honor him at the Kodak Theater in 2002, he told them, "I pray that evolution, professional and personal, will not conclude in this rented hall. If you can feel like a good man in your forties, you can feel like a better man in your fifties, a superman in your sixties—and maybe a Spider-Man in your seventies."

Excel at your life's work. Honor the sacrifices your elders made in the service of a seemingly impossible goal. Embrace your passions. Treat women with respect. Worship in the church of baseball. Use the right tool for the job. Don't dwell on the road not taken. Remember that Shakespeare will tell you the truth. Value your friends but accept your loneliness. Stand up for what you believe. Excel at your life's work. Honor the sacrifices your elders made in the service of a seemingly impossible goal. Embrace your passions. Treat women with respect. Worship in the church of baseball. Use the right tool for the job. Don't dwell on the road not taken. Remember that Shakespeare will tell you the truth. Value your friends but accept your loneliness. Stand up for what you believe. Excel at your life's work. Honor the sacrifices your elders made in the service of a seemingly impossible goal. Embrace your passions. Treat women with respect. Worship in the church of baseball. Use the right tool for the job. Don't dwell on the road not taken. Remember that Shakespeare will tell you the truth. Value your friends but accept your loneliness. Stand up for what you believe.

Section Two

The Ten Commandments of Tom Hanks

BREAKING-NEWS SHOCKER: TOM HANKS didn't always have a sunny, upbeat outlook on the world. Check out his POV circa 1985: "I'm a pessimist, pure and simple," he said. "I guess it's based on experience, on a certain amount of wisdom that you acquire by the school of hard knocks. I always expect everything to stink to high heaven. That way you don't get disappointed."

Fast-forward sixteen years, and ask Hanks if he's an optimist. "Shamelessly so" is his answer.

Let's stipulate that some very good things happened to Tom Hanks in those intervening years. Not only did his up-and-down movie career go up, and then up, and then up some more, he went from the throes of a miserable divorce to domestic bliss. But for most people, pessimism isn't easily dislodged, no matter how much good news comes along. In a psychological study, lottery winners and people who were rendered paraplegic by car crashes proved to be roughly as happy as one another—the likely culprit is hedonic adaptation, meaning that human beings will get used to just about anything, and soon return to their usual baseline level of daily joy and misery.

Tom Hanks, however, given overwhelming affirmation that his life was going well, learned to embrace the good news. Asked if he was happy, he replied, "It's a choice I make, yes." Astonished by how joy had overtaken him, he said, "I apologize to my friends and family because I say it all the time, but if you told me in 1966 [when he was ten years old] that I'd be an actor and make movies, I would have thought that you were insane. If you had told me in 1966 I'd be married and have four great kids, I could never have imagined it."

The personal is the political in many ways, including temperament. Hanks continued, "I look at the United States of America now, underneath the Stars and Stripes banner and all the hokey stuff that goes along with it, and despite the problems we have, and the constant strife we go through, I think we are undeniably at a better place as a country and as a people than we've ever been, and it's because of who we are."

Life is complicated; glasses are simultaneously half-full and half-empty; optimists and pessimists will always have a wide range of evidence that can reinforce either point of view. Weeks after Hanks said that, terrorists hijacked four planes and crashed them into the Pentagon and the World Trade Center, killing thousands of people. The strife in the USA showed no signs of reducing.

In good times and bad, if you ask Tom Hanks to summarize his philosophy, this is how he does it: "Life is one thing after another."

Sometimes he says that with exasperation, like at the end of a bad day when a woman on an elevator asked him how it felt to sit on top of the world and he replied, "Look, lady, life is just one damn thing after another, no matter where you live." Sometimes he says it as an expression of joy, like when he summarized his marriage to Rita Wilson thus: "We knew it was going to be one damn thing after another, but they were all good damn things."

But most often, Hanks says it as an acknowledgment of the vicissitudes and crosscurrents of human existence. He describes life as "something good jammed up right next to something bad that's followed by something good that's followed by two things that are bad that's followed by seven things that are good that's followed by something that's bad. It is one damn thing after another. Which is actually wonderful, in its constant variety."

How does any human being make sense of that constant clamor and chaos, which adds up to weeks, years, and eventually a life? Hanks figured out what worked for him and then resolutely applied those principles to his daily existence. He's not descending from the mountain with ten commandments on stone tablets, full of interdictions and prohibitions for the rest of the human race—but by studying the choices he's made, we can learn from his hard-won wisdom.

These commandments are how one of the most admired people in the world has chosen to govern the unruly abundance of his own life. Following them won't turn you into Tom Hanks. But if you follow his example, you might find yourself leading a better life, with more joy, more good news, more meaning. Let Hanks predict your future: "It's still going to be one thing after another, some of them so horrible that you'll weep for all humanity, but then others so magnificent and beautiful that you'll say, 'Well, I'm going to keep going because that's possible.'"

THE FIRST COMMANDMENT
Excel at your life's work.

• • •

THE SECOND COMMANDMENT
Honor the sacrifices your elders made in the service of a seemingly impossible goal.

• • •

THE THIRD COMMANDMENT
Embrace your passions.

• • •

THE FOURTH COMMANDMENT
Treat women with respect.

• • •

THE FIFTH COMMANDMENT
Worship in the church of baseball.

• • •

THE SIXTH COMMANDMENT
Use the right tool for the job.

• • •

THE SEVENTH COMMANDMENT
Don't dwell on the road not taken.

• • •

THE EIGHTH COMMANDMENT
Remember that Shakespeare will tell you the truth.

• • •

THE NINTH COMMANDMENT
Value your friends but accept your loneliness.

• • •

THE TENTH COMMANDMENT
Stand up for what you believe.

THE FIRST COMMANDMENT

Excel at your life's work.

• • • • • •

Tom Hanks' chosen line of work, of course, is acting. Here's how he started: On a family car trip, young Tom heard a bird, and announced that fact by adopting a Shakespearean delivery and saying, "Hark, a mourning dove!" It got a laugh, as he hoped. So he spent the rest of car ride trying out variations on it: "Hark, some cows!" "Hark, I need to go to the bathroom!" Fortunately for all parties, he eventually developed some new material.

Being the wiseass looking for the punchline at all costs carried Hanks through high school and his sitcom career. Gradually, he toned down his comedic desires in favor of his dramatic training. But the back-of-the-classroom cutup never went away entirely: that's why Hanks is one of the most coveted talk-show guests in the world and why he hosted *Saturday Night Live* nine times (the fifth-most-frequent host ever) between 1985 and 2016, fully committing to characters ranging from a terrible Olympic ice skater to Mr. Short Term Memory. When he played an Aerosmith roadie, he adjusted microphones with uncommon intensity, getting laughs just from the way he said "sibilance."

In 1989, after making *Joe Versus the Volcano,* Hanks was asked how he approached comedy. "Blindly," he said. "I think it takes care of itself." He explained that his attitude was more than the confidence of the seasoned professional; it derived from his belief that if everybody did their jobs, the comedy would emerge. "It's an assumption the actor has to make—and then pay no attention to it," he said. "You have to go on to the more specific tasks of actors: to actually walk in the world, to reflect what's going on in society, to be a breathing character others can recognize. I consider myself an actor before I consider myself a comedian, but I'm certainly aware that I'm funny and that my movies are comedies."

Hanks added, "To be funny when you're not supposed to be funny is a crime. But to *not* be funny when you're supposed to be, that's a fucking sin. You don't do that. No matter if it's Chekhov, Ibsen, you just don't do it. Pretty highfalutin talk from a guy who dressed up like a woman on network TV, huh?"

After Garry Marshall cast Hanks in *Nothing in Common,* he congenially asked his star how he liked to be directed. Hanks told him that he preferred to avoid lengthy, abstruse discussions of motivations, and responded well to basic comments like "louder," "softer," "slower," "faster," "lighter," "darker," "smarter," "confused," "aware," or "not aware." "You can do a whole movie with Tom just by using those words," Marshall said.

Some years later, Marshall recalled, Hanks confided that a director on another film had told him, "I see this scene as chartreuse."

"So do I," Hanks readily assented, although he had no clue what the director was talking about.

Hanks was open to different working methods with different directors. Clint Eastwood famously liked to shoot just one take; Penny Marshall preferred to rehearse until everybody's brain cells hemorrhaged. Hanks didn't even mind if a director tried to "trick" him: if surprising him with an unexpected element in the middle of a scene got the desired performance, he could roll with that. He insisted that some of the most valuable feedback he'd ever gotten was: "That was terrible. I didn't believe a moment of that. You're horrible. You call yourself an actor?"

The one thing Hanks really wanted: the shooting schedule. If he knew in advance that he had a major scene coming up, he could prepare and pace himself, making sure that he would have the necessary energy and focus.

For a big scene—one where he cries, for example—Hanks used to confine himself to his trailer, isolating himself, trying to stay at a boiling point of intensity, which would get harder and harder as one hour of waiting stretched into four. "You attack and it's finally done and you're spent and going 'I can't keep doing this to myself,'" he remembered. "Now it's a matter of, 'Look, I've done the work, I understand that when the time comes it's gonna be alright.' In the same way that I'm aware that if the kid has a bloody nose, there's an easy way of taking care of it, as opposed to [high-pitched scream] 'Oh my god, he's got a bloody nose!'"

Scott Shepherd, who played opposite Hanks in *Bridge of Spies,* had one day on the set where he decided to focus on Hanks' technique. It was a scene where Hanks' character was arguing before the Supreme Court; Shepherd's character was in the crowd of people watching. "I was basically an extra in that scene," Shepherd said. So while Steven Spielberg filmed elaborate tracking shots of the justices, Shepherd watched Hanks deliver the same speech over and over. "I loved trying to figure out what his thing was, because it wasn't obvious," Shepherd said. "Other people, they put on headphones between takes, they've got some kind of routine going." One thing Hanks did was to start the scene before the assistant director had finished saying the word "action."

Shepherd noted, "That's professional and efficient, but it's also a good way of not overthinking—you're already in the speech and you have to negotiate your way out of it before you have time to make a plan."

Shepherd said, "I have a hard time not falling into the trap of 'That was almost perfect—do all that again and just change one thing.' But if you do that, you stop being creative. He would come at the scenes different ways—he felt free to get rid of whatever he had just done."

Hanks wasn't a chameleon or a wizard with accents, and he understood that he was more naturally suited to playing a wacky zookeeper than a bare-knuckled drill instructor. Again and again, though, he pulled off the magic trick of making it look like he was hardly acting, just saying his lines in a natural fashion. Only after the fact did you realize how much distance there was between, say, his HIV-positive lawyer, his marooned efficiency expert, his simpleton millionaire, and his washed-up baseball manager. Not just in their professions or their superficial appearances, but in their beliefs, their rhythms, and their emotional lives. Hanks did the hard work of constructing a full life for all those characters—and many more—so that the slice of each one that appeared on screen would feel organic.

Hanks would never ask a director for his character's motivation—as far as he was concerned, it was the actor's job to come up with that. "Because if you don't get up from the desk and cross to the window, we won't see that there's a bad guy in the phone booth across the street. So *you* have to figure out why you're getting up and walking over to the window—even though it seems incredibly fake, even though there's no reason to do it, *you've* got to communicate the reason why you're getting up and going over to the window."

He didn't belong to the school of clenched-jaw Method acting, and dismissed actors who tried to stay in character for the duration of a film shoot. "Call me by my character's name," he said mockingly. "Then what are you doing in the makeup trailer?"

Asked about what memories he channeled when he had to look haggard on screen in *Cast Away,* he scoffed, "You mean when I crossed my eyes and thought about my dog that died when I was seven? It didn't work like that. It was just acting. That's what they pay me to do."

Nora Ephron, who directed Hanks in *Sleepless in Seattle* and *You've Got Mail,* said, "The older I get, the more interested I am in people who are not going to tell you their innermost hopes and fears. It's what he's pulling all these performances out of. But he isn't going to tell anyone about it, partly because it's none of your business and partly because it's bad manners. It's America at its finest, at its most absolutely pre-Freudian finest."

Sally Field, his costar in *Punchline* and *Forrest Gump,* put it a little differently: "You know, underneath there's somebody else. Somebody dark. And it's a man. Not a boy, but a man who I sense has a lot of anger in there. And he doesn't feel he has to hide that on the screen; he just hides it when he's not on screen."

Asked directly, Hanks acknowledged there was truth in what Field saw, but declined to discuss it further: he preferred to keep some areas of his life private. He claimed that he had extracted every easy ounce of emotion from his own memories long ago. "You can only mine these things so many times," he said. "I'm running out of emotions in my own life. I've got to get some more stuff."

Through a combination of life experience, inner darkness, and hard work, Hanks reached the point as an actor where he could consistently achieve the focus necessary for the job. Some actors get bent out of shape if somebody steps into their "eye line" on a movie set (famously, Christian Bale had an epic tantrum over that issue on the set of *Terminator: Salvation*).

"If you're paying attention to the artificiality of it all, then you aren't in character," Hanks said. "Your concentration has to be this protective snow bubble, a sphere all around you."

Sometimes members of a film crew would ask Hanks, "Am I okay here? Am I in your light?"

He always told them, "I don't even see you."

Hanks' hard work at his job produced visible results: over the decades, he steadily improved as an actor. But he found it difficult to judge the effectiveness of his own performances in the moment: "I've worked on a set where I would go home and say, 'Man, I nailed it today.' And you see it in the movie and it lies there like a dead fish. And there've been days where I said, 'I don't know what I was doing today. I couldn't even remember the lines.' And you see it in the movie and it's the greatest scene." He concluded, "Anybody who says they know is lying or demonically possessed."

THE SECOND COMMANDMENT

Honor the sacrifices your elders made in the service of a seemingly impossible goal.

• • • • • •

Conan O'Brien gave Tom Hanks a gift for his forty-sixth birthday: something special that would encompass his love of outer space and his fascination with World War II. The talk-show host told him, "We had a painting commissioned of astronauts storming the beach at D-Day."

Once the painting was unveiled and Hanks stopped laughing, he commented, "What a day in history that was, Conan." He reenacted the scene with sound effects and mimed weaponry: "That's one (*bang, bang*) small step (*kaboom*) for man (*ratatat*)!"

Hanks' fascination with the space program and the military derived from a common source: "Astronauts, test pilots, Army Rangers all adhere to a kind of self-government that is infectious. They become a spiritual class—part family and part competitive—that's undeniable." That admiration was sincere, but it had a hint of self congratulation: film crews are also formed of elite technicians coming together as a short-term family to execute a mission. Hanks was quick to quash any implication that he was putting himself on that level. "The fact is," he said, "I have no inner discipline, and Americans rigorously training to perform public service is inspiring to me."

The two events that remade the world for young Tom Hanks, opening up new frontiers of human possibility: the advent of the Beatles and the moon landing. When he was in the third or fourth grade, his school wheeled a huge black-and-white TV into his classroom so everyone could see a Gemini launch. "Two guys side by side, up in the vacuum of space—it was romantic," Tom remembered. He felt a personal connection because commentators kept saying that the capsule wasn't much bigger than a Volkswagen: "My dad drove a Volkswagen."

Hanks watched the Apollo 11 moon landing when he was visiting his mother at her home in Red Bluff, California. He owned an action figure of Major Matt Mason, the astronaut manufactured by Mattel. He had built the models of the lunar module and the command module, sold by Aurora and Revell. Twelve years old, he lay underneath his mom's coffee table with his belly on her oval hooked rug, playing with his toys and models, waiting for Neil Armstrong to make history. Hanks said, "Then, of course, when it came on, you could hardly see the damn thing. The camera angle wasn't very good—and it never changed."

At that age, Hanks had a dim secondhand understanding of World War II, filtered through his father's experiences working on the navy's hydraulic systems. "Growing up, I always knew Dad was somewhere in the Pacific fixing things," he said. "He had nothing nice to say about the navy. He hated the navy. He hated everybody in the navy. He had no glorious stories about it." But even though his father had contempt for his military experience—he was sent to a war zone thousands of miles away and had to put his life on hold for years—Hanks noticed he still carried his battered navy dog tag on his keychain.

Hanks grew up in a navy town, so many of his friends had fathers who had served in the Pacific theater. Not that he cared about it when he was a kid: "When it came to understanding history, I nodded off."

His perspective changed when he was nineteen and he was "convinced that things were harder on me than they were on anybody else in the world." He said, "I was trying to get to school on time; I was trying to have this part-time job as a bellboy at a hotel. The Vietnam War was scary and I was having problems with a girlfriend." Every day at the hotel, Hanks would briefly interact with an older guy, about fifty years old, who worked for a dry cleaner—in the morning, he picked up the guests' garments, and in the afternoon, he dropped them off. Then, for one week in June, the dry-cleaning man was replaced by another guy.

When the usual guy returned, Hanks asked him where he had been. The answer was France—but it hadn't been a vacation. Hanks learned that the dry-cleaning man had been a paratrooper who jumped into Normandy on D-Day; he fought for about a hundred days before he was wounded and knocked out of the war. Decades later, he had returned with some other members of his platoon to visit the battlefields where they struggled and the gravesites of their friends.

"When he left that day, I had perspective on my life that I had not had before," Hanks said. "Here's a guy who jumped into France and ended up sleeping in a hole, watching his best friends get killed. And on top of that he had to kill other kids like himself." Hanks was learning that the world was bigger than his personal corner of it, even if he didn't know what to do with that knowledge yet.

It was years before Hanks really explored the history of World

War II, but eventually, spurred by his role in *Saving Private Ryan* (directed by Steven Spielberg), he went deep. He devoured volumes of history, grilled any veteran he could meet, and visited the actual sites of battles. On Omaha Beach, he said, "I walked where they died, where some put on dry socks for the last time." Alone and overwhelmed by emotion, he had to lie down on the spot and take a nap.

When Hanks and Spielberg decided to follow up *Ryan* by collaborating on a WWII miniseries for HBO, they each had a favorite Stephen Ambrose book they wanted to adapt. Spielberg touted *Citizen Soldiers,* but Hanks prevailed with his choice of *Band of Brothers,* tracking the progress of Easy Company (part of the 506th Parachute Infantry Regiment) through the war. Hanks didn't just lend his name as executive producer and make a cameo as a paratrooper, he punched up scripts, sat in on marathon casting sessions, and directed the pivotal fifth episode, "Crossroads." He also got involved in tracking down vintage army materiel, which is part of why the miniseries was filmed in England. "You can't find Sherman tanks in the U.S. We brought this stuff over here in the 1940s and didn't bother taking it back," Hanks observed.

"I feel like I've been working on my historical doctorate," Hanks said. Searching for on-screen verisimilitude, he did enough research to earn "a PhD in paratroop experience in Northern Europe."

Hanks was interested in the larger strategic decisions of the war, but what he really cared about was the grunt's-eye point of view—that was where he found the details that brought history to life. It was one thing to read that it was cold when E company defended the town of Bastogne in Belgium. "You think, 'Well, I've been outside on a cold winter's day for, like, seven hours, which is pretty unpleasant, man,'" Hanks said. It was another thing to understand what that meant on a visceral level: "You're telling me that these guys didn't even get inside, literally didn't have a roof over their heads or a hot towel passed over their bodies for forty-nine days? It was so cold that they had to piss on their machine guns to unfreeze the mechanisms! *That's* cold."

Having gained that understanding of what American soldiers went through, Hanks wanted to pass it on, and became a major supporter of both the World War II Memorial on the National Mall in Washington, DC (sterile, but moving), and the National WWII Museum in New Orleans (top-notch—if you get to visit, don't miss "Beyond All Boundaries," the Hanks-narrated multimedia extravaganza).

With the space program, Hanks followed the same path: a starring role in a hit movie (*Apollo 13*) that led to a successful HBO miniseries (*From the Earth to the Moon*). Hanks could hold forth on the arcane points of the different NASA logos (nicknamed "the meatball" and "the worm" by insiders) or the health of Apollo 7 astronauts ("Wally Schirra was cranky because he had a cold"). He had been immersed in the details of space exploration since he was a kid, but now he got to go deeper than he had ever dreamed.

In 1994, Hanks stood next to the crew of the shuttle *Endeavor* as they boarded their vessel and prepared to launch. Museums took the Plexiglas off exhibits so he could climb into actual historic capsules. He experienced weightlessness on NASA's high-altitude training plane, the "Vomit Comet." What was originally going to be a single research trip on that plane turned into 612 separate "flight parabolas," meaning that a significant chunk of *Apollo 13* was filmed on the plane in twenty-five-second takes; by the time the shoot ended, its principals had logged four hours of weightlessness, more than most astronauts get before they go into space.

Ron Howard, director of *Apollo 13,* worried that his cast might need some extra coaching to get the job done. He said, "I remember talking about bringing in a mime to help what I call the 'actronauts' achieve the illusion of weightlessness during heavy dialogue scenes where we couldn't use our zero gravity simulation aircraft very effectively and I remember Tom being vaguely negative about it but the notion stuck with me. And I brought up the mime concept a couple of times until finally Tom took me aside and said, 'Ron, please, we can hack this. I've been dreaming of being weightless my whole life. I used to stick a brick in my pants so I could suck a garden hose in the bottom of a pool and pretend I was taking a spacewalk, for God's sake. If you really follow through with this idea of yours, Ron, I'm warning you, I might have to kill the mime.'"

Sometimes Hanks expressed his profound awe for the space program with vaulting rhetoric: "How dare we have such faith in ourselves and in each other? We can dare, and we can dream of such things, because from December 1968 to December 1972, twenty-four different human beings not all that different from you or me made the impossible yet divine voyage from the earth to the moon. And Lord knows, if we can do that, there is nothing we cannot do."

Other times, as an aesthetic man trying to express the magnitude of a scientific accomplishment, he compared the Apollo program to the crowning artworks of humanity, like the Sistine Chapel. Or he'd say "it was a combination of Shakespeare, Sophocles, and T. S. Eliot." On a fundamental level for Tom Hanks, the astronauts would always be the Beatles.

Hanks urged anybody fortunate enough to cross paths with an Apollo astronaut to remember that although they flew into space, they were mortal men. "Made of flesh and sinew, of blood and brain, and when allied with hundreds of thousands other like-minded human beings, they helped make a fact where there had only been fiction." It was true of space travelers and soldiers alike—and it was a particularly powerful alchemy for somebody who spent his life making fiction out of fact.

Interlude

PETER SCOLARI,
BOSOM BUDDY

"TOM HANKS IS A HERO OF MINE," PETER SCOLARI says before he even orders a cup of coffee. "He's a role model to me—I spend most of my life finding my way to being like him."

Scolari met Hanks in 1980, on the Paramount Studios lot in Los Angeles. The occasion was the sixth day of an eight-day production, during which they would rehearse and shoot the pilot for a new TV series, *Bosom Buddies*. The show was a sitcom about two best friends working at an advertising agency in New York City who get evicted from their apartment and disguise themselves in dresses and wigs so they can live in a women's-only residency hotel (still a thing in 1980, but just barely).

Scolari was a last-minute replacement—the original costar wasn't working out. "They thought they had lightning in a bottle with this series but there was a piece missing," Scolari says. "I immediately felt like I was plugged into something and I had to step up. Tom felt like a show unto himself, almost swaggering. His confidence was shocking." When they did a read-through of the script, Hanks "was ad-libbing off the page, saying things that weren't there. I picked up the cue and started doing the same thing. We had instant chemistry, which was very exciting."

Just as important, though, was the lunch Scolari and Hanks shared that first day. "We almost immediately started talking about our family histories: what we had struggled with, when did your father die, and what were you like in high school? He was so deeply personal with me right away, and I think we kind of fell in love with each other."

That real-life friendship was the foundation of the show: audiences could see the pleasure the two young actors took in goofing on each other, riffing together, and dialing into each other's rhythms. Scolari remembers the vibe on *Bosom Buddies* as being like a "sleepover party: we're up late and we're watching TV and drinking lots of Diet Coke." He grins. We're sitting in a diner on the Upper West Side of Manhattan; Scolari's grown a bit grizzled with the years, but he still has a youthful glint in his eye. "Well, not Diet Coke in our era. Real sugar."

The show's premise required most of the women at the Susan B. Anthony Hotel to be oblivious to the fact that their neighbors Buffy and Hildegarde were actually men in drag. "We objected, week in and week out, to not letting some of the girls in on the secret," Scolari remembers. "We said, 'How stupid are we making these girls out to be if they don't know it's us?'"

The big reveal came early in the second season, at a reception at a Latin American embassy where Hanks' cis male character Kip tells his secret to Donna Dixon's character Sonny—and when a curtain is drawn at an inopportune moment, to most of the rest of the cast. Hanks set up a practical joke with the show's makeup artist Michael Westmore (also famous for *Raging Bull* and *Star Trek: The Next Generation*): underneath his dress, he was wearing not just falsies, but a realistic latex prosthetic women's chest. So at the crucial moment, Hanks didn't pull off his wig and declare, "Ain't this a shocker?" He ripped his dress open and told Dixon, "I'm half a woman." She was looking into his eyes, so she didn't notice his breasts at first. Hanks improvised a monologue about his life as a hermaphrodite while his bosom heaved in a most un-buddyish fashion.

"It's on the gag reel," Scolari says, laughing. "The gag reel's full of the two of us making the other laugh. I always won. I could control parts of my face that the camera wouldn't see." Scolari demonstrates: he can maintain a normal expression on half of his face while he makes the other half of it twitch like he has epilepsy. Sometimes Hanks had to play a whole scene with a partner who had the off-camera side of his face jerking and convulsing. Scolari brags, "The only way he could get me to laugh was to have already broken himself. And then his destruction would make me laugh."

That friendly one upmanship continued off the set when they made joint public appearances. For example, when appearing on *The Merv Griffin Show* (a popular daytime talk show) in 1980, they did a bit where Scolari juggled and Hanks provided narration. Then Hanks felt like he needed to up the stakes, so he suddenly announced, "I do Superman." He ran off-camera before returning to view in a dive, arms stretched in front of him as if he were flying parallel to the floor. He got a big laugh, but landed hard on his chest and hips.

When they got offstage, Scolari quietly asked him, "How bad?"

"I'm hurt," Hanks conceded.

"What are you *doing*?" Scolari thought. "But as a performer, the guy would go for it. I didn't understand how that would manifest and he would become a meaningful dramatic actor. I didn't see it coming." In fact, at the time, Hanks scoffed at serious material. "When he had touching scenes where his character was contrite about misunderstanding a girl on a date or being insensitive in a relationship, he was not happy. He would say, 'This is a sitcom! What are we doing with this? Let's do the jokes!'" Hanks and Scolari had a running gag about one of the characters getting cancer on "a very special episode of *Bosom Buddies*."

Away from the camera, Hanks and Scolari were building a bond beyond their mutual love of antic comedy. "He didn't get deeply personal with people," Scolari says. "There seemed to be this special relationship that we carved out with each other. One day he said to me, 'You might be surprised to know that when I was in high school, I used to do Bible study.' And that's not something we'd readily share in 1981. We're hip guys—most of the star actors at Paramount and ABC television are doing cocaine, smoking weed, partying, and going from troublesome relationship to troublesome relationship. Not Tom. I was so entrenched in my father's atheism that it was a nonstarter for me, but I wondered what that must be like, what kind of critical thinking you have to suspend to be a man with a god in his life." Scolari chuckles. "All these years later, I pray and meditate almost every day."

Scolari chews on a bit of toast. "In our mid-twenties, we were both really challenged to make sense of ourselves as young men."

ABC cancelled the show after two seasons, leaving Hanks and Scolari to look for acting work (and hoping it would be roles that didn't involve cross-dressing). Soon Scolari was a regular on the TV show *Newhart* while Hanks kick-started his movie career with *Splash*. "Everything he ever did was effortless," Scolari says, "but it still did not prepare me for when he began to become a star. He was not yet in a riptide, but he was in an undertow. It was difficult for me, because a false equivalency gets set up. In the extreme, you've got a Johnny Depp and Richard Grieco on *21 Jump Street*. Michael Keaton and Jim Belushi did a TV series for a while," he says, alluding to *Working Stiffs,* a short-lived 1979 CBS series where they played janitor brothers. "Who stays? Who disappears? My self-esteem was so horrible, I was always worried about disappearing. But my ego would suggest to me that I'm going to catch fire and I'll have a career like Tom's. That's never happened. *Nobody* has a career like Tom's. *Oscar winners* don't have careers like Tom's."

Many show-business relationships are intense but fleeting, forged in the long hours of a shoot but ending when the production shuts down. Hanks and Scolari stayed friends, however, getting together periodically to have lunch or play golf. Hanks was new to golf and had "no solid technique," according to Scolari. But he was a quick study, as always: when Scolari taught him to juggle, Hanks went from zero skills to being able to pass six clubs in front of a live TV audience two weeks later. One time in 1988, Scolari arranged a golf foursome with himself, Hanks, Bob Newhart, and Tom Poston (who played George Utley on *Newhart*). "Bob and Tom were thrilled to meet him"—Hanks was on the cover of *Newsweek* that week—"and he was star-struck, which was so adorable."

The group reached the tenth green at the Bel Air Country Club. "You're hitting this long shot on a par three over a ravine. And Clint Eastwood and Bill Bixby come out of the grill to perch on the rail and watch people fail." Newhart teed off first: the best golfer in the bunch, he got over the ravine cleanly. Scolari cleared the ravine but hooked the ball into a sand trap. Poston hit the ball well but a little short. Then Hanks stepped up to the tee.

"With a huge movie star and Bob Newhart watching, he just got loosey-goosey," Scolari marvels. "And he had been watching the real golfers play for nine holes—so he was starting to become like them. He made a beautiful idiot-savant golf swing that was correct in so many ways." The ball sailed over the ravine and landed on the green 215 yards away. "Look at you, you son of a bitch," Scolari said.

The moral of the story, other than "If you're hoping to get cast by Clint Eastwood in *Sully* twenty-eight years later, play your best golf"? Scolari thinks that it's this: "He gets out of his own way. He lets himself be free. And that's the ultimate acting lesson you get from Tom Hanks. Your willingness to get out of your own way and look at the greater good, that really matters more than anything else. It's a gift from God, but what we say in my neck of the woods is 'God will steer, but he won't row.'"

There were bumps along the way in their friendship: Scolari once told a reporter that he could have had Hanks' career, if he had caught a break. Hanks was offended. "I realized that he pays attention," Scolari says, wincing a little. "I have a cross to bear that I'm a Bosom Buddy who didn't go on to be an iconic figure. But I'm also his friend and confidant, so I take that very seriously. We've had big heart-to-hearts about it."

When Scolari got nominated for an Emmy in 1987, for his *Newhart* role, nobody was more excited than Hanks. "He made a huge fuss about it, calling me and cursing—'that's goddamn fucking right!' It was a win for him. To this day, he wants me to have a better career than I do. And I have a nice career! I really do—I won an Emmy [for *Girls*] last year."

Over the years, Hanks kept making sure there were roles for Scolari: he cast him as a hotel clerk in an episode of the Showtime noir anthology *Fallen Angels* and as the host of a TV variety show in *That Thing You Do!* When Hanks starred in *Lucky Guy* on Broadway, he and Scolari played rival newspaper columnists. "He tossed himself into it with a playground enthusiasm that in another actor might have been undignified," Scolari says. "I thought, 'He's going to kill this thing because he has no embarrassment.' His stagecraft developed as the rehearsals came along. He started by being big and gangly and goofy, and I'm like, 'Wow, those are some bold choices.' And he winnowed those down to give you just enough of the enthusiasm of the columnist Mike McAlary, just enough to steal your heart and break it into a million pieces."

Scolari now treasures every opportunity he gets to work with Hanks. "I didn't see how profoundly gifted he was while we did *Bosom Buddies*." But what he values even more is Hanks' friendship. At Scolari's wedding, Hanks toasted him, telling the guests that they should all try to be more like Scolari—because he never gives up. And in rough times, he made sure that Scolari lived up to that toast: "When I was in the throes of difficulty in my personal life, he'd be calling me—and then calling me back if he didn't like the way I sounded."

Now, looking back at *Bosom Buddies,* Scolari concedes, "It was just a silly TV show, really. But it starred one of America's most important actors—I don't mean in his time, I mean in all time. And I kept up. I returned serve. And it laid the foundation for this deeply sentimental, deeply personal affection that we have for each other that embarrasses me."

Scolari's forgotten about his lunch. "I continue to be ever-so-slightly a misfit, while he still makes me think he's that uber-confident, swaggering, clever, funny, larger-than-life guy, when in fact…" He lowers his voice and leans forward. "I think he's very quiet, very calm inside because he needs to be. Otherwise the life force moving through him would be nearly unmanageable—he'd tear the tops off of fire hydrants."

He continues, "I'm glad he has all the success that he has. He truly deserves it. And that's a message to all of us: Do you want all these things that you want? Earn it, deserve it. You should be worth it, you should be humbled." Scolari grins. "So I am."

THE THIRD COMMANDMENT

Embrace your passions.

• • • • • •

It's easy to tell when Tom Hanks is excited about something. He doesn't conceal his enthusiasm, or affect hipster indifference: he gets louder, his vocal pitch rises (ending up around the same place he uses for Woody in the *Toy Story* movies), sometimes he even waves his arms. When he's fired up about *Star Trek* or *The Godfather*, he hopes that you share his mania—but the underlying message is just that it's worth getting excited about *something*. These are some of Hanks' favorite things; some of them might be yours, but whatever you care about, don't be shy about it. Passionate obsessions make life worth living.

STAR TREK

Hanks grew up on the original *Star Trek*. Although he was more enthralled by the real-life space program, "My entire family worshipped at the feet of *Star Trek*. Those guys are having so much fun. Look at those phasers, man." In Hanks' neighborhood, the show was syndicated daily at 6:00 p.m.—he would often watch the reruns on the phone with a friend, engaged in a contest to see who could identify the episode and shout out its name first.

Years later, when Hanks was working on the sitcom *Bosom Buddies*, it filmed on the Paramount lot at the same time that *Star Trek II: The Wrath of Khan* (still probably the best of the Trek movies) was being made. So during a break, Hanks and his costar Peter Scolari snuck over to check out the sets. Every step of the way, they expected to get busted, but they made their way onto the soundstage. "And there was the bridge of the Starship *Enterprise* right before us," Hanks said. Captain Kirk's chair was occupied—but not by William Shatner. An electrician was working on it with a soldering gun. He looked up, noted the two visiting actors, and welcomed them to the twenty-third century: "Hey, guys."

Hanks and Scolari scuttled away and found the set of the transporter room, where they pretended to beam on and off the ship until they had to return to *Bosom Buddies* for hair and wardrobe (on their show, that usually meant wigs and dresses).

Hanks kept up with the franchise as it evolved. Patrick Stewart, who played Captain Jean-Luc Picard in *Star Trek: The Next Generation,* said that when he met Hanks in 1994, "he told me he doesn't just watch the show, he stays to read all of the credits. Tom knows the name of every Trek character, past, present, and I think future. His one regret is that he wanted to be in *Generations* or on a *Next Generation* episode, but he didn't have time."

Hanks held out hope that he might end up in the twenty-first-century reboot of the franchise. His request? "Let me play a peaceful Romulan."

SURFING

Hanks never got on a surfboard as a teenager, but he embraced the sport's soundtrack. "There was a lot of really cool stuff: the Hondells and the Rip Chords, the Chartbusters, the Trashmen, of course. Then it all disappeared into some haze."

By the time he caught a wave, he was thirty-two years old. Somewhat to his astonishment, Hanks had a home in Malibu. Producer Brian Grazer, who knew Hanks from *Splash,* said, "I remember Tom sitting on the beach, holding the sand tight in his fist, and saying, 'I can't believe this is my place.'" Since Hanks was so close to the Pacific Ocean, he tried surfing—pretty soon he was doing it four days a week.

As with many aspects of his life, he learned to embrace the uncertainty and to roll with events beyond his control. "You're out there and you get scared," he said. "Then you realize there's no reason to be scared. The waves throw you down and you're underwater. You can't fight it. You have to learn to be comfortable down there."

Once Hanks got comfortable, he found the beauty of the salt-water world, saying, "There's really a placidness to it. It's other-worldly. Then you come out of the surf and you're tired and you're cold. Recently, I was out there and there were these squadrons of pelicans flying all over the place. They looked like prehistoric beasts. They were flying low, just a few feet over your head, *vreeeem,* all around you, and these little, tiny fish—I have no idea what kind of fish they were—but hundreds, thousands, *millions* of them all around you, shimmering, and other fish feeding on them, so there's a rippling on the water, and all of a sudden, they just *jump* out all at once and chase each other in and out...A rush, one of the greatest feelings I know."

He brought a journalist (David Sheff of *Playboy*) along to the beach one day, offering him a towel and coffee from a thermos. Hanks hit the water, and Sheff sat on the sand, watching as the movie star missed wave after wave, with lots of futile paddling. He wrote, "There he was, paddling about and missing waves—his legs flailing behind him, his hair sticking up on top of his head— and it was becoming funny. I found myself laughing out loud." Sheff decided that this was the essence of Hanks: "He was doing something with the utmost sincerity and was by turns endearing, charming, silly and goofy just being himself."

Three years later, Hanks alluded to that article in a different interview. "A guy wrote about me surfing once, and he said if you were to watch this guy surfing, it would make you laugh," he said. Hanks accepted Sheff's reaction with the good humor of a man who instinctively knew how to slip on a banana peel. "I naturally make people laugh," Hanks conceded, "although not necessarily out loud."

RANDY NEWMAN

Tom Hanks and Randy Newman intersected professionally on the *Toy Story* franchise—Hanks voiced Woody, while Newman did the music. But Hanks favored the darker, weirder side of Newman, especially *Good Old Boys,* his 1974 concept album about the American South, simultaneously ironic and heart-wrenching, famous for songs like "Rednecks" and "Louisiana 1927." Hanks said, "Through each illuminating track on the record, Newman kept creating these characters. Some of them were hilarious. Some were trapped by their culture of ignorance. Some were at the mercy of the river. Some were assholes. This was not music that dealt with large, all-consuming themes like war, love, or the generation gap. Newman's music was about human behavior, how each of us are products of influences beyond our control—individual like snowflakes—and that each of us has the intellect, though not always the desire, to respect each other."

BLASTING CAPS

Running jokes can start—*should* start—with the unlikeliest of sources. For Tom Hanks and his brother Larry, it was a public service announcement recorded by baseball great Willie Mays circa 1962, when he was the All-Star centerfielder for the San Francisco Giants. In his high-pitched drawl, Mays warned kids against the dangers of…blasting caps. (You might know them better as "detonators"—they're small explosive devices designed to set off much larger explosions.) "I'd never seen blasting caps in my life!" Tom said. "But I guess there was a lot of development in the '60s going on, housing developments that kids played in."

In the minute-long spot, Mays warned kids, not always completely coherently: "Baseball is a game of playing to win but playing it safe and so is life. You can play hard, but play it safe. If you kids find anything that looks like those [image of blasting caps], don't touch them. Those are blasting caps—remember now, don't touch them. Blasting caps are used almost every place explosives are used, like in the construction work, but you can take your arms and hands and legs and save your eyes. If you see a blasting caps, remember now, don't touch them, tell the police or a fireman where it is. Have fun like I do, with those [image of bat, ball and glove] and not these [image of blasting caps]."

Tom and Larry were convinced that they would be blown up by blasting caps if they walked anywhere near a construction site. They saw the PSA maybe three times, but it was so bizarrely memorable that they quoted it endlessly, dissecting its nuances. "Have fun like I do": be one of the most famous baseball players in the world?

Larry is now a successful entomologist, on the faculty of the University of Illinois at Urbana-Champaign, where the Hanks Lab specializes in Cerambycidae (longhorn beetles). But neither Tom nor Larry ever forgot about the danger of blasting caps. For half a century, they've reliably been able to crack each other up by riffing on the PSA: "Here, this coffee is hot," one brother will tell the other. "Be careful, don't touch it."

READING

As one of America's most beloved popular historians, David McCullough was frequently approached by people who wanted to option his books for movies. He grew accustomed to the glad-handing rituals of Hollywood, and he knew the script they usually followed. First a producer would tell him how much he loved one of his books. McCullough would thank him and engage him in conversation, at which point it would become abundantly clear that the producer hadn't actually read the book.

So when McCullough agreed to meet Tom Hanks at a diner in Sun Valley, Idaho (home to the Sun Valley Film Festival), he had low expectations. Hanks told him how much he loved *John Adams* (one of two McCullough presidential biographies that have been awarded the Pulitzer Prize). "Oh yeah, here we go," McCullough thought.

Then, however, Hanks fished out his own copy of *John Adams:* well-thumbed, full of Post-its sticking out the sides. McCullough said, "He opened it to various pages, and not only had he read it, he had underlined it and made margin notes. And he wanted to go through it and ask me if various scenes were important."

McCullough granted an option on the book to Hanks; the resulting miniseries, produced by Playtone, starring Paul Giamatti and Laura Linney, aired on HBO and won so many Emmys it couldn't go through the twelve-awards-or-fewer line at the supermarket.

Hanks was a voracious reader—in our modern world, that made him not just an unusual movie star, but an unusual American. But when he got interested in a topic, he wanted to learn as much about it as he could. Sometimes that curiosity meant that he plowed through an entire book about the history of cod, or the history of the potato. (Two books that together, told the story of fish and chips.) "I could go to HBO and say, 'The most important thing ever pulled out of the ground is a potato. I see a six-hour miniseries,' and I bet you we could at least get a couple of scripts written," he joked. "I'm such a dope, I can be intrigued by anything." But he wasn't reading because he was always looking for his next miniseries—those projects naturally emerged from his book-fueled obsessions.

Hanks said, "Some of the best vacations I've had have just been in a tent, up in the mountains with a book." His reading list skewed toward history and science fiction: authors he's named as particular favorites include Anna Funder, Bill Bryson, John Hersey, James Baldwin, Maeve Binchy, Sarah Vowell, Ada Calhoun, Bill Bryson, Dave Eggers, Alan Furst, Philip Kerr, Amor Towles, and John Scalzi. (Scalzi said that being publicly name-checked by Hanks didn't seem to have any significant impact on his sales. "But it made my editor, publisher, and mom happy, which is nice.")

Five books Hanks particularly recommended: 1. *The Aspirin Age: 1919–1941,* a compendium of twenty-two essays edited by Isabel Leighton. "A collection of stories about events and personalities between 1919 and the war. You read 'The Forgotten Men of Versailles' and you just see politics in a nutshell." 2. *Stoner* by John Williams. "It's simply a novel about a guy who goes to college and becomes a teacher. But it's one of the most fascinating things that you've ever come across." 3. *Davita's Harp* by Chaim Potok. "He weaves a glamorous world out of these settings and the family superstructures and out of the social era… almost always painfully, painfully sad." 4. *A World Lit Only by Fire* by William Manchester. "You learn so much, not just about the Dark Ages but all this stuff that puts it into purely human terms." 5. *Sapiens: A Brief History of Humankind* by Yuval Noah Harari. "That fellow connected an awful lot of dots in that work. I thought the book would be a dense read, a slog, with a struggle for my brain on every page. I had a highlighter ready to mark the more pavement-thick paragraphs I'd have to go back and re-ponder. Instead, I flew through it like it was a nonfiction *The Thorn Birds*. Does that mean I'm getting smarter?"

Hanks was the kind of guy who said "I went on a reading rampage." This was inaccurate only in that it implied there were times when he wasn't devouring a book. He kept his books stacked up: three columns, each six or eight books high, a mountain that he was perpetually wearing down, one volume at a time. "And when someone tells me they finally read a book they could never crack, I take a whack out of a sense of a challenge. That's how I finally read *Moby-Dick,* the book everyone pretends to know," he bragged. "In 2011, I finally made it from 'Call me Ishmael' to 'It was the devious-cruising Rachel, that in her retracing search after her missing children, only found another orphan.'"

NUDITY

Tom Hanks is large, he contains multitudes. He's a performer who, through dint of years of hard work, has made himself into one of the most famous people on the planet. He's also an incredibly private person who prefers to reveal as little about his personal life as possible. Are you looking for a perfect real-world metaphor for the reticent exhibitionist? Hanks likes to walk around on hotel-room patios naked. (He rarely strips on film—although you might be able to catch a quick glimpse of his butt in the hot-tub scene in *Charlie Wilson's War.*) Hanks explained his hotel nudity thus: "That's as close as I can get to a feeling of anonymity and power."

THE BEATLES AND THE DAVE CLARK FIVE

On February 9, 1964, the Beatles went on *The Ed Sullivan Show,* tore up every single American living room with "She Loves You," and nothing was ever the same. Tom Hanks, just seven years old, imprinted on the Fab Four: the music, the deadpan wit, the unimpeachable cool. As an adult, he said, "If I had my way as far as fashion and style and everything else like that went, I'd look like the Beatles did on *The Ed Sullivan Show* in 1964. I'd be in a skinny-lapeled suit with a white shirt and a black tie and pointed shoes. That to me is the absolute be-all and end-all of what I think is glamour."

Not that he ever wore those clothes as a seven-year-old, but he could still fantasize about joining the band. As a kid, he imagined that he would become such a good drummer that for some reason, when Ringo left the band, John, Paul, and George would invite him to join them on tour.

Hanks loved the Beatles—but he also loved the Dave Clark Five, the British Invasion rock band who were even more frequent guests on *The Ed Sullivan Show* (making eighteen appearances, compared to the Beatles' four). He said, "I was convinced that the Dave Clark Five was *way* better than the Beatles. They had this string of very catchy, beat-heavy songs that just kept coming."

In 2008, Hanks gave an impassioned speech inducting the Dave Clark Five into the Rock and Roll Hall of Fame, talking about hearing their songs "blare from a speaker the size of the bottom of a soda can on your sister's clock radio, connecting you to a world beyond that cheap but clean rental apartment."

Transporting himself back to an elementary-school world of AM radio and individual jukeboxes in diner booths, he preached, "The result was more than just audiences filled with screaming teenagers and schoolyard arguments over who was better, this quintet or that quartet from the northern part of the Queen's Isle, no—the true product was joy. Unparalleled, unstoppable, undeniable joy, the joy to be alive, the joy to be young, the joy to get a Sunmark transistor radio for your birthday so you could carry the British Invasion with you."

THE GODFATHER

One of Hanks' favorite movies in his youth, alongside Stanley Kubrick's sci-fi epic *2001: A Space Odyssey* and *One Million Years*

B.C. (cavemen, dinosaurs, scantily clad Raquel Welch), was *The Godfather*. He noted that he became a hardcore movie fan as a teenager "at probably the best time for American movies, which was the 1970s. You can't make 90 percent of those movies now. You can't make *Five Easy Pieces*; you can't make *Chinatown*; it would be hard probably to get *The Godfather* made now."

Hanks paid tribute to *The Godfather* in *You've Got Mail* (just as he paid tribute to *The Dirty Dozen* in *Sleepless in Seattle*). In a scene that has his thumbprints all over it, he informs Meg Ryan that *The Godfather* is like the *I Ching* for men: there's always a relevant quotation. "*The Godfather* is the sum of all wisdom," he tells her online, adopting a Marlon Brando facial expression as he types. "What should I pack for my summer vacation? 'Leave the gun, take the cannoli.'"

TELEVISION

Like many kids, Hanks grew up with the TV set always on: he knew what time it was by what program was broadcasting. "Bad TV was great in our day," he complained. "Bad TV is so terrible now."

Hanks observed, "It's become cheap and profitable to merchandise the worst aspects of our nature. That's been going on in a lot of movies for a long time. It's all guns, it's all confrontation, people yelling at each other. It's all *The Jerry Springer Show*! Who knew that when Geraldo got hit in the face by a chair thrown by that Nazi that that would be the moment in TV everybody wants to emulate now?"

So Hanks became somewhat more discriminating in his television consumption, but he still watched it, both when he was working out on the treadmill and when he was hanging out with his wife. He enjoyed many of America's favorite shows, including *The Sopranos, Friends, Mad Men,* and *Breaking Bad.* He also spent a lot of time with MTV (back when it still played videos), various sporting events, and the news (BBC, CNN, NBC).

He did, however, get sucked into "three fabulous reality TV shows," all of them testosterone-heavy examples of the genre. Hanks enumerated them: "Number one: *Deadliest Catch.* Now, there is not a man in the world who doesn't feel like the biggest pussy on the planet when he watches *Deadliest Catch*…I adore *MythBusters* because it's actual science and physics. And I must say the guilty pleasure I have is *Storage Wars.* Oh my God, I love *Storage Wars.*"

RED VINES

In 1995, Tom Hanks gave a speech to the movie-theater own ers of America at their annual NATO/ShoWest convention. He explained that for him, the moviegoing experience didn't center on the quality of the sound system, or even the quality of the film. It boiled down to one question at the concessions stand: did they have Red Vines, or did they have Twizzlers?

"I've never actually tasted a Twizzler," he conceded. "I've never purchased Twizzlers. I've never opened a package of Twizzlers. I've never chewed on Twizzlers. I don't go for Twizzlers. Why? Because I am a Red Vine man. Twizzlers might be delicious, they might be delightful—hell, they might even be good for you—but I will never know. Because I am a Red Vine man."

Hanks said, "The lack of Red Vines will not ruin the movie for me, it just alters my night out. They can be showing a triple bill of *2001: A Space Odyssey, A Hard Day's Night,* and *The Best Years of Our Lives,* and what I will remember most is 'No Red Vines.'"

He grew more impassioned. "I am inspired by the works of filmmakers from all over the world. And I revel in the beautiful light that cuts through the darkness of your cinemas, and projects the human condition up there on your screens. I can be moved to tears and to laughter, and to the investment of all my emotion toward whatever story those movies tell. But when I get home, and the question is asked 'How was the movie,' I will say, 'The movie was sensational. But they didn't have any Red Vines.'"

He concluded, "My point is not to campaign for the placement of Red Vines in all the theaters in the country—although I would not be against that. I only want to say that in our shared efforts to get people into theaters, the work you do is of paramount importance—and of course, it's very important to Paramount. We keep trying to make good movies. Our efforts may fail more often than they succeed. You, however, can guarantee a good time for everyone, every night, just by keeping the floors from being too sticky, keeping that frame in focus, and by keeping the counter stocked with Red Vines."

THE FOURTH COMMANDMENT
Treat women with respect.

● ● ● ● ● ●

"I graduated from high school in 1974, so I was operating with a relatively modern view of the world," Tom Hanks said. Society hadn't magically transformed into a feminist utopia, but people were breathing the notion of gender equality into their lungs: the Equal Rights Amendment passed both houses of Congress in 1972 and was sent on to the state legislatures for ratification (it would narrowly fall short, needing approval in thirty-eight states and gaining only thirty-five). The magazine *Ms.* started monthly publication the same year; in 1973, Billie Jean King beat Bobby Riggs in a game of tennis billed as the "Battle of the Sexes."

"I never thought of my relationship to women in terms of a feminist point of view, because what's to think about it?" Hanks asked. "By the time I was an adult, I didn't have to make myself respect women."

He added, "The ideas that were put forward by the great feminist thinkers—and I don't even know who they are—were just part of my life." That was the Tom Hanks approach to feminism: he wasn't intellectually rigorous about it, but he had internalized the movement's ideals. He summarized that regular-guy ethos in two sentences: "I think I'm a gentleman, you know. But a sloppy one."

Hanks was a keen enough observer of humanity that he could see when other people were working out their gender issues. Discussing why he so often had beautiful women overcome by desire for him in his 1980s movies, despite not being much of a sex symbol himself, he posited, "There are a lot of writers who aren't very attractive but who are fairly funny and want to have sex a lot, so they write about these guys who are not very attractive, but they're funny and *do* have sex a lot. So I guess I'm the chief beneficiary of that."

Some of Hanks' favorite subjects—World War II, the space program—are too often considered to be the exclusive achievements of men. But when he covered the history of the space race in the miniseries *The Earth to the Moon*, Hanks wanted to make sure that it wasn't a big steaming mug of testosterone tea, and devoted an episode to the wives of the astronauts. "The wives are pretty much always treated as if they are somehow outside the experience of their husbands," Hanks complained. "But by and large they are equal partners. What they went through was just as arduous and just as stressful."

When Hanks made *Big*, directed by Penny Marshall, he repeatedly got asked something that surprised him: What was it like being directed by a woman? "I didn't understand the question," he said. It was premised on the notion that there was something inherently male about having the artistic ability and authority to direct a film. "Her personality was very unique," he allowed—but it wasn't as if Hanks thought her sense of humor or her indecipherable mumbling derived from her genitalia.

"The most commercially successful movies I have done have all been directed by women," he pointed out, accurately. (At the time he said that [1994], he had three movies that had grossed over $100 million in domestic box office: *Big* and *A League of Their Own*, both directed by Penny Marshall, and *Sleepless in Seattle*, directed by Nora Ephron.) "They were in charge. They made the movies!"

Asked what the male equivalent was for Hollywood actresses who aged out of leading roles, he said, "Unfairly, I don't think there is one. But here's what you can do: you can fat yourself out. If you're fat, you can't play an astronaut. Take a look at the guys who are still working; they're in really good shape. Otherwise, they become character guys. So that's possible. But it's not the same as with women. With women, the biggest problem is that there's usually a fraction of women in a movie compared with the number of men. There's only ever one girl in an action movie, and it's like, 'Hi, I'm mysterious, but I'm hot.' That is literally the template for an awful lot of women in film."

In 2017, the #metoo movement revealed just how widespread sexual harassment and assault were in almost every walk of American life—but an especially bright light shone on Hollywood. "We all left town and joined the circus," Hanks said of people in the movie business. "There's a number of reasons people go into this line of work that I'm in, essentially trying to come up with stories that people will pay to see. One is because it's ridiculous amounts of fun; two is if you can make it stick, it can be a pretty good living." But sexual predators, Hanks observed, did it because they got off on power—specifically, when they had it and their victims didn't.

Hanks said that he'd seen people, inside show business and outside it, who felt entitled by their achievements. They "love hitting on, or making the lives of underlings some degree of miserable, because they can," he said. "Somebody great said this, either Winston Churchill, Immanuel Kant, or Oprah: When you become rich and powerful, you become more of what you already are."

Taking stock of his own transgressions, as many men did, Hanks realized he needed to be careful about his language. "I know that I have participated in crude humor worthy of a baseball locker room on the set," he said (which didn't mean "locker-room talk" in the unusual sense of "bragging about sexual assault"). He had previously assumed that there was some sexual harassment in Hollywood, just because it was part of human civilization, but was stunned to learn how pervasive it was.

Hanks declared, "There's no reason not to view this as a reckoning that is going to make us a better society."

THE FIFTH COMMANDMENT

Worship in the church of baseball.

• • • • • •

Baseball is about cycles, about generations, about epic journeys that bring you back home. So the story of Tom Hanks and baseball begins with an ending.

On a Sunday afternoon in 1973, the Oakland Athletics and the New York Mets played a game of baseball. Specifically, game two of the World Series, on October 14, 1973—a wild twelve-inning game that was longer than any World Series game that came before it. Roaming the stands of the Oakland Coliseum for all twelve innings, selling bags of peanuts: a seventeen-year-old Tom Hanks. On the field, making his final appearance in center field in a major-league game: the forty-two-year-old Willie Mays. One of the greatest players ever, famous for the joy he brought to the game and how he would chase down impossible fly balls with such alacrity that his cap would fall off, Mays was a shadow of his former self on this day, even losing two balls in the blinding sun. But he also got the last hit of his career, punching a single up the middle in the twelfth inning to give the Mets the win. "I wish I'd had a little camera in my pocket at the time," Hanks said. "I'd love to have captured that moment."

Hanks is an avid baseball fan. As he put it, "Baseball is the perfect metaphor for life. Football is a metaphor for war and basketball for struggle, but baseball is life." When Hanks wanted to describe how sad his character in *Splash* would have been if he hadn't fallen in love with a mermaid, the zombie-eyed purgatory he described was "a bitter guy sitting on a park bench who doesn't even come alive for baseball season." The 1970s Oakland A's were a great team for a kid to grow up on, full of stars as colorful as their green-and-gold uniforms, like country-boy pitcher Catfish Hunter, the bombastic slugger Reggie Jackson, and the gloriously mustachioed relief pitcher Rollie Fingers. Owner Charlie Finley was a brilliant blowhard; the A's won three straight World Series. But when Hanks started working at the Great Lakes Shakespeare Festival in 1977, he was on the market for a new team, because Finley had spitefully dumped the contracts of most of Oakland's best players. (Hanks called him "that bastard Charlie Finley.")

Just up the road from the festival were the Cleveland Indians, who hadn't won the pennant since 1954. The Tribe played in the cavernous Cleveland Municipal Stadium, a multipurpose facility known as "The Mistake by the Lake." It held almost 80,000 people, but when Hanks attended games, he "would be there on a given night with 4,800." Hanks fell in love with a hapless fifth-place baseball team, and discovered that losing could be more beautiful than winning.

Rooting for a losing baseball team tests character. You learn to appreciate the elegance of a sacrifice bunt or the aesthetics of a hot dog, to savor the rituals of the game unsweetened by victory. At a moment when it wasn't obvious where Hanks' life was going to take him, this was a powerful lesson: persistence and attention could be their own rewards.

Aside from the blemish of the designated hitter, Hanks loved Cleveland baseball. "Cleveland has no built-in national affection factor, which clubs like the Dodgers and the Cubs have. People in Denver don't say, Hey, how about those Indians? But they are not completely anonymous either, like the Mariners, which even the people in Seattle don't care about. Cleveland can finish last and the local crowd still loves 'em."

"Our friendship revolved around baseball," said actor and author Clive Rosengren, who was an intern at the Great Lakes Shakespeare Festival alongside Hanks in the late '70s. "I had a Chevy Vega that I called 'Lope de Vega,' in reference to the Spanish playwright. We'd go to the ballpark, have a couple of brews, listen to Herb Score do the recap on the way home. Before the era when ushers and stadium personnel would direct you to your correct seat, we'd sit in the upper deck." Surrounded by empty seats, Hanks and Rosengren would entertain each other with impressions of the public address announcer introducing players such as Mike "The Human Rain Delay" Hargrove.

"During the summer of 1979, Cleveland had a big, burly guy by the name of Cliff Johnson," Rosengren remembered. One game, Johnson got hit by a pitch and looked as if he might charge the mound to confront the pitcher; calmer heads intervened. On the ride home, the friends listened to Score interviewing Johnson about the incident. "I don't know what everybody's getting so riled up about," Johnson protested. "I'm just playing a good, clean Christian game."

That fall, after Rosengren had returned to Minneapolis and Hanks to New York City, Rosengren got a letter from Hanks. It included an ode to baseball, titled "A Good Clean Christian Game: An Epic Poem." The fourteenth stanza (out of fifteen):

> *But soon the Cactus League will start*
> *And the pulse will grow in each fan's heart.*

We'll count our dead and shoot our lame
And head to the park for a good, clean game.

Living in New York, and later in Los Angeles, Hanks kept the Tribe close to his heart. When he had trouble falling asleep at night, one of his tricks for nodding off was "the little-boy fantasy of imagining I'm a ballplayer." Inside the imaginary game, he could calm his mind and his soul. "I always play for Cleveland. Center field. That's where the grace is."

For a time, Hanks had season tickets at Dodger Stadium— section 227, a covered area behind third base. He spent as much time at the ballpark as he could: "I don't root for the home team. I don't root for the visiting team. I root for baseball to last as long as possible. I root for extra innings. Let's go fourteen!"

Hanks' love for baseball was mostly vicarious, even as a kid, but sometimes he got a chance to run the bases. In the fall of 1985, Hanks was in Chicago filming *Nothing in Common*. One weekend, the moviemakers played a doubleheader against the cast and crew of *Ferris Bueller's Day Off* (also shooting in Chicago). They played "fatball," a local baseball variation with a large ball and no gloves. "Lots of broken fingers," Hanks said.

"I won the first game when I came up with the bases loaded and clobbered a big fat hanging pitch, high and inside—cleared the right fielder's head by a mile and just kept rolling to the fences as I circled the bases," Hanks recalled fondly.

"In a bizarre fluke, I came up with a chance to win the second game, but the catcher said 'Don't give him anything high and inside,' and I popped out in the opposite direction." The moral of the story? "You always remember your grand slams."

Jimmy Dugan, Hanks' manager character in *A League of Their Own*, hit 487 home runs, which would have ranked number four of all time in the movie's era, but none of them happened on-screen. Hanks did get to drill some line drives in a scene where he took batting practice against a pitching machine—and he spent his summer wearing a baseball uniform, being entertainingly cranky on camera, and periodically giving speeches about the philosophy of baseball. The most famous is the "there's no crying in baseball" monologue, but the one that comes closest to Hanks' own horsehide beliefs is when he tells Geena Davis, the star player who's leaving the team he manages, "Baseball is what gets inside you. It's what lights you up. You can't deny that." When she replies, "It just got too hard," he says, "It's supposed to be hard. If it wasn't hard, everyone would do it. The hard is what makes it great."

As Hanks grew older, the game remained part of the fabric of his life. In 2006, when he turned fifty, he gave himself a birthday present: a bus tour of baseball stadiums, hitting seven games in seven different parks in seven days, with stops including Baltimore, Cincinnati, and of course, Cleveland. He brought about twenty people along for the ride, including his brother, his brother-in-law, Rosenberg, Ron Howard, and Dennis Miller—and he gave everyone custom baseball jackets to commemorate the trip.

Some of the trappings had changed since the days of Lope de Vega. When Hanks goes to a game these days, he likes to sit in a private box. This not only means he can enjoy the game without being hassled for autographs—it lets him keep score on a portable typewriter. He keeps score because it helps him focus on the game, and he does it on a typewriter because, well, he likes typewriters. (Looking like a sportswriter for the *New York Herald-Tribune* circa 1955 is just a fringe benefit.)

According to Hanks, the greatest joy of typed scorekeeping comes when an opposing player strikes out, an action traditionally noted with a "K." Or in Hanks' case, "Big fat capital K, dash, parentheses, 'sit down,' period period period, backspace backspace backspace, shift-8, apostrophe apostrophe apostrophe—because that makes an exclamation point, you see—close parentheses. I think whoever it is, walking back—'Gee, I struck out, I should have caught that, I didn't get it, I struck out'—they hear me typing that up in my little box."

The Cleveland Indians have punctuated decades of futility with moments of glory. They were American League champions in 1995 and 1997, and then again in 2016. That last pennant matched them up in the World Series against the Chicago Cubs, another franchise that had spent many years in no danger of burdening themselves with the logistical complexities of hosting a championship parade. "I know the entire world and three-legged dogs and orphan children are all rooting for the Chicago Cubs," Hanks acknowledged.

Hanks himself couldn't cheer for any outcome other than a Cleveland victory, with one exception: the possibility of a seventh game, tied in the bottom of the ninth, when a high fly ball that might determine the championship would instead be interrupted by divine intervention. As Hanks detailed the scenario: "Armageddon, four horsemen of the Apocalypse, earthquakes, lightning, toads raining down. God brings the world to an end because he can't quite root for whichever team." This was weirdly prescient. The World Series actually went to seven games, and it was tied in the bottom of the ninth, at which point it was interrupted by weather (albeit an ordinary rainstorm). In the tenth inning, the Cubs won and the Apocalypse did not happen— bad news for Indians supporters, good news for fans of human existence.

It ends with a beginning: teenage Tom Hanks is watching Willie Mays play in the World Series. They have more in common than either of them could have imagined. Years later, Hanks mused, "You know, the sporting analogy for an actor is that you're the center fielder. You're standing out there and you start moving on the windup. If the batter's swinging, you're making a judgment on the speed of the pitch. Even with just that, you have this innate sense of where the ball will go. It's all so fast and instinctive. The difference between leaning the right way and the wrong way is the difference between Willie Mays making a catch or not." The contradiction of baseball is the contradiction of Hanks' own life as an actor: "You have to be completely prepared and completely instinctive."

Interlude

RANDOM ACTS OF HILARITY
AND KINDNESS

WHEN ACTOR SCOTT SHEPHERD FIRST MET TOM HANKS, on the set of *Bridge of Spies,* the actor loomed larger than he had expected—and by more than a few inches. "He seemed like a Macy's Thanksgiving Day Parade balloon," Shepherd said. "He's like an American superhero—it took a while to realize he's a regular guy."

Shepherd watched Hanks in action, being friendly with the other actors, accommodating to total strangers, and generally finding ways to make his immediate vicinity a good place to be. When Hanks senses that strangers want to approach him but are too nervous, he'll often walk up to them instead and introduce himself, and find a way to be funny or generous. Sometimes he's both: sharing a joke can bring more joy than sharing a selfie. "He's developed this amazing grace about it," Shepherd said. "He's perfected the art of taking well the joke of being Tom Hanks."

Tom Hanks has over fifteen million followers on Twitter, and another four-million-plus on Instagram. With this humongous audience, what does he post again and again? Photos of solitary gloves, lost on the street someplace. A typical caption: "Single at night. Ain't right." Or: "Beside the road. In the gravel, weeds and rocks. A workman's glove. Was it lost? Or tossed? Think about THAT!"

Hanks joked that the posts, each one individually signed "Hanx," constituted "the absolute best use of worldwide social media."

Sometimes, he's branched out to abandoned umbrellas, stray shoes, or lost keys—and once in a New York City park, he found the student ID of a young woman named Lauren, a psychology major at Fordham. Lauren had dropped the card when she pulled out her phone to take pictures of the fall foliage. Hanks tweeted a picture of the ID (with his thumb over Lauren's last name), telling her to get in touch with his office if she wanted it back. Lauren didn't have a Twitter account, but one of her professors did—so he was the one to alert her that her lost ID had gone viral. She got the ID back with a note from Hanks, advising her, "Hold on to this!"

Usually, Hanks didn't have any expectations that his posts would lead people to reclaim their lost property. "It's really kind of a visual haiku of separation, loss, maybe freedom, maybe loneliness in the big city," he explained.

"A lost glove looking for its mate, isn't that just the way of the world? Aren't we all just lost gloves?" he asked. "If we're a left hand aren't we looking for our right hand?"

Ken Levine, one of the screenwriters of *Volunteers,* crossed paths with Hanks periodically after the movie's release. "We were at a restaurant in Westwood and I noticed that Tom and Rita were sitting in a booth across the restaurant. I didn't want to disturb them, but when Rita got up, she spotted me—'Tom, it's Ken'—and they walked across the restaurant. We were helping my daughter, who was in high school at the time, with some history paper, so Tom and Rita stood there, pitching in with ideas on U.S. history."

Another time, Levine and his writing partner David Isaacs were overseeing a couple of young writers who had come up with a TV pilot, and were meeting them at the Coffee Bean and Tea Leaf in Century City to give them feedback. "This guy comes up to us in a baseball cap: 'Ken! David!' It was Tom Hanks." Levine observed, "They took our notes a lot more seriously after that."

Tom Hanks once said awards "are kind of like the door prizes at a pancake breakfast—if they're going to give them away, it would be nice to have one." And he's gotten his fair share, including four Golden Globes, eight Emmys, the ShoWest Convention's Box Office Star of the Decade honor, the Kennedy Center honors, and the Presidential Medal of Freedom. And, of course, two Academy Awards (for *Philadelphia* and *Forrest Gump*)—he's been known to dress the Oscar statuettes up in doll clothes so they look like Santa Claus.

Hanks demonstrated his awards-show sangfroid at the Golden Globes in 2018: he didn't win the award he was nominated for (Best Performance by an Actor in a Motion Picture—Drama, for playing Ben Bradlee in *The Post*), but somebody snapped a photo of him delivering a tray of martinis to the other people at his table, including Steven Spielberg. "I was at the table and I was told to get martinis," Hanks said, as if he were occupying a natural spot on the actor/waiter continuum. "It was like I was one of those truckers on mountain roads with a load full of nitroglycerin. I had never been more nervous carrying something through a crowded room."

Hanks' most entertaining award-show moment actually came after the cameras stopped rolling at the 2012 Emmys. Having won an award for the Playtone-produced political movie *Game Change,* he didn't just stick it on a mantel—he got a roll of packing tape, attached the trophy to the hood of his Lincoln Town Car, and then took Emmy for a joyride.

Joe Mantegna said, "My show, *Criminal Minds,* I'm number one on the call sheet, you understand what that means?" (We do: it means that he's the top-billed talent on the hit CBS show, and so the shooting schedule tends to flow around his availability and needs.) "We do a reading before every episode. We'll still be shooting the previous episode, but at lunchtime, we gather in this big trailer, bring in the cast, including the guest cast, and we do a read-through of the next script." Often, that's the only chance everyone on the show gets to meet each other—if you don't have scenes with a particular actor, you probably won't see them again that week. So Mantegna makes a point of walking around the table, greeting everyone and welcoming the newcomers to the show.

"This one young guy comes up and says, 'I want to tell you how much we appreciate that you did that.'" Mantegna thanked him, told him he'd been doing it for the eleven years he'd been on the show, and said that he learned it from Tom Hanks, when Mantegna made a guest appearance on *Bosom Buddies* (playing a sheik at a casino in Monte Carlo). Even at the beginning of his career, Hanks was a good host. "He walked around the table at the read-through and greeted everybody. Jesus, he even said hello to the extras. You've got to be number one on the call sheet to pull that off—you set the tone. Show business, we're all blessed to be doing it. The hours are tough, the new people are nervous, so let's start off right." Mantegna laughed. "He was young, but he was one of the good guys—good to the point that I learned something from him."

Tom Hanks was visiting Los Altos, California, in early 2015 for the most Hanksish of reasons: he was taking his son Truman, a student at nearby Stanford University, to a local shop to get his typewriter repaired. (Once he got to the shop, Los Altos Business Machines, he ended up buying two vintage Smith-Coronas for himself.) As he walked down the sidewalk, he passed three Girl Scouts—Addyson Andrade, Claire Chen, and Anushka Srinivasan—who recognized him and ran down the sidewalk after him.

Asked if he was Tom Hanks, he acknowledged that he was. He posed for pictures, bought four boxes of cookies, and donated an additional twenty dollars. When another family walked by, they asked if they could take a picture with him, too. Hanks told them, "Only if you buy cookies from these young ladies."

Benedict Taylor, the British actor who costarred with Hanks in the 1986 movie *Every Time We Say Goodbye*, filmed in Israel, remembered:

Whenever I go on location, I really try to immerse myself in the place that I am. So I hired a car while we were filming, and every evening I'd head out into the desert and visit places. There's a wonderful place called St. George's Monastery right near Jerusalem—it's this Christian Greek Orthodox monastery, clinging to the side of this ravine with these cave dwellings where the Coptic monks almost entomb themselves, for years at a time.

One day, Tom said to me, "Hey, Ben, where do you go in that little car?" I said, "Well, I collect some firewood, I go into the desert, I make a little fire, and sometimes I make a bit of flatbread in the sand, and sometimes I make some coffee, and I watch the sun go down. And I listen to the Bedouin women ululate, they do that *woooooo* thing in the distance. I watch the stars come out and it's a nice way to unwind after a day's filming."

He said, "Do you mind if I come?"

I said, "Sure, Tom, jump in. Bring a coat, it gets colder later."

So we drove off an hour or two to an absolutely beautiful spot in the desert and we made a little fire and we were having a nice chat. But as the light started to dwindle and the sounds of the desert started to increase, the conversation came round to talking about how Americans in particular were beginning to feel increasingly nervous in Arab countries because things had changed internationally.

You know what it's like when you're a kid and you're telling stories—the more you tell these fearful tales, the more you scare yourself. And suddenly we'd got to that point in the evening where it was getting quite dark and the sounds seemed to be almost closing in. At first we didn't say anything, like we were in denial. But it became apparent that we were surrounded by Bedouin voices and they were getting closer.

All of a sudden, we heard these footsteps really close, behind some nearby rocks. We froze and went very quiet. There was crunching on the gravel as it got closer. And out of the gloom came this large, dark, hooded shape. We held our breaths for a moment as he stepped into the firelight, and then there was this Swedish voice: "Hello, I wonder if you can help me? I'm a Swedish ornithologist and I've lost my way."

We laughed our heads off and said, "You don't know how scared you made us. Come and sit down." So we shared the fire, and talked about bird-watching for half an hour, and then we gave him a lift back to Jerusalem.

Before he directed a feature film, Hanks went behind the camera for a few TV shows, including the network-television adaptation of *A League of Their Own*. In his assigned episode, the script had a plot point where a chimp was killed by a batted ball—which at least had the virtue of novelty. Hanks told the showrunners, Lowell Ganz and Babaloo Mandel, that when he met Italian film legend Federico Fellini at the Oscars and described the episode to him, the director told him a story about the time one of his movies featured the death of a monkey. Preview audiences in Milan were dismayed by the untimely simian death; Fellini insisted he couldn't let Hanks make the same mistake. The whole story was pure fictional monkeyshines, but Hanks sold it so convincingly, Ganz and Mandel changed the script. The kicker, according to Ganz, was that after the revisions, the episode worked "a lot better!"

In the spring of 2013, Adam Ryon was visiting his friend Dustyn Gulledge backstage at the Broadhurst Theatre—Gulledge was lucky enough to be making his Broadway debut, acting in *Lucky Guy* alongside Tom Hanks. "I feel this presence behind me: Tom Hanks is standing right there," Ryon said. "If you consider yourself to be a true New Yorker, you don't allow yourself to get starstruck. You just ignore them, but I lost full control of my body and mind. He walks in, Dustyn introduces us, and he puts his arm around my shoulder and says, 'Well, any friend of Dustyn is a friend of mine.' In my mind, I'm thinking: *I'm friends with Tom Hanks. We're best friends.* It was a brief encounter, but he was so gracious, so friendly—I walked away from that night with the biggest grin."

Pop singer Carly Rae Jepsen, most famous for her blockbuster 2012 single "Call Me Maybe," was worried about a hummingbird. She was attending the wedding of her manager; the hummingbird had flown into one of the tents, and a guest was wielding a broom, trying to guide it to freedom. Having had a couple of drinks, Jepsen was perhaps overly worried about the hummingbird's safety—which is how she found herself running across the tent, grabbing Tom Hanks' arm, and shouting "Don't hurt the bird!"

Jepsen said, "We laughed about it, and we kind of had a

cocktail and talked for the rest of the night. So it was all good, but it was an awkward beginning, for sure." The groom, Scooter Braun, a friend of Hanks, also managed Justin Bieber—which meant that the Biebs posted video of Hanks, in a yarmulke and a prayer shawl, singing along at the wedding reception to Montell Jordan's 1995 single "This Is How We Do It."

Some months later, Braun and Hanks were having dinner, and Braun mentioned that since Jepsen's next single, "I Really Like You," had a sweaty-palm teenage-crush vibe, they were thinking of doing something totally unexpected for the video, like having it star an older man. "Why didn't you guys ask me?" Hanks said. "I would do it."

Which is how Hanks ended up in New York City on a freezing cold winter day, lip-synching lyrics like "who gave you eyes like that?", walking down the street fist-bumping passersby and autographing a Ping-Pong paddle, and pretending to text with Jepsen in the back of a taxi. (Fun detail: she sends him the emoji for "Run Forrest run.") The video ended with a choreographed routine on the streets of Soho—the most dancing Hanks had done on-screen since *Bachelor Party*—where he was joined by Jepsen, Bieber, and about thirty dancers.

The single barely scraped into the Top 40 in the United States, but it was huge in some other countries, including Japan, South Africa, and Scotland—where it went all the way to number one.

Richard Kaufman, a violinist and symphony conductor, was given the job of teaching Hanks how to play violin well enough that he could look like a professional on-screen in *The Man with*

One Red Shoe. They lived a few blocks away from each other in the Studio City neighborhood of Los Angeles, so every day, Hanks would come over for his lesson. "It's not easy to teach somebody to do something physically they've never done. You can't do it unless they're really committed," Kaufman said.

There were advantages to having Hanks as a neighbor: "One night he called me and said he had a telescope in his backyard— he and his kids were looking up at something. He said 'You got to come over.' I threw my clothes on, ran over to his backyard, and stood there looking through the telescope."

For the movie, Hanks specifically needed to be able to simulate playing Rimsky-Korsakov's symphonic suite "Scheherazade," and to do it well enough that he could keep going when the seams on his jacket busted. But he had a few requests of his own. First he wanted to learn the themes to *My Three Sons* and *Leave It to Beaver.*

"Most of the time when I work with an actor, they're miming what they're doing," Kaufman said. "In fact, you put soap on the hair of the bow so people don't have to suffer through the sound." But because the movie was filming in Washington, DC, and Tom's brother Larry (who played guitar) was working on his PhD in entomology just outside the city at the University of Maryland, Tom said, "I'd love to play something with my brother when I go to Washington." So Kaufman got a Beatles songbook. "We picked one of the easier pieces, 'Yesterday' or 'Michelle,' and Tom actually learned to play the song. And when we went to Washington, he visited his brother and they played music together."

*   *   *

When Tim Meadows came to 30 Rockefeller Plaza for a job interview with Lorne Michaels at the *Saturday Night Live* office—he
hadn't officially joined the cast yet—Tom Hanks was hosting,
so they met on the floor of Studio 8H. "Lorne introduced me: I
was like, 'Wow, Tom Hanks!'" Meadows said. Then, when he was
talking with Michaels in his office, three of the writers—Conan
O'Brien, Bob Odenkirk, and Robert Smigel—interrupted so they
could run through the script of the "Five-Timers Club" sketch,
which involved Steve Martin and Paul Simon welcoming Hanks
to the elite tier of *SNL* hosts. "Somebody wasn't there to read one
of the roles, so Lorne asked me to read it in the room," Meadows said. "So it was me, Steve Martin, Tom Hanks, Paul Simon,
Conan, Robert, Bob Odenkirk, and Lorne Michaels. And this was
my first time; I didn't even know I had the job." Hanks, who was
seeing Meadows for the second time in the same day, told him,
"Hey, Tim, you're moving up pretty quick in show business!"

New York City cabdriver Manny Anzalota, cruising down Park
Avenue, heading back to the garage after a shift ended, saw a man
hailing him: red scarf, eyeglasses, receding hairline. Anzalota
pulled over and asked the man where he wanted to go. The
answer was Seventy-Fourth Street; Anazalota regretfully told him
that was too far away.

"Thanks anyway," the man said, walking away.

Anzalota felt bad because "hey—I got a conscience." So he
called the man back to the cab, turned on the meter, and headed
uptown. His passenger got in and was immediately chatty: "all

excited, all animated, and he's talking about all these things." But he had a cap pulled down low, so Anazalota couldn't see his eyes. Eventually Anzalota figured out what you already know: the man was Tom Hanks. So at the next red light, Anzalota turned around in his seat, looked him in the eye, and screamed: *"Wiiiiiiilllsssooooooon!"*

Hanks burst into uproarious laughter. The name of the volleyball in *Cast Away* is the single thing that strangers shout at him most on the street, but rarely is it done at such close quarters with such panache. He noticed that Anzalota was wearing a Ferrari shirt and cap, and for the rest of the ride, called him "Mr. Ferrari."

At Seventy-Fourth Street, Hanks and Anzalota took a quick selfie together, which seemed like the end of the story. Except that over the next few weeks, Anzalota told the tale of his Hanks encounter to everyone who stepped into his cab, which was how he found out that he was picking up lots of passengers with random connections to Hanks: people who worked with him, people who had acted alongside him. In each case, he gave them the same instructions: "Tell Mr. Hanks that Mr. Ferrari says hello."

One day, Anzalota got a text from one of those passengers. It said that Hanks wanted to invite him to see him in his Broadway show. "So I bring my lady to the show, and we get to go backstage and everything, and after the show we're waiting for him in his dressing room, and he walks in and screams, 'Mr. Ferrari!'" Anzalota said. "Can you believe that story? And you wanna know the craziest thing? The name of his show was *Lucky Guy*. How crazy is that? 'Cause that was me. A lucky guy!"

*   *   *

Amy Poehler set up the joke while hosting the Golden Globes, deliberately mispronouncing Tom Hanks' name as "Tam Honks." In the audience, Hanks played along for the camera with a dismayed reaction shot and a mouthed "Really?"

A year and a half later, a fan asked Hanks for an update on the alleged feud, and the actor was happy to concoct one: "I haven't spoken to Amy since we broke up in the '80s. We shared a small apartment in Eagle Rock for about six months. Before I met Rita, of course. Amy didn't like my dog, and she stole some of my good records when she moved out (without so much as a goodbye). I'm happy for her success, but would not walk across the street to say hello to May Epolher, as I know her." Hanks concluded that Poehler still owed him copies of Jackson Browne's *Running on Empty* and The Who's *Live at Leeds*.

Hanks costarred in *Nothing in Common* with the *Honeymooners* star Jackie Gleason. "The Great One," as Gleason liked to be known, was sixty-nine and suffering from terminal cancer—it was his last movie. He expected to be treated like the legend that he was, so when the air-conditioning in his trailer broke down on a hot summer day, he was not a happy man. (His trailer was a Winnebago that served as a dressing room on wheels.) Since it would take hours to get a replacement, time during which Gleason would be too cranky to work, Hanks volunteered to give up his own trailer.

Director Garry Marshall said, "Besides being a nice guy, Tom was not one of those actors who used his trailer like a bear uses a cave in winter. Tom didn't really care much about his trailer. He preferred to spend time in between scenes throwing a ball around with the crew."

Gleason, however, didn't want to accept Hanks' offer. "I don't want to take the kid's trailer," he grumped. "He'll be a star someday. That's not the way things work."

So Marshall and Hanks agreed on a plan: the prop department painted over Hanks' name on his door. Then a Teamster drove Hanks' Winnebago around the block; rolling back onto the lot, he announced, "I have a new air-conditioned trailer for Mr. Gleason!"

"Jackie was happy," Marshall said. "Tom was happy. And we could all go back to work."

A hungry movie set is an unhappy movie set, so Tom Hanks established a tradition of providing a special meal for his coworkers once a week. "It's amazing," Frank Darabont, director of *The Green Mile,* said. "On Friday evenings a couple of sushi chefs would show up. Or the In-N-Out Burger truck. You were looking at well over one hundred people, so it wasn't cheap. More than the generosity, though, was the thoughtfulness."

On *Bridge of Spies,* for a cold all-night shoot on the titular Glienicke Bridge in Berlin, Hanks hired a sausage vendor for the night, so everybody had free (and hot!) sausages. The production was using fake snow for the shot. "It's made of paper," actor Scott Shepherd said, "but it's so convincing, you feel like your feet are wet." Some German extras were playing the soldiers on the western side of the bridge, manning a booth at the checkpoint. The booth had a huge perk: there was a small heater. "In between takes, the local German guys were in this super-warm booth," Shepherd said. Meanwhile, the principal actors made do with heat packs tucked into their costumes. "Finally, there was one time, just one time, when Tom told those guys they had to get out of the booth and let us sit in there," Shepherd said. "It was always fun when he asserted his higher status because he so rarely did it."

The actors were standing around silently when one of them— Shepherd thinks it was Mark Rylance—said "Don't be a cunt, Scott." Shepherd cracked up, because he hadn't been talking, or doing anything at all—the randomness of Rylance's outburst was what made it funny. Hanks, having missed the moment, asked what Rylance had said, and Shepherd told him.

Later on, Hanks repeated the joke, trying to turn the line into a running bit. Out of nowhere, he told Shepherd, "Don't be a Cub Scout."

"He had misheard what the joke was!" Shepherd said. "It had gone through the Tom Hanks filter and become more G-rated and All-American."

Fame is intoxicating but weird, even in small doses. Tom Hanks got the celebrity multivitamin, and early in his career, he griped about its side effects—when a teenage boy approached him for an autograph in front of a reporter in 1987, Hanks glared at him and said, "I don't usually do this. If I give my autograph to one person, I have to give it to everybody, and everything is ruined." He signed the autograph anyway.

As the years went by, Hanks came to accept the rough justice of twenty-first-century American celebrity: he got to have a pretty great life, but in return, people would not only act like they knew him, but like he owed them something. He was friendly to strangers, finding ways to disarm them before they could get flustered. Asking only that people respect his space when he was spending time with his family, he reported, "Ninety-nine percent of the people respect it very much and one percent of the people are the biggest assholes in the world."

Since Hanks had figured out that nobody wanted to hear him complain, it fell to the people around him to explain just how surreal his life could get and marvel at how he maintained his grace in the eye of the hurricane. "I've traveled with Tom," his brother Jim said, "and I see the crap that he goes through. But he's incredibly gracious about it."

Even Leonardo DiCaprio was flabbergasted by Hanks' public life. DiCaprio, *one of the most famous people in the world,* told Hanks, "I often wonder what it must be like for you, because people view you as so personable and such a nice guy they must think they can come up to you all the time and say whatever the hell they want."

Sean McGinly had only a brief working relationship with Tom Hanks—he directed *The Great Buck Howard,* a 2008 movie that featured a cameo by Hanks and a lead performance by his son Colin Hanks. He reported:

> One of the most surprising things about working with Tom Hanks was how many people got in touch with me over the years because they wanted a favor from Tom Hanks— despite the fact that I had such a thin connection to him.

It was numerous people from all walks of life. Some had a charity event they wanted me to tell Tom Hanks about. Others had scripts or books or manuscripts or movies. There were even people with real estate deals. Some were people I knew. Others were distant acquaintances or friends of friends of my parents. Some were total strangers who tracked me down online or who I randomly met at film festivals. At one point two filmmakers from Norway or Sweden got in touch to ask me if I'd be interested in directing a movie they had set up. But they wanted Tom Hanks to play the psychotic villain in this movie (which was ridiculous and bizarre) and thought I might be able to get the script to him. When I told them that Tom would never play this part and I would never show it to him regardless, they disappeared.

I've worked with Malkovich and Paul Rudd and Emily Blunt and other great people and nothing like this ever happened.

And people were always a little put off when I told them I couldn't approach Tom with any of their ideas. Several times these people actually got angry with me. The feeling was that Tom Hanks was their friend—they were sure that if he just knew about whatever thing they were pushing, he would surely be interested and help them. And I was standing in the way.

This kind of thing happened a lot, to the point that I began to expect it when a strange person seemed interested in me. And it made me think that it must be kind of exhausting to be Tom Hanks.

Hanks shrugged it all off with a smile, believing that most people were happy with a handshake and a few quick words. "By and large, that's all everybody wants: they just want some validation that we were in the same room at the same time," he said. Despite getting pestered sometimes and being unable to visit a shopping mall, Hanks refused to "walk around with a phalanx of bodyguards. It's just no way to live."

Even after a childhood spent on a carousel of divorce, Tom Hanks was a big fan of marriage—so long as you find the right person. Although other people marveled at the longevity of his union with Rita Wilson (thirty years and counting!) the couple mostly hung out with other married couples, and he said that their domestic life seemed entirely ordinary to him.

When he could, Hanks gave his blessing to young couples crossing the matrimonial threshold. "I think that anybody who gets married is partaking in an act of bravery," he said.

In 2008, Hanks was on location in Rome, filming a scene for *Angels & Demons* outside the historic Pantheon (a church, formerly a second-century temple, with an awe-inspiring dome inside). Good news for Columbia Pictures, bad news for a twenty-seven-year-old British woman named Natalia Moore, who needed to get to her own wedding at the Pantheon but was blocked by the film crew.

Hanks spotted Moore in her wedding dress and stopped filming so he could escort her (and her father) to the steps of the Pantheon. As they walked across the Piazza della Rotonda, Hanks draped her dress over one arm so it wouldn't get dirty. He told

Moore she looked stunning and asked her father whether the groom was a suitable husband. At the steps of the Pantheon, they parted ways—Hanks told her, "I've got a film to make and you have to go and get married."

A decade later, on a lark, Kristen Jerkins and Joe Dobrin sent Hanks an invitation to their wedding in Nashville—he didn't show up, but he did type out a note of regret explaining that he would be stuck in Los Angeles rehearsing for a play, and enclosed a Polaroid picture where he held up their wedding invitation. The note concluded: "congratulations you kooky kids. Throw deep."

While on tour for his book *Uncommon Type* in 2017, Hanks finished a Q&A session and told a packed house in Austin, Texas, that he had a question of his own. He produced a slip of paper and said the question was actually on behalf of a man in the audience, Ryan McFarling, for Nicki Young. "Nicki, will you marry me?" Hanks asked.

McFarling produced a ring and Young said yes. Hanks told the crowd, "We can all see this is a very lucky man. We can also see that she could do a little better."

In 2016, Hanks was out for a jog in Central Park when he spotted a couple, Elisabeth and Ryan, posing for their wedding pictures. He cruised into the frame, photographer Meg Miller said: "He leaned in close as he took off his hat and sunglasses and said, 'Hi, I am Tom Hanks,' while reaching out to shake the groom's hand."

"It was pretty surreal," the groom reported. "I was shell-shocked."

Hanks offered to administer the couple's vows, explaining that he was an ordained minister, but was informed that they had just completed the ceremony. So he posed for some photos—the newlyweds in their finery, Hanks in shorts and a hoodie—and jogged on.

The previous year, Hanks actually had officiated at the wedding of Allison Williams and Ricky Van Veen. Williams asked Rita Wilson—who played her mother on *Girls*—to sing at the wedding, and mentioned they were still looking for an officiant. "We just wanted someone with charisma, who's good at reading a crowd, who has, like, gravitas," Williams said.

Wilson volunteered Hanks, who'd spent thirty-five dollars to become ordained. "If you want to call me the Right Reverend Tom Hanks, I think you should," he joked.

Hanks came through in front of a crowd that included Bruce Springsteen, Katy Perry, and Seth Myers. "He should marry everyone," Williams said. "He is the most ideal officiant of all time. As good as we thought he was gonna be, he was just so great. He was so excellent."

The Right Reverend Tom Hanks was down with this new career plan, joking, "I'm for rent. If you can afford the honorarium, I'll be there for ya."

Hanks knew that love can crash and burn—and that it was worth seeking out anyway. Asked if he agreed that there was no difference between a wise man and a fool when they fall in love, he flipped the jaundiced premise of the question on its head and found the bliss concealed within. His answer: "Both have beaten the odds."

THE SIXTH COMMANDMENT

Use the right tool for the job.

• • • • • •

Consider a letter from Tom Hanks. Not an email, but a physical document—and one that was composed on a typewriter. Using a typewriter was unusual for most people in the twenty-first century, but for Tom Hanks, it was part of his daily routine.

At the top, the letter was dated "31 August 2 o 1 7," with extra spaces separating the numbers in the years, emphasizing the moment it was written. The letter was on Hanks' personal stationery: the bottom had his name printed on it, while the top was emblazoned "PLAYTONE" and "Film Television Music Typewriters." While those four words were presented as the areas where his production company has chosen to do business, they could just as easily be considered as the pillars of Hanks' belief system.

The heyday of typewriters lasted a hundred years, from the late nineteenth century to the late twentieth century. Tom Hanks wasn't a Luddite—he owned and used computers—but he didn't believe in casting aside a well-made machine when it remained an ideal tool for many writing tasks. As the years passed, he became Earth's leading advocate for typewriters having value in a word-processor world.

"There's something about the clean mechanics of the hammer striking," Hanks said. "This ribbon rises up. The hammer strikes it. It goes through. It's quaint. It makes you think a bit slower and strike a little more definite. So you end up, like, composing, so it comes off as a brand of poetry almost. You don't have the added bonus of, like, going up to a different font and italicizing. The most you can do it capitalize and underline and put in quotes."

Hanks still did as much of his writing as possible on typewriters. When he pressed a wrong key, he didn't use Liquid Paper, Wite-Out, or Ko-Rec-Type to remove evidence of the mistake; he overstruck it with the letter that he intended and moved onward. The flaws in the document—like the capital B raised a half-step above the rest of the line—were the fingerprints that provided proof of its human Hanksian origin. The time he spent writing three paragraphs was an evanescent moment that would flicker away, but he left behind physical evidence.

Writing on a typewriter is a different experience than writing on a word processor, and not just because of the pleasing tactile details: the percussive clack of the keys, the emphatic thud of a carriage return, the periodic chime of a bell. Without spell check or the ability to cut and paste chunks of text (unless you actually use scissors and glue), the typewriter enforces a forward momentum, one that's conducive to the creative state of flow. That's true even when the typewriter is being used for something mundane, like a letter to an aspiring biographer, a grocery list, or a thank-you note.

"I hate getting email thank-yous from folks," Hanks said. " 'Hey, we had a great time last night.' 'Hey, I really appreciate it.' Really? You appreciated it so much you took seven seconds to send me an email? Now, if they take seventy seconds to type me out something on a piece of paper and send it to me, well, I'll keep that forever."

That was a quiet evangelism, one that led to people who wanted to correspond with Tom Hanks using a typewriter for the first time in decades (pro tip: many public libraries have a typewriter stashed in a corner) and experiencing that state of writerly flow for themselves. Some people went to greater lengths: when the producers of the *Nerdist* podcast invited Hanks to do an interview, they typed a letter on a Smith-Corona portable, left it on the platen, and shipped him the whole shebang as a "typewriter-o-gram."

Hanks responded (with a few typos), "Just who do you think you are to try to *bribe* me into an appearance on your 'thing' with this gift of the most fantastic Corona Silent typewriter made in 1934? You are out of your minds if you think…that I…wow, this thing has great action…and this deep crimson color…Wait! I'm not so shallow as to…and it types nearly silently…Oh, OKAY! I will have my people contact yours.…"

Sometimes the evangelism was louder: Hanks gave away typewriters from his collection to friends who expressed even casual interest in using one. But if he visited them and found that the typewriter had reverentially been placed on a shelf as an art object, he would insist that they haul "that bad boy" down, put it on a desk, and make it part of their life. "I've tried to foster a community of typewriting people," he confessed. "It hasn't quite worked."

Doug Nichol, who directed the compelling documentary *California Typewriter* (which prominently features Hanks), witnessed an hour Hanks spent with some troubled high school kids in Colorado (he was visiting the Telluride Film Festival on behalf of *Sully*): "He said, 'If you give me your name and address, I will send you a typewriter.' And he sent every one of those kids a typewriter with a typewritten note."

Hanks could spare the machines. At his peak, he owned close

to three hundred typewriters, 90 percent of them in perfect working order—"let's call it a harmless vice, shall we, as opposed to an addiction," he said—although he gave away so many that he reduced the collection to about 180. Looked at from a certain angle, the Playtone offices were a typewriter storage facility with a film production company attached. Hanks had his favorite machines—there was a Smith-Corona he was particularly fond of—but he rotated through them to keep as many as possible in regular use.

"My desire is to eventually only have about thirty typewriters scattered across the country," he said. "There's not a lot of reasons to own a typewriter, which means there's absolutely no reason to own more than three. After that, man, it's overkill. I overkilled it a long time ago."

Hanks had reasons for choosing typewriters as his medium of excess. He rhapsodized, "There is a wonderful way to spend time, typing. You get to think about it. You get to romantically sit back and ponder what your next words are going to be, and that is a pleasant tactile action. It actually turns writing or composing into a very specific physical process that has a soundtrack to it." Hanks did what he could to promote those aesthetics—he developed and gave away the "Hanx Writer" app, which simulated a typewriter on your phone and encouraged users to find "a cadence and rhythm that is yours alone, be it bang bang, KLOCK KLOCK-KLOCK, or tix-tix tix-tix." But he knew he was recruiting soldiers, ten fingers at a time, for a battle that already had been lost.

"The truth is no good typewriters are ever going to be made again," Hanks admitted. "No matter how much of a premium you're going to want to pay for them, no businessman in the world is going to open up a factory and say 'We are going to make the finest typewriter that will last absolutely forever and anybody who is willing to pay the seventeen thousand dollars for a Hanks typewriter, they're going to pass it down....' No. You might do that with a watch, there's always going to be a new iPad that's coming down the pike, there's always going to be good cars and things like that, but no one is ever going to make the great typewriter ever, ever, ever again. Boo-hoo."

Tom Hanks' typewriter obsession had an origin story, like Hal Jordan finding the ring that turned him into Green Lantern. In the summer of 1978, when Hanks was working at the Great Lakes Shakespeare Festival, hoping that he might be able to make a life as an actor, he took his malfunctioning Sears portable typewriter to a local repair shop. "An old German man said, 'I vill not fix zis typewriter. For zis is not a typewriter, it is a toy!'" Instead, he sold Hanks a used Hermes 2000 typewriter, made in Switzerland a couple of decades before. "This thing, it was the Mercedes-Benz of portable typewriters," Hanks remembered. "It was smooth, it was crisp, it had this fabulous action on it. Everything about it was solid. It had a tension bar on the keys so you could make them either really firm or really light, and that was my typewriter for the longest time."

Hanks fictionalized that encounter in his short story "These Are the Meditations of My Heart." He set the action in the present day and made his narrator a young woman who's recently split with a boyfriend she calls "the Knothead," but the machine that uncages the poetry inside her is still a Hermes 2000. "Along with cuckoo clocks, chocolate, and fine watches, the Swiss once produced the finest typewriters in all the world. In 1959, they made this one. The Hermes 2000. The apex, the state of the art in manual typewriters, never to be bested," the old man at the repair shop tells her. "The typeface is Epoca. Look how straight and even it is. Like a ruled line. That's the Swiss."

The story appeared in Hanks' 2017 collection of short fiction, *Uncommon Type*. The book's eighteen stories were united thematically in that each of them contained a cameo appearance by a typewriter, whether it was the teenager waking up in the same room as a busted Olivetti-Underwood or the single mother who spots her astronomer neighbor tinkering with a nineteenth-century model on his backyard picnic table.

Hanks was an engaging writer with a keen eye for the foibles of humanity. His tone wobbled at times and the book could have been pithier—issues that he would have grown out of if he had spent the bulk of his professional life writing instead of acting. When he published a story in *The New Yorker* in 2014, he got offered a publishing contract and then spent about three years hammering out the rest of the book. He dedicated the volume to his family and to Nora Ephron; before she died in 2012, she had been a constant source of writerly encouragement and dauntingly rigorous advice.

Hanks was happy to have a public venue for what had previously been a private process of storytelling: "As an actor in movies, you assemble as intricate a backstory for your character as possible, so that any time you have a moment that you have to create on-screen, you know where it's coming from. You don't tell anybody those stories, you don't write them down, you don't have a meeting about it, you don't go over it and okay it with the director. You keep it completely to yourself."

Hanks carried around some of his stories for decades, not knowing what would happen to them. After filming *Saving Private Ryan* in 1998, he periodically would tell interviewers about a scenario he imagined where a returning World War II soldier watches a young child playing with a train set on Christmas morning and has to reconcile domestic bliss with the horrors of combat—that became "Christmas Eve 1953." "Go See Costas," the story of a resourceful young man fleeing communist repression in Eastern Europe, arriving in the United States without resources or paperwork, and making his way as an immigrant in New York City, was inspired by the history of his in-laws.

For much of the book, Hanks followed the maxim "Write what you know." His own experiences as a surfer colored "Welcome to Mars," in which a nineteen-year-old boy discovers on an early-morning trip to the beach that his father is having an affair. "Who's Who?" evoked the humiliation and frustration of being a young actor getting nowhere in New York City in 1978 (although, again, Hanks turned the narrator into a young woman).

The opening story was "Three Exhausting Weeks," told by a semi-retired man who has a whirlwind romance with a female friend but discovers he can't keep up with her regimen of jogging, acupuncture, and miscellaneous self-improvement. "Being Anna's boyfriend was like training to be a Navy SEAL while working full-time in an Amazon fulfillment center in the Oklahoma Panhandle in tornado season," Hanks wrote. Since the narrator has the regular-guy tone of Hanks himself, you might imagine that was the character most like him in the story—but you don't make dozens of feature films by being a slacker.

His old friend Mary Beidler Gearen commented, "He really gets into the female psyche in a powerful way. As I read that story, I remember thinking it's a duality in his nature, being the guy who wants to hang and that incredibly motivated exhausting person—in my presence, he was never idle. Whether he's hyperactive or not, I can't diagnose—I'm not a psychiatrist. But the pace of his life is a powerful one. I once asked him, 'How in the hell do you survive this?' He said, 'You know me, I'm a beast.'"

When you sit down to write and ask "What happened before that?" and "What came next?" sometimes magic happens. Truman Capote famously dismissed Jack Kerouac by saying "That's not writing, that's typing"—but for Hanks, the two activities were often one and the same. The surprise twist: because he was a man who recognized the limitations of a philosophy and believed in using the right tool for a job, he wrote most of his book on a laptop.

Even if Hanks didn't use the typewriter all the time, he pulled it out as often as he could, finding other jobs that it was perfect for. As he said, anybody with a typewriter can create a document that will last forever—"and if the idea on it is a good one, the idea can last forever too."

TOM HANKS

MAJOR MATT MASON

THE SEVENTH COMMANDMENT
Don't dwell on the road not taken.

• • • • • •

If you're a Hollywood actor, one of your greatest sources of power is the ability to say "no." Turning down ill-conceived roles and miscellaneous hackwork helps you burnish your reputation and shape your career—but can also require you to play a waiting game that extends over month or years, holding out for a quality project, even when you need to be earning some money or just want a good reason to get out of the house.

As one of the most bankable actors in Hollywood, Hanks spent years as a big dog who could have his pick of just about any hot screenplay making its way around town. (I have it on good authority that one of his peers, an award-winning name-brand actor about the same age as Hanks, similarly gifted in both comedy and drama, typically referred to his rival as "Tom Fucking Hanks"—because it seemed like every time the actor fell in love with a script, Hanks snarfed it up for himself.) An odd side effect of that status is that Hanks has turned down lots of movies that got made anyway.

"I've read plenty of things that other people have gone off and made that I didn't react to," Hanks said. "Somebody else went off and made them and sometimes they turned into great movies and other times they didn't and that's fine. It's hard sometimes to say no, because it is so attractive—because they are going to make the movie, and it is going to be these fantastic people, and it is going to vie for the attention span of the national populace. Because it's a movie, you see, and jeez, *don't you want to be part of it?*"

You can't do everything in life; sometimes you have to choose one of two parties happening simultaneously on the opposite ends of your town, or you need to decide between two distinct career options. But you probably don't have to deal with the career option you turned down becoming a major motion picture playing at a movie theater near you, earning millions of dollars and a slew of Oscar nominations. That happens to Tom Hanks with some regularity, but he's learned the art of moving forward gracefully, not looking over his shoulder with regret.

Oliver Stone wanted him to play Nixon in his biopic (a role that eventually went to the Welshman Anthony Hopkins). Hanks was offered key roles in *Dead Poets Society* and *Field of Dreams,* which ultimately went to Robin Williams and Kevin Costner, respectively. Another Costner movie that could have starred Hanks was the post-apocalyptic *The Postman,* with Ron Howard directing instead of Costner. Hanks was attached to the remake of *Shall We Dance,* in a role that Richard Gere took over, and to *Night and the City,* as a small-time lawyer who gets in over his head when he becomes a boxing promoter. After Hanks left the project, Robert De Niro stepped in—reversing the sequence of recasting from *Big* a few years earlier.

Hanks almost teamed up with Julia Roberts a decade before *Charlie Wilson's War* to make *Benny & Joon*—which would have made it a very different film from the one that featured Johnny Depp and Mary Stuart Masterson. Harold Ramis offered Hanks two lead roles, one in the forgettable *Multiplicity* (Michael Keaton), one in the immortal *Groundhog Day* (Bill Murray). Who knows how either of them would have turned out had Hanks accepted? Hanks, for one, believed that *Groundhog Day* would have been less effective with him at the center: as Ramis related the story, Hanks told him, "Audiences would have been sitting there waiting for me to become nice, because I always play nice. But Bill's such a miserable S.O.B. on and off screen, you didn't know what was going to happen."

A movie that Hanks was attached to for a long time was called *Significant Other.* The screenplay, by Al Franken and Ron Bass, was a black comedy about a man with an alcoholic wife. Hanks hung out for hours in Bass' backyard, helping to polish the script, coming up with jokes and lines. Bass said, "There's a style of talking, of almost a way of looking at the world that just pours out of him, that is a uniquely consistent character, witty, intelligent, and it all sounds funny." Hanks stayed with the project for years, even as original costar Michelle Pfeiffer dropped out, to be replaced by Debra Winger. Ultimately, he had to move on, too—the movie was finally released with most of the comic elements stripped away, starring Andy Garcia and Meg Ryan, under the title *When a Man Loves a Woman.*

The role that Hanks most famously passed on was Jack Stanton in *Primary Colors*: basically, President Bill Clinton with a new haircut and a quick coat of paint. Hanks was widely expected to star in the Mike Nichols adaptation of the political satire written by an anonymous author (actually Joe Klein); when he dropped out, it became a nationwide news story. There was speculation that it was because Steven Spielberg had talked him out of it for ideological reasons or that Hanks couldn't stomach the job after becoming friendly with the Clintons. Hanks insisted that the problem was a full schedule: *Primary Colors, Saving Private Ryan,* and his HBO miniseries *From the Earth to the Moon* all came to fruition faster than expected, and he didn't have time to do a good job on all three. John Travolta took his place.

Cameron Crowe offered Hanks the title role in *Jerry Maguire,* having written the screenplay with him in mind. Hanks conceded, "Well, I will say without question, that is a great movie and it would have been fun. But I was already doing *That Thing You Do!* and I was too much infected with that to even be able to qualitatively say a yes or a no. It's kind of embarrassing, because they went off and made such a great movie. I would feel like George Raft saying, 'Hey, I could have been in *Casablanca.*' Boy, that would have been a bad movie with George Raft, don't you think?"

For his part, Crowe remembered Hanks calling him on the phone to let him down gently: "It was one of those passes where you hang up and you go, 'Wow, that was a great phone call,' and somebody says, 'Is he going to do it?' and you go, 'No, he passed.' Tom Hanks could hold a seminar on how to say no to a project with class. I felt great and yet had no movie." (Things worked out fine with Tom Cruise, obviously.)

Every day in Hollywood sees vast amounts of effort expended on movies that will never actually exist. Despite industry buzz and breathless announcements in Hollywood trade papers such as *Variety,* Hanks never costarred with Sylvester Stallone in a movie called *Brotherly Love* or with Tim Allen in *Jungle Cruise* (an adaptation of the Disneyland ride). And in 1992, he and Meg Ryan were committed to star in a Lawrence Kasdan romantic comedy called *The Inns of New England*; it never happened because Kasdan pulled the plug. That left both performers with a hole in their schedule—which got filled with Nora Ephron's *Sleepless in Seattle.*

The most revealing unmade movies are the one Hanks tried to will into existence but never quite succeeded: they're shadow-box versions of his beliefs and obsessions. Take, for example, *Lonely Hearts of the Cosmos*—Hanks had the project in development for years without ever convincing a studio to green-light it. Neal Jimenez wrote a script; Jonathan Demme was mentioned as a potential director; it would have been an adaptation of a non-fiction book by Dennis Overby about the twentieth-century history of astronomy and the men and women whose work led to the discovery of black holes and quasars. There's poetry in the story of earthbound scientists looking up at the stars, grappling simultaneously with the mysteries of the universe and their intramural squabbles. Hanks has never actually played a scientist, but it would have been fascinating to see what that field meant to him.

On the other end of the outer-space spectrum was *Major Matt Mason,* based on the Mattel action figure of the same name that went on sale in 1966, when Hanks was in elementary school. Circa 2012, the movie was planned as a $100-million 3-D spectacular with Robert Zemeckis directing. Hanks even cowrote the screenplay with Graham Yost. Reportedly there were no aliens or other antagonists; the plot centered on Mason trying to survive when he's trapped on the Moon. It never came to fruition—and since *Gravity* and *The Martian* both covered similar territory, it seems unlikely that it ever will.

Another adaptation of a science-fiction totem from Hanks' youth was *Stranger in a Strange Land,* which would have been the movie version of Robert Heinlein's 1961 cult novel about a charismatic superpowered man born on Mars who returns to Earth, where he starts his own religion and spreads free love. The book introduced the world to the concept of waterbeds and the verb "to grok." A few years after *Heathers*, Hanks commissioned its screenwriter Daniel Waters to write a *Strange Land* script—the freewheeling result appears to have been an effort to do a comic sci-fi journey through the American landscape. "It's definitely the creepy side of *Forrest Gump*," Waters said. The screenplay, somewhat incoherent, was quickly shelved.

Hanks always wanted to make a Vietnam War movie, but never really succeeded (both *Forrest Gump* and *The Post* have sequences set in Vietnam, with the obligatory Creedence Clearwater Revival song playing on the soundtrack, but neither film has its center of gravity there). The closest he came was *Khe Sanh,* about the months-long siege of a U.S. Marine base by the Viet Cong, as told from the perspective of Ray Stubbe, a chaplain in the U.S. Navy who was stationed there. William Broyles Jr., who wrote *Cast Away* and cowrote *Apollo 13,* tackled the script—despite being in development for the better part of a decade, the movie never got made.

Another true-life story was *A Cold Case,* an adaptation of the acclaimed nonfiction book by Philip Gourevitch about a New York City police detective who, before retiring, decides to track down the man who murdered his best friend twenty-seven years ago and bring him to justice. John Sayles and Eric Roth wrote the script; Mark Romanek was ready to direct the film; Robert De Niro had agreed to costar with Hanks. And then in preproduction they had what Romanek called a "life-rights crisis," meaning

that they couldn't get permission to depict some of the real people in the movie. "I'm going to start crying," Romanek said when
asked about it years later. "It was going to be this beautiful, dry
procedural. I hope to make it someday, and in a way, it's a part
for Tom Hanks that might be a lot more affecting when he's older.
Like if he played it in his sixties or something, so we may come
back to it someday."

Hanks would have turned fifty around the time *A Cold Case*
was released, if it had been made. Becoming eligible for AARP
membership is a natural time to think about mortality, how you
have affected the planet during your time on it, and what you
want to accomplish in your final years. So around the same time,
Hanks seriously considered starring in a remake of *Ikiru,* the 1956
classic by Akira Kurosawa; Richard Price would have written the
screenplay and Jim Sheridan would have directed. The original
movie tells the story of a Tokyo bureaucrat who has been toiling
ineffectually in a municipal job for decades. When he discovers
that he's dying from stomach cancer, he searches for a way to give
his final months meaning, and decides to cut through the red
tape so a cesspool can be turned into a playground.

Another attempt to explore the legacy we leave behind was a
potential collaboration with director Gus Van Sant: *How Starbucks Saved My Life,* an adaptation of Michael Gates Gill's mem-
oir of how, after his career and marriage both collapsed, a barista
job taught him what was really important.

Hanks tried to collaborate with the legendary Martin Scorsese
more than once. They were planning on having him star as gossip
columnist Walter Winchell in a movie that could have played like

a real-life version of the arsenic-cookie classic *The Sweet Smell of Success*. But they waited too long and got beat out by a competing Winchell biopic on HBO, directed by Paul Mazursky and starring Stanley Tucci (who won an Emmy for it).

So they switched gears. Scorsese owed a movie to Warner Bros.; he had spent years prepping a script on composer George Gershwin, but in the wake of the hep-cat success of *Swingers,* the studio told him they'd rather have a movie about singer Dean Martin. "Nick Pileggi and I killed ourselves working on that script," Scorsese said—they were adapting Nick Tosches' dark biography *Dino*. Hanks agreed to play Martin, heading up an all-star cast that would have included Jim Carrey as his partner Jerry Lewis, John Travolta as Frank Sinatra, Hugh Grant as Peter Lawford, and Adam Sandler as Joey Bishop. But when the picture was delayed—there were legal issues and problems with the script—Scorsese decided to make *Gangs of New York* for Miramax instead, a production that ended up taking nearly three years. "The story of Dean Martin is very difficult," Scorsese explained later. "Ultimately he pulls back in life…the active ones were Sinatra and Sammy Davis." Although the studio wanted him to focus on the Rat Pack years, Scorsese believed the stronger story was the history of Martin's partnership with Lewis.

Hanks' talent and popularity has granted him a lot of Hollywood juice, which is exciting and terrifying—as he once explained, "When somebody says, 'Tom, you could turn this napkin into a film,' I'm just shaking my head." He's discovered the limitations of his clout many times: for example, when he tried to star in a movie about Dean Reed, who had a teen-idol singing career in the 1960s. Hanks described Reed as "a third-rate if not fourth-rate version of Elvis meets Ricky Nelson. He wasn't a very good actor, he wasn't a very good singer. He was drop-dead gorgeous. But in his mind, he viewed himself as an intellectual socialist. He was seeing no success in Hollywood whatsoever despite his good looks and then he found out that he had the number-one record in Chile, so he got on a plane and flew down to Chile." Reed spent years as a star in South America before ending up in East Germany, where he became the biggest rock star in the Soviet bloc. This "fascinating, ultimately tragic" life played perfectly into Hanks' personal Venn diagram of obsessions—it covered politics, adult compromises, and 1960s rock 'n' roll—but, he said, it "turned out to be a movie absolutely nobody wanted to pay to see." (Or more precisely, a movie nobody wanted to pay to make.)

When you have dozens of movies on your IMDb page, it's not healthy to spend too much time dwelling on the ones that got away. (But it's an object lesson for the rest of us—the careers of even the most successful people are pockmarked with false starts and failed efforts.) Looking at other movies, Hanks has named a few parts he would have loved to play, characters a bit darker than his usual fare: Kevin Spacey's role in *American Beauty* and William H. Macy's role in *Fargo*. And there's one improbable bit of casting he wished had happened, something that would have given him a rare chance to chew the scenery, roll it around in his mouth, and spit it out again: "I never got a shot at any of those Batman villains, and that would have been fun, don't you think?" he complained. "They didn't even ask."

Interlude

STEVEN SPIELBERG AND
THE BOND OF BROTHERS

Tom Hanks calls Steven Spielberg "The Boss." Or "El Jefe." Occasionally, "The Governor" or "Mon General." Or, because they are good friends who have made five feature films together, sometimes he goes with "Mr. Smartypants."

For his part, Spielberg has enthused, "Tom is an Everyman because every man would like to be him, just as every woman would probably want to be with him. He has the kind of face Norman Rockwell would have loved to depict in a painting like *Freedom of Speech*. I think Tom's secret weapon is his speaking voice, his gently measured cadences. Add to all that, he's a brilliant actor who, quite possibly, could have been the only actor to have made Spencer Tracy jealous." But, Spielberg added, "For an Everyman, he's pretty damned opinionated."

Hanks, a decade younger than Spielberg, knew who the director was from early on, just like any film fan with a carotid artery—as a teenager, Hanks read about Spielberg's 1971 TV movie *Duel* and made sure he was home, sitting on the couch, to watch it when it aired. By 1977, Hanks was living in Sacramento, sleeping on a friend's floor, working as a stage manager and building sets at the Civic Theater. He had a rare morning off when he got a phone call from a friend, inviting him to a 10:20 a.m. showing of *Close Encounters of the Third Kind,* a film that basically made their skulls explode. "We had never really seen a movie where a guy who worked for the power company met the aliens," Hanks remembered.

For his part, Spielberg thinks he might have run into Hanks at an early '80s awards show, but he didn't watch *Bosom Buddies*— the first time the director paid attention to Hanks' work was when he saw *Splash.* Two years later, Spielberg was an executive producer on a movie that starred Hanks, *The Money Pit,* and found the actor commanded his attention: "When I was watching dailies, his comic timing and his willingness to laugh at himself were remarkable. I thought, 'This person's going to be around for as long as he wants.'"

Years before Hanks and Spielberg worked on a movie set together, their wives, Rita Wilson and Kate Capshaw, beat them to it. The two families lived in the same coastal neighborhood and sent their children to the same nursery school. Wilson and Capshaw became "bestest friends," as Spielberg put it, and one morning, they ran into each other at school while dropping off their kids. Capshaw told Wilson about a script she was considering for a short film. They read it together, sitting in Capshaw's Land Cruiser, and agreed they would make the movie: *No Dogs Allowed,* a twelve-minute short directed by Linda Rockstroh.

The families spent a lot of time together, even though Spielberg and Hanks were homebodies who would rather watch TV than go out to a restaurant. "So often, if we are dragged by our wives into a room together, we get along great," Spielberg said. They discovered that they could even enjoy companionable silences.

"The nice thing about being with Tom is that when he feels comfortable around you he doesn't feel a responsibility to spearhead the conversation," Spielberg said. "You know that Tom is your friend, and you his, when you can sit in a room independently reading, or doing other things, and not speak to each other for an hour. I know that I've grown closer to Tom and Tom's grown closer to me when we don't feel we have to *invent* conversation. There's no nervousness. And I think when you can get rid of the nervousness in a friendship between two guys, then it does become a...well...*older* kind of relationship."

What the two men discovered they had in common: they both loved history. "We were always reading biographies or histories, searching out the documentaries we'd never seen," Hanks said. They were constantly alerting each other to cool discoveries: "Did you hear about this?" "Did you read this?" "Did you see this?" "Are you reading that now?"

According to Spielberg, the reason they got along was that they both had an old-fashioned suburban-dad approach to life—"car pools, barbecues"—and, he added, Hanks "completely, unerringly, loves his wife."

They both received the script for *Saving Private Ryan* on the same day. Hanks had some issues with the lead role in that draft—"Captain Miller was a stock one-dimensional war hero who'd won the Medal of Honor and chomped on a cigar and said, 'Come on, you sons of bitches'"—but called up Spielberg to see if he wanted to make the movie together.

They were both at the top of their respective A-lists, but they had never worked together, so before they started, they sat down to talk about how they would handle the multitude of potential conflicts that come when you make a feature film. Spielberg said, "We decided our friendship came first, and we both agreed not to disagree."

Easier said than done—except it turned out that the two friends were on the same page not just temperamentally, but artistically. They both believed less is more, and were always looking for ways to pare a movie down to its essence. One morning on the shoot, Spielberg told Hanks that he had gone through the screenplay the night before and cut out twenty lines of the star's dialogue that seemed superfluous. Hanks produced his own marked-up copy of the script: the night before, he had gone through it and removed the same twenty lines.

Spielberg said, "We have a shorthand. We don't do a lot of talking, and we don't spend time analyzing. We work in a more instinctive way, which kind of bypasses a lot of conversation."

For all this harmonious agreement, there was one thing the director couldn't get the star to do: watch the playback of the scene on the on-set monitor. If Spielberg pulled Hanks over to the monitor, Hanks would just say, "Hey, Boss, I felt good about the last take," and walk away. Hanks explained his aversion to the monitor: "It makes me self-conscious. And that's the death of acting."

After *Saving Private Ryan,* they became partners on two HBO miniseries about World War II, both serving as executive producers on *Band of Brothers* and *The Pacific.* (A third HBO miniseries, about the air battles of WWII, is slowly moving forward. It's based on Donald L. Miller's book *Masters of the Air,* although there are rumors it might be renamed *The Mighty Eighth.*) And over the next twenty years, they made four more movies together: *Catch Me If You Can, The Terminal, Bridge of Spies,* and *The Post.*

Hanks and Spielberg have proved over and over that mainstream movies, made with inventive spirits and mastery of craft, can appeal to mass audiences and illuminate the human condition. *The Terminal* aside, the movies they've made together reflect the fundamentals of their characters: deeply interested in the nuances of history, comfortable with long silences, and groping toward a better version of humanity.

"He only sees the honesty in people's personalities, attitudes, and philosophies," Spielberg said of Hanks. "Everything that comes through Tom is about honesty. His love for family and this country are two of the reasons audiences love him; that's where his honesty comes from. People across America and around the world trust him. In that sense, I know of no other actor who sees that kind of loyalty among fans."

For his part, Hanks praised Spielberg for his attention to detail, even with small roles, so that a day player delivering an on-screen telegram gets an interesting beat. "Steven will want them to come in with a great idea," Hanks said. At the top of the call sheet, Hanks felt that pressure, only magnified exponentially. He joked that "sweat and anxiety" fuel his working relationship with Spielberg: "You don't want to go to work in the morning and have Steven Spielberg disappointed in the work that you did."

On their last couple of films, Hanks served as the director's self-appointed deputy: before shooting started, he got together with the other actors and gave them a crash course on Spielberg's working methods. "Guys, this is what I know about the Boss," he told them. "He will have an idea of where the camera is going to be, but everything else he's looking for is to come. He wants to be inspired by everybody. So let's be armed for bear."

Tom Sizemore, who also starred in *Saving Private Ryan,* said the director and actor have congruent temperaments. "Tom Hanks is a great person, a serious person; he's dissatisfied in a very likeable way, in a very discreet way," Sizemore observed. "Steven Spielberg is similar in his discretion and drive."

That seriousness of purpose doesn't mean the two of them never goof around. Doing international press for *The Terminal,* they found themselves in the same Berlin hotel room where Michael Jackson had dangled his infant son Prince Michael II (aka "Blanket") over the edge of the balcony, to the shock of onlookers. So they did what came naturally: Spielberg got out his camera and Hanks starred in an impromptu home-video parody of the incident.

Scott Shepherd, who starred in *Bridge of Spies* opposite Hanks, spent many days witnessing the Hanks-Spielberg dynamic. His conclusion: "They talk on a different level because they understand each other."

THE EIGHTH COMMANDMENT

Remember that Shakespeare will tell you the truth.

• • • • • •

Reynaldo isn't one of the plum roles in the Shakespearean canon. A servant to Polonius, he has thirteen lines in *Hamlet,* including "I will, my lord," "Very good, my lord," and "My lord, I did intend it." Nevertheless, playing Reynaldo in 1977 was a formative experience for Tom Hanks; it elevated his craft, and not just because, as he put it, learning acting by performing Shakespeare was like "learning to play the violin on a Stradivarius."

In this production, Reynaldo was onstage when Hamlet gives his instructions to the theatrical troupe he engages to perform *The Mousetrap,* the play-within-the-play with which Hamlet plans to catch the conscience of the king. So for dozens of rehearsals and performances, Hanks listened intently to Hamlet warning the players "suit the action to the word, the word to the action" and "do not saw the air too much with your hand."

Hanks said, "You know, 'Speak the speech, I pray you, as I pronounc'd it to you, trippingly on the tongue'—that's important. But theologically, philosophically, Hamlet also tells the players to hold the mirror up to nature. That stuck with me. I really think that's what the actor's job is, no matter how silly or space-age or fantastic the project is that you're doing."

"Hold, as 'twere, the mirror up to nature, to show virtue her own feature, scorn her own image, and the very age and body of the time his form and pressure," Hamlet says: in other words, he wants the actors to perform in a way that provokes everybody in the audience to reflect on their personal characters, and that tells the truth about the era they all live in.

Hanks took Hamlet's advice. Reversing the plot of *Big* (unless he was referring to the final scene), he said, "Look, I played a guy who magically turns into a little boy, okay? That doesn't happen in real life. But there is a way to hold the mirror to human nature to reflect the authenticity of being alive. *That* is the actor's job."

Hanks has played Shakespearean roles including Bottom in *A Midsummer Night's Dream,* Dogberry in *Much Ado About Nothing,* and Falstaff in *Henry IV.* He was Sir Andrew Aguecheek in *Twelfth Night* in high school, and returned to the part more than forty years later. But the character he's dreamed of tackling for decades is Iago, the villain of *Othello.* Hanks periodically mentions the part as a dream role, even calling the character "hip."

In case you haven't seen the play lately: Iago, a soldier resentful that he has not been named the second-in-command by the Moorish general Othello, embarks on an elaborate campaign to destroy his superior officer by making him believe that his wife Desdemona has been unfaithful. Iago succeeds; Othello ends up killing both Desdemona and himself. Iago is brilliant but sadistic, a black-hearted malefactor who wants to recast the world as a sick joke. Evidence suggests that Othello is the first play Shakespeare wrote after he retired as an actor, and he poured his new identity as a full-time playwright into Iago: the character creates his own world within the play and gulls his audience into believing his version of events. (Milton's Satan in *Paradise Lost* owes a lot to Iago.)

Hanks claimed that a large part of the appeal of playing Iago was just that, while he found the motivations of many bad guys inscrutable, he understood Iago: he "lost out on a promotion." But you have to connect with the material on a more primal level to be able to recite the following monologue from memory, as Hanks can:

We cannot all be masters, nor all masters
Cannot be truly follow'd. You shall mark
Many a duteous and knee-crooking knave,
That, doting on his own obsequious bondage,
Wears out his time, much like his master's ass,
For nought but provender, and when he's old, cashier'd:
Whip me such honest knaves. Others there are
Who, trimm'd in forms and visages of duty,
Keep yet their hearts attending on themselves,
And, throwing but shows of service on their lords,
Do well thrive by them and when they have lined their coats
Do themselves homage: these fellows have some soul;
And such a one do I profess myself. For, sir,
It as sure as you are Roderigo,
Were I the Moor, I would not be Iago:
In following him, I follow but myself;
Heaven is my judge, not I for love and duty,
But seeming so, for my peculiar end:
For when my outward action doth demonstrate
The native act and figure of my heart
In compliment extern, 'tis not long after
But I will wear my heart upon my sleeve
For daws to peck at: I am not what I am.

"When I first heard that," Hanks said, "it just sent me right through the stratosphere and made me want to become an actor." And "I am not what I am" is a good summary of the trickery of an actor, who puts on masks and makes people believe that they're human faces. Or, as Hanks sees it, "I am what I am not."

Another way of considering the knotty truths that emerge from this fictional character is that Shakespeare provided Iago with an overabundance of motivation, trusting that the actor playing the role would find a way of making it coherent—and in so doing, gave the opportunity for the audience and the actor playing the role to be equally surprised as events unfold. The malignant imagination of Iago can conceive of almost anything except the places his hatred takes him to. Iago uses deception to crush the lives of those around him. Hanks employs as much artifice as an actor and a public figure—to put himself, and his audience, in touch with other lives. Iago is not complete without an actor like Tom Hanks; Tom Hanks can't do his job without having some Iago inside him.

Every year since 1990, Hanks and Rita Wilson have hosted an event called "Simply Shakespeare": they pick a Shakespeare play, recruit some of their actor pals (William Shatner and Martin Short are regulars), have a table read and a dress rehearsal in a single afternoon, and do a staged reading that evening. Tickets, which can run one thousand dollars, benefit the Shakespeare Center of Los Angeles, a nonprofit that brings the Bard to schoolkids and veterans. (Wilson was in one of the organization's plays back in the late 1980s, playing Celia in *As You Like It*. Apparently, they cast her unaware that she was married to Hanks and were stunned on opening night when her husband was in the audience, along with a bunch of their other Hollywood pals.)

Being loose and unrehearsed is a large part of the point of "Simply Shakespeare," Hanks said: "The whole message is 'This is not medicine. You do not have to work at this.'"

One year, Hanks invited Sir Anthony Hopkins to join them, but the classically trained actor said, "Look, I'm asked to do this all the time, and it's absolutely dreary. It's a hideous occasion with a bunch of snooty people."

Hanks told him, "Tony! We rip it up! We play everything for maximum laughs."

"Oh, alright," Hopkins assented. "That sounds like fun."

The benefit can be fun for non-celebrities too. John Frankenheim, a man unconnected to show business who made a donation to the Shakespeare Center and thereby stumbled into an annual backstage visit at "Simply Shakespeare," reports:

> An error on my 2008 tax return, just a stupid mistake on my part, resulted in an unexpected windfall that I wanted to give to a single charity for maximal impact. I felt I could trust the Shakespeare Center, as both Rita Wilson and her husband were longtime members of the board. If you can't trust Tom Hanks, whom can you trust?
>
> In appreciation, I was invited to fly to Los Angeles to join in a celebrity fundraiser a few days later. Alongside the winner of an eBay auction, I was given a supporting role in *The Taming of the Shrew*.
>
> Rita took a break from rehearsal to show me around the theater. She pointed out each cast member in a humorous

running commentary—William Shatner, Annette Bening, with Warren Beatty close at hand, Arte Johnson, and David Schwimmer—everywhere you looked there was another wonderful performer. Tom Hanks, the heart of the action, remained busy until rehearsal broke for the cast photo. I hesitated, staying off to one side. Tom, noticing me for the first time, waved me over to join him. I was touched, but Rita whacked him over the head with her rolled-up script for calling me by the wrong name. So we were already laughing the first time we met. I call this my Emperor Zurg photo, as I am right between him and Tim Allen.

My role was Curtis, servant to Tom's Petruchio. Stephen Root played Grumio, his other servant. At the beginning of Act IV, when the script calls for mutton, I was instructed to bring Tom a platter of artificial fruit instead. Petruchio, displeased, throws the food back at his "heedless joltheads." I was a bit stiff, I suppose, so Tom delighted in throwing the fruit at me, one piece after another bouncing off my chest. To his surprise, I decided at one point to catch an apple and toss it behind his back to Stephen, whose comic instincts prompted him to slip it back onto the platter in Tom's lap. Amused, Tom kept the cycle going, hurling piece after piece for me to catch and toss to Stephen for underhanded returns to the platter. This went faster and faster until Stephen began to fall behind, fumbling and dropping the fruit. Tom feigned anger at his clumsiness, with Stephen affecting tears even as he still bobbled the fruit. All of a sudden, swept away by the sportive absurdity of it all, I found myself saying, "Are you crying? There's no crying!

There's no crying in baseball!" Everyone froze. Quite a faux pas, I was to learn: you don't quote famous lines around the actors who said them. After a few moments, Tom, nodding sagely, broke the tension. "The kid's right: There's no crying in baseball!" And the silliness began anew.

After the cast party, I assumed that a once-in-a-lifetime experience had come to an end. I had no idea that I would be welcomed every year since. Tom kids me about returning to the stage, but after my third go I knew the audience was the place for me. The year after that, Tom wandered from the stage with a pizza during a performance of *The Merry Wives of Windsor*. Faith Hill had not wanted a slice, nor had Kenneth Branagh, nor Tracey Ullman, so he worked his way through my row looking for takers, comically incensed that there were none. Then he reached me. Finally! I tipped him a dollar, which he held up proudly.

In 2013, I was among a very few allowed to sit in for rehearsals for *The Two Gentlemen of Verona*, during which musical guest Paul McCartney played about fifty more songs than he would during the actual performance. At one point, the two gentlemen, played by Jason Alexander and Eric McCormack, were traveling through a forest represented by four cast members standing abreast, their outstretched hands holding almost-bare branches. Tom, not in the scene, had taken a seat by himself in the right center orchestra to watch them rehearse. Although loath to disturb him, I whispered what I thought was a worthwhile idea. Rita Wilson, Val Kilmer, Lily Rabe, and Thomas Sadoski had been holding their branches at random, but Tom, leaping to the stage, was now directing them to match an image he had called up on his cell phone. Paul, curious, approached from stage left, then chuckled when he saw Tom recreating the album cover of *Help!* by positioning the actors' arms into the same flag semaphore. Tom, bless him, pointed me out from the stage, giving me full credit. Paul gave me a wink and a happy little wave, which I will never forget.

Once, on an empty stage, in an otherwise empty theater, Tom wandered back after a performance to what had served as a bar in a western saloon. I watched him pick up a glass, raise it to his eye, hold it aloft against the light, spit into it, raise the hem of his apron to polish it, study it again, appear satisfied that it was clean, put it back down, and then walk off the stage. Except there was no glass, and there was no apron. He had created them entirely through expression, gesture and movement, by himself, for himself. I once heard him say that he only really feels like an actor when he is on stage. That cannot be true, but I came close to believing it that day.

In addition to what he has given us all, Tom Hanks has meant, for me, the beginning of a more charitable life. I have had so much fun in his company, have learned so much, and have stories to dine out on for years. Don't get me wrong—we're more kindred spirits than bosom buddies. In his life, I am just a bit player in a cast of thousands. But for all that Steven Spielberg or Barack Obama can tell you about him, I can tell you something else: Tom Hanks will treat an unknown like a star.

THE NINTH COMMANDMENT

Value your friends but accept your loneliness.

• • • • • •

"All the great stories are about our battle with loneliness," Tom Hanks said. "That's what I always end up being drawn toward." That wasn't Hanks' only unified field theory of literary value— he'd also opined that all great works of literature are witty—but loneliness was a theme he returned to again and again.

For example: "The cinema has the power to make you feel not lonely, even though you are. You can go in a lonely human being and you can see something that, for two hours and however long the afterglow lasts, can make you feel as though you actually belong to something really good."

If you suspect that maybe Tom Hanks was not purely detached and clinical when he talked about profound loneliness, you're absolutely right. It's a hard topic to discuss head-on, so he usually couched his isolation in the past tense or recast the feeling as the yearning for a grand purpose. He's said that the roles he chooses reflect "this desire to belong to something bigger than ourselves— otherwise we're lonely. We all fight the battle of loneliness."

Hanks is a convivial and warm human being; he had a broad cross-section of acquaintances and work pals and people whose company he enjoyed. But that wasn't the same thing as having bedrock friends. While his family with Rita Wilson occupied a large part of that emotional territory, he was still aware of the empty spaces in his life. "I have no best friend," he declared.

That wasn't something that slipped past him by accident—Hanks put some serious thought into what it would mean to have a true, close friend. "The requirements," he said, "are that it has to be someone who has known you a really long time, that you've kept up constant, almost day-to-day contact with, and has been a part of all of the good and all of the bad. Well, I've got to tell you, there is nobody on that list. That's the bad part. The good part is that I'm always able to pick up where I left off with people. But that loneliness thing has always dictated that it has been my choice when to do that. And that's not fair to them. I don't hold up my end of the friendship bargain with an awful lot of people."

Hanks deliberately chose a definition of "friend" that guaranteed he didn't have any. Even if you considered people he worked closely with and cared about for decades, like Peter Scolari and Steven Spielberg, he hadn't stayed in daily contact with them. Many adult men lack those intimate bonds with other men, but the lifestyle of a professional actor makes the problem worse: for a few months at a time, you are intensely bonded with the people you're doing a movie or a play with, but once it's over, everyone scatters and moves on to the next project, maybe halfway around the world. (One exception in Hanks' filmography was the main cast of *Saving Private Ryan*—after the movie wrapped, their bond was so strong that they got together regularly. Even that tradition lasted only three years before it petered out.) Hanks could usually count on his family, at least, to stay in one place.

Even if all the logistics had been easier to navigate, Hanks still might have pushed people away. He confessed, "I can pretend to be very good friends with people and then not have anything to do with them for eighteen months." Only Hanks knew for sure whether that was a defense mechanism he learned from his childhood: if you move around all the time, you better be ready to cut off ties at a moment's notice with anybody who isn't a blood relative. In real life, it turned out, making a new friend wasn't as easy as drawing a face on a volleyball.

As Hanks got older, and his children moved out of the house, he made more of an effort to spend meaningful time with the people he cared about, regardless of whether he gave them the ceremonial "best friend" title. When a buddy of his got married, the bachelor party was a two-night camping trip. "The next year we went for three nights," Hanks said. "Every year we do it, we add an extra night because you can truly decompress. And you get all smelly."

And in 2016, Hanks organized a reunion of the Great Lakes Shakespeare Festival interns, class of 1977 and 1978. The actress Bairbre Dowling, the daughter of the festival director Vincent Dowling, had died unexpectedly, and Hanks declared, "We better do this now or there won't be anybody to reunion with." About twenty of the former interns flew into Cleveland—other than Hanks, the most famous was Jose Rivera, a playwright (*References to Salvador Dali Make Me Hot*) who was nominated for an Oscar for the screenplay of *The Motorcycle Diaries*.

They all hopped on a luxury bus Hanks had hired. "We tooled all over town in this bus, taking in the old haunts," Lucy Bredeson-Smith said. One stop was in Lakewood (a neighborhood right next to Cleveland), visiting the house they had nicknamed "Parkwood Manor," which Hanks had shared with some other interns. Nobody was home—but when the next-door neighbor pulled up on a motorcycle, Hanks took a bunch of selfies with the neighbor, leaving behind proof for the current residents of Parkwood Manor that he had visited.

They took over their old favorite pizza place, Angelo's. The former interns got to see how Hanks moved through the world as a mega-celebrity, marching up to a few customers who weren't part of their group, saying, "Hey, how you doing?" and taking it in stride when they burst into tears. The whole time, Hanks' assistant (who had organized the trip's logistics) and bodyguard discreetly hovered in the background.

"He would never say this, but he has to be very careful for his safety," former intern Mary Beidler Gearen said. "I know when he did *Philadelphia* he got hate mail, and there's still loonies. And people feel like he's their long-lost brother, and he loves that, but we have to be really protective of him. It's a challenge to keep a guy secure who's in love with people."

The bus ended up back at the Lakewood Civic Auditorium, a stage attached to a local high school, where the Great Lakes Shakespeare Festival used to perform. (The festival has thrived; it now has a year-round repertory schedule and a state-of-the-art playhouse, and has renamed itself the Great Lakes Theater.) The Civic was happy to open their doors free of charge for its most famous alumnus, even providing a tour guide and an electronic greeting on the sign outside the building.

The former interns got onstage, the way they used to late at night after they had finished moving all the scenery around for the next day's show. People took turns telling jokes and performing monologues. But while everyone was milling around onstage, Hanks spotted an American flag on the side of the stage. "People were reacquainting themselves with the stage," Beidler Gearen said, "and all of a sudden, here's Tom, sixty years old, running across the stage with the flag."

Hanks wrote everyone a letter after the reunion, reminiscing about their summers full of innocence and potential, and letting them know how much he valued the time they had spent together, in the past and in the present day. He had to admit he had good friends, no matter what he called them.

For his part, Spielberg said that he didn't think of Hanks as a lonely person—he just made choices that included a certain degree of solitude. "I think he needs to spend time alone getting familiar with that part of him that he needs as an actor, as an artist," Spielberg explained. "Tom is just really in touch with himself and you can't be in touch with yourself if you are always serving others."

THE TENTH COMMANDMENT

Stand up for what you believe.

• • • • • •

Philadelphia, released in 1993, changed Tom Hanks' life—and not just because he received his first Academy Award for his performance. Hanks said the movie "politicized me, which is a pain in the ass."

Before making it, Hanks had been a vaguely progressive guy, having internalized the values that came along with growing up in Northern California in the 1970s. He didn't think about politics too hard, and didn't want to make any public statement more ideological than "we're all kind of questioning ourselves as a nation and a species." In fact, he argued that it was a bad idea for actors to do so.

"I think we have no responsibility whatsoever and that we hold no clout whatsoever," he declared in 1989. "And I think that we do no service by throwing ourselves into causes. I will vote at my polling place and be very vociferous about my opinion around my kitchen table. But elsewhere, it's nobody's business. And I don't expect anybody to be swayed because Tom Hanks says vote no on Proposition B or something like that."

Four years later, when Hanks starred in a movie designed to change American attitudes toward homosexuals and AIDS victims, he didn't just accept the responsibility that came with the role, he embraced it. Hanks sharpened the underlying message of acceptance in *Philadelphia* into a lethal point, challenging interviewers with statements such as this: "Having thought about

AIDS a good deal for quite a while now, I've come to think of it as a test of us as a civilization, among other things. Is man more enlightened than he was during the Black Plague in Elizabethan England? I don't know. I do know there are still a lot of people who think this disease is about hedonism and therefore deserved. All I can say about that is that's not a very Christian response to suffering."

After *Philadelphia,* Hanks found he couldn't flip the switch back to being politically disconnected, even if he wanted to. Some of his movies touched on issues he'd have to discuss (like *The Green Mile* and capital punishment—Hanks was for it in some situations), while others seemed apolitical, sometimes determinedly so (like *Forrest Gump,* which careened through decades of American history without taking a stand).

Hanks recognized that his artistic choices had political dimensions, even when they weren't obvious. So he expressed his opinions: he was a moderate Democrat who believed that the government could make people's lives better in ways that extended beyond building roads and bridges. And he did what he could to push the USA to live up to its ideals, to be "the promised land for the whole world."

Hanks said, "We examine our failures more than any society in the world, it seems like. And we beat ourselves up about them. But by and large, when the lights go out because there's an earthquake or the blizzard shuts down the city, suddenly you're knocking on your neighbor's door saying 'Is everything okay?' And it's almost to the point where when the lights come on, it's like 'What a shame. The lights are on, so we've got to go back to our own life.' But there is a kind of spirit of pulling together."

Hanks discovered that one side effect of being a famous, trusted, articulate celebrity who touts the greatness of American values is that people wonder if you're running for something yourself. When Hanks was asked about his political future in 1998, he said, "My image is a really good one. I made a nice acceptance speech on TV a couple of times. I handle myself pretty well in the glare of the entertainment media. The actual ideology that anyone can glean as projected by my appearances on TV is that America is good because we are all so different and respecting each other is not so hard a thing to do. Not a bad platform, I suppose, to run for some office."

Whether that was just idle musing or a deliberate trial balloon, it quickly became a huge news story—which was a problem, because Hanks didn't actually want to run for office (at least, not anytime soon). He quickly walked the statement back, aggressively stamping out speculation with unambiguous statements like, "It's an asinine, ridiculous idea. It's nonsense. The whole idea of politics bores me to tears. I'd rather have flu than discuss it."

Once Donald Trump moved into the White House in 2017, it seemed less improbable that somebody else with a high Q rating but no political background might follow suit. (As it happens, Hanks is distantly related to Abraham Lincoln, via Lincoln's mother, Nancy Hanks: he's the third cousin, four times removed, of America's sixteenth president.) Hanks found himself mentioned as a political contender alongside folks like Mark

Zuckerberg and the Rock, but he maintained that he had no interest in giving up his acting career for a presidential campaign. "I wouldn't want to answer the phone calls," he said. "I'm not trying to be flip. What would I have to offer other than I can make a speech every now and again? I mean, Clooney's a guy to run. Talk to him. Oprah!"

If he had made those stump speeches, they likely would have reflected Hanks' core political principle: you should respect people who have opinions different from your own. This was partially good manners, partially the actor's instinct of wanting to get inside the motivations of other people, and partially the belief that American society was a long-term project that required a robust spectrum of opinion, not just two tribes lobbing insults at each other. Hanks complained, "You can be the biggest policy geek in the world, you can watch every conceivable mass-media representation of politics today, and you're still going to get only two polarized sides arguing with each other, as opposed to a whole."

Hanks, for example, strongly opposed Proposition 8, a 2009 California ballot initiative that outlawed gay marriage in the state. (It passed, but was ultimately overturned by the courts.) He even criticized the financial backers of the ballot measure, many of them organized by the Mormon church, as "un-American." His language not only offended the anti-gay activists but stuck in his own craw—given a few days, he decided he regretted creating "more division when the time calls for respectful disagreement." He made a statement that didn't back off his convictions. "I believe Proposition 8 is counter to the promise of our Constitution; it is codified discrimination," he wrote. But, he allowed, "Everyone has a right to vote their conscience—nothing could be more American."

Those hyperpartisan local conflicts, writ large, became the daily story of the United States—a trend that accelerated and then reached terminal velocity under the presidency of Donald Trump. Like many people (including Trump himself), Hanks didn't think there was any chance the reality-show host would win the presidency. Here's how he dismissed the possibility: "Well, you know what? Then aliens are going to land on my front lawn and dinosaurs will wear capes." A year after the election, he revised his hypothetical: "Neo-Nazis are going to hold torchlight parades in Charlottesville and Pocahontas jokes will be said in front of the Navajo code-talkers—that would have been just as hellacious in imagination."

With hindsight, Hanks blamed Trump's election on political "doublespeak," collective national exhaustion with the "Bush-Clinton continuum," and the work *The Apprentice* did to make the Trump Taj Mahal casino in Atlantic City look glamorous even though it was shoddy and infested with mold. But he pointed to the pivotal moment back in 2016 when Congressman Joe Wilson interrupted Barack Obama making an address to Congress by shouting "You lie!" Hanks could see lots of evidence that bipartisan comity was dead—and yet he believed it was worth working for, as one of the fundamental values of the United States.

Another one of the nation's basic tenets is freedom of the press. Tom Hanks has done his bit for the First Amendment, not only playing a newspaper publisher as a hero (his portrayal of Benjamin Bradlee in *The Post*); he consistently went the extra mile for the Fourth Estate. On Memorial Day weekend 2004, during the George W. Bush presidency, Hanks was touring the White House with his family when he discovered that the briefing room lacked a coffeemaker. He arranged for a top-notch Illy espresso machine to be delivered to the beat reporters with this note: "I hope this machine will make the twenty-four-hour cycle of news a bit more pleasant. Add water, insert pod, press button and REPORT. All good things, Tom Hanks."

The caffeine-deprived press pool was grateful. Ron Hutcheson, president of the White House Correspondents' Association, sent a note to Hanks telling him, "I can't promise favorable coverage if you ever run for president, but you have at least earned the gratitude of the White House press corps with your generous gift."

Hanks returned to the White House in 2010 for a screening of his HBO series *The Pacific,* and dropped by the briefing room to check on his espresso machine—which had gotten grimy in six years. "Let me see what I can do for the poor slobs in the Fourth Estate here," Hanks said, inspecting a dirty coffee filter. "You know you are supposed to clean this after every use!"

Nevertheless, Hanks declared, "We're just trying to combat sleep deprivation," and sent the press corps a replacement machine.

In February 2017, after having been president for less than a month, Donald Trump declared the press to be "fake news" and "the enemy of the American people." Hanks promptly showed his support for the White House reporters the way he knew best: with a brand-new espresso machine. This one was a Pasquini model retailing for about $2,200, and it came with a signed note from Hanks: "Keep up the good fight for Truth, Justice, and the American Way. Especially for the Truth part."

The daily news cycle is a crucial tool for making sure that the nation's representatives in government remain accountable. But it can also be a buzzing, spinning distraction—not just from daily life and art and loved ones, but from the issues confronting the nation in the decades ahead. For example, Hanks wanted people to consider how best to counter fundamentalist Islam: "Is there some brand of Western intellect, achievement, freedom, and self-determination that can become so important and so glamorous and so universally understood that everyone wants to participate?" Or maybe, he acknowledged, the important concerns were competing with China and India, or how to combat global warming—but ignoring any of those big questions wouldn't make them go away.

Hanks asked, "Is the United States of America still on the cusp of discovery and change? Are we still at a place where some new version of manifest destiny is coming down the pike? And are we still naturally inclined to pursue that? I'm not so sure we are."

He had put some thought into the question of who might lead the nation out of its twenty-first-century morass, the modern equivalent of the elite souls who served as astronauts. "You'd be looking for folks who are smart, competitive, sacrificing and tested. They'd be taking jobs that are taxing on the body and soul. Jobs that require training and risk. Jobs that don't require that you kill anybody," he said.

You don't have to be a combat medic or a movie star to make a difference. As Hanks pointed out, every day you wake up, you make a choice: "Do I make the world better today somehow, or do I not bother?"

Section Three

The Films of Tom Hanks

TOM HANKS UNDERSTANDS THAT HE'S A PUBLIC FIGURE—which is why he's always zealously guarded the boundaries of his private life. More than one journalist has come away from an interview with Hanks frustrated that although the actor was friendly and engaging, he elegantly sidestepped any substantive discussion about his personal life. For years, he didn't even disclose the names and ages of his children.

The flipside of that reserve is the full-body commitment and emotional exposure he brings to his film roles. Watch Tom Hanks' movies and you'll have a good picture of the man: his passions, his joy and his grief, his trajectory through the world. So this filmography isn't just a viewing guide or a critical compendium (although it wouldn't be a bad thing if you watched *Big* or *Captain Phillips* tonight)—it's an alternate history of Hanks' life, as it played out on soundstages and at location shoots around the world.

He Knows You're Alone

(1980, Elliot)

> *"I'm most interested in fear, the emotion of fear."*

Hanks began his career at the bottom of the popcorn bucket. This cheap slasher film, made quickly on Staten Island, is a barely competent knockoff of *Halloween*. The concept: a serial killer is murdering brides-to-be just before their weddings, plus other random characters as necessary to hold the audience's interest. If you enjoy seeing an unbelievably fake severed head submerged in a tank of tropical fish, then you're watching the right movie.

The only real points of interest in *He Knows You're Alone* for modern audiences are the period details (a pack of cigarettes costs sixty-five cents!) and the screen debut of a twenty-four-year-old Tom Hanks, who is gawky but entertaining in a supporting role. Hanks plays the love interest of Nancy, the best friend of Amy (the killer's primary target). He's a psychology student who spouts off on the psychology of fear (a forerunner of the know-it-all character played by Jamie Kennedy in the *Scream* series): "Horror movies and the roller coasters and the house-of-horror rides—you can face death without any real fear of dying. It's safe. You can leave the movie or get off the ride with a vicarious thrill and the feeling that you've just conquered death."

You wouldn't peg Hanks as a future star from this movie, but he delivers self-conscious meta-dialogue like that winningly enough that you'd expect him to work again. (Although the movie paid him only eight hundred dollars, it got him his SAG card, meaning that as a member of the Screen Actors Guild he was qualified to audition for other, better movies.) Hanks ad-libbed some dialogue in a scene at an amusement park, announcing that he didn't have money and getting his date to pay. Director Armand Mastroianni said that originally Hanks' character was supposed to be one of the victims, but "we liked him too much. We didn't want to kill him."

Mazes and Monsters
(1982, Robbie)

"I am Pardieu, the holy man. In reaching the ninth level, I have acquired many magic spells and charms, the greatest of which is the Graven Eye of Timor. But I also have a sword, which I only use should my magic fail me."

Mazes and Monsters—also known as *Rona Jaffe's Mazes and Monsters,* which tells us that novelist Rona Jaffe had a really good agent—was a made-for-TV movie that aired on CBS in the final days of 1982. It's the story of a (thinly disguised) Dungeons and Dragons game at the fictional Grant University that gets out of control when one of the players loses himself in the fantasy world, made in an era when people thought that D&D might lead to Satanic worship rather than social awkwardness and too many R. A. Salvatore novels. (Jaffe based her novel on a sensationalized news story about a suicidal student who disappeared into the steam tunnels at Michigan State University.)

The result, occupying the previously unexplored intersection between Erich Segal and Gary Gygax, is an overwrought campus drama. *Mazes and Monsters* was apparently a production where somebody said "it's important to flesh out the characters" but then came up with the solution of "have one of them wear a different hat in every scene." For fans of role-playing games, this movie is just bad enough to be enjoyable, especially when the police detective Martini delivers his lurid warning about the dangers of RPGs: "Mazes and Monsters is a far-out game: swords, poison, spells, battles, maiming, killing."

Hanks plays the central role of Robbie, who proves to be too psychologically fragile for the game. He gets so fully into his alternate identity as a cleric that he breaks off a romance, gives away his possessions, and has mystical visions about his brother (who vanished years earlier, apparently for reasons not related to wyverns or umber hulks). Robbie starts wearing a hood that makes him look like Debra Winger in *The Sheltering Sky*, and eventually snaps, heading to New York City, where he stabs a mugger and almost hurls himself off the World Trade Center.

Twenty-six years old when *Mazes and Monsters* aired, Hanks was believable enough as a college student. But at this point in his career, his primary assets as a performer were good timing and a smart-ass attitude. This role didn't make many comedic demands; the real problem, however, was that Hanks didn't have enough chops as an actor to transcend the material. Since his dialogue included lines such as "There's blood on my knife! And it's on my hands! I think I killed somebody!" he really needed to rise above it.

Splash

(1984, Allen Bauer)

"All my life I've been waiting for someone, and when I find her, she's a fish."

If you're going to make a fish-out-of-water comedy, why not take the metaphor all the way? *Splash* is a charming, well-executed romantic comedy about a young man who falls in love with a mermaid (who has grown legs to pass as human on dry land). Hanks has the central role in the movie, and when he's given a comedic set piece, he executes it well: check out the scene where he's an usher at a wedding just after he's been dumped by a girlfriend. Hanks has to toggle between pitying himself, putting on an affable front as he guides guests to their seats, and expressing increasing snappishness to friends who ask him where his girlfriend is, until he yells, "She left me! She moved out and my life's a shambles! Okay? That's the news, you want the weather? Anywhere but the first three rows!" Somehow, Hanks makes this channel-flipping display of emotions seem natural.

But for most of the movie, Hanks plays straight man to Daryl Hannah's mermaid Madison: on dry land, she doesn't know humanity's customs, and is confused by everything from television to ice skating. When he takes Madison to a fancy restaurant so he can propose marriage, she picks up a lobster and bites through the shell sideways, devouring it. His job is to gaze at her with more loving tolerance than embarrassment and tell the other diners, "She's *really* hungry." And when she's not on-screen, John Candy is bulldozing his way through the movie as Hanks' lecherous drunk brother, who likes to bring a cooler of beer to a racquetball match and to drop loose change as a way to look up women's skirts.

Hanks plays a character without many eccentricities; the most memorable thing about Allen Bauer (other than his amphibious girlfriend) is his job as a fruit and vegetable wholesaler. Hanks nevertheless managed to make him not boring. He also proved to have excellent instincts for when to take charge of a scene and when to remain still, letting his acting partners shine.

Splash was a big sleeper hit, immediately establishing Hanks as a film actor. It was also a career-making movie for Hannah, Howard, and the screenwriting team of Lowell Ganz and Babaloo Mandel, proving that a rising tide lifts all mermaids.

Bachelor Party

(1984, Rick Gassko)

"I am not complaining, but I usually don't like my filth this clean."

Looking back at *Bachelor Party* five years later, Hanks said, amiably and accurately: "The movie is just a sloppy rock 'n' roll comedy that has tits in it." It's famously raunchy, with gags involving a donkey snorting cocaine and a male stripper who offers up his wiener in a hot-dog bun. But what made the movie more than a string of over-the-top yuks is that it has heart: if you don't buy that the central couple, played by Tom Hanks and Tawny Kitaen, are crazy about each other, the whole premise falls apart. Director Neal Israel knew that, which is why a week into production, he fired his original leads, Paul Reiser and Kelly McGillis, for lacking chemistry, and hired Hanks and Kitaen instead.

We know it's the 1980s because Hanks shows up wearing fingerless gloves and a bandana around his neck. He plays Rick, a school-bus driver who sasses the nuns and tells the kids, "Thank you for being Catholic and for choosing the St. Gabriel school bus." In the mode of Bill Murray in *Stripes* or Chevy Chase in *Fletch*, Rick is an anything-for-a-laugh guy who gets salty with any authority figure in sight—including his fiancée's parents—while the moviemakers trust that their lead actor's charisma will excuse any antisocial behavior.

Three years before she became famous for doing splits on the hood of a car in Whitesnake's "Here I Go Again" video, Kitaen played the fresh-faced Debbie, who extracts a promise from Rick that he won't cheat on her during his bachelor party. And despite his friends' best efforts, he doesn't. (The narrative logic of making Rick a jerk before the party starts is that he can remain faithful at an orgy without coming off as a milquetoast prude.) Hanks spends most of the movie presiding over a bacchanal that's more like a Huey Lewis video than a Caligula feast, in a hotel suite crammed full with everyone from punks to businessmen to basketball players. While his friends are getting laid, Hanks is doing the pony on top of the piano and refereeing an indoor volleyball game. Enthusiastic without being dweeby, Hanks makes a likable-if-lightweight leading man.

As ribald as *Bachelor Party* is, there was apparently even bawdier material that got left on the cutting room floor, either because Neal Israel was worried about getting an X rating or because he had a mother he had to kiss with that mouth. "We had so many funny scenes that were hysterical—none of it was even saved and shown on the DVD," complained costar Adrian Zmed. "There was this one scene where the party is not going well, and I'm the one who put it all together, and I grab Tom in the hotel room and I go, 'Come on, let's go downstairs and get something to eat.' Cut to the scene, and I throw him into a booth at the café in the hotel lobby, and then all of the sudden, you hear a zipper sound. There's a hooker underneath the table who's, you know, servicing him. And I go, 'My gift to you.' And he starts to moan and groan, and the minister who's going to marry him walks into the café, and I go, 'Oh, Father, over here! Over here!' The minister comes up, and Tom starts to bang on the table with his hand: 'Oh, mother of God, Mary, mother of Joseph.' And he's getting louder and louder and louder and the table starts moving up and down. And I say, 'He likes to say grace just before he eats, Father.' And eventually, Tom can't take it anymore. He gets out and runs away, and I say, 'Father, sit here. It's the best seat in the house,' and then I take off. Then you hear the zipper sound, and it's a close-up on his face. It's a shame that one didn't make it in."

"You have to explore your past to do a part like this," Hanks said sarcastically at the time of the movie, mocking the idea that there was any Method to his performance. "Rick is sort of like Tom was in high school," he explained a little more seriously, lapsing into the third person. "Except Rick has seen a little action. Which I certainly never saw in high school."

The Man with One Red Shoe
(1985, Richard)

"Walk tall! You're in the string section!"

This movie, probably the worst in Tom Hanks' career, is a flailing adaptation of a French spy farce, *Le grand blond avec une chaussure noire* (which translates as *The Tall Blond Man with One Black Shoe*—apparently, the shoe color and the hair color of the protagonist weren't the only things that got lost in translation). The story, such as it is: two rival factions of the CIA are scheming against each other. One faction picks a random man out of a crowd and ostentatiously makes contact with him, knowing that will cause the other faction to squander their resources chasing after him. The patsy is a concert violinist named Richard (Hanks), who is largely oblivious to the machinations and gunplay happening around him, but ends up falling in love with one of the agents (the fetching Lori Singer) sent to investigate him.

The plot is ludicrous, which isn't necessarily a problem. Most of the best spy comedies are broad affairs: *Austin Powers, Top Secret!, Burn After Reading*. But since this movie is populated by dimwits and cardboard cutouts, it's impossible to care why anybody does anything. Hanks is game enough, but like his costars Charles Durning and Dabney Coleman, he doesn't have anything to sink his teeth into. As plot coincidences and dead bodies pile up around him, he's required to remain oblivious. Comedic set pieces—like Hanks discovering that the CIA has modified the plumbing in his bathroom so that when he flushes the toilet, water squirts out of the sink—are dead on arrival but shamble laughlessly on anyway.

A spark of life comes in the interactions between Hanks and Carrie Fisher, another musician in the symphony. Their big scene together betrays the movie's French origins: she's the wife of his best friend, now trying to seduce him. Fisher is cast against type, playing a bespectacled femme fatale who strips down to leopard-print underwear and gets turned on by Tarzan ululations. But despite the absurd setup, the two performers clearly respect each other's intelligence and have an easy rapport together.

"Not a very good movie," Hanks said after he had recovered from the experience. "It doesn't have any real clear focus to it. It isn't about anything in particular that you can honestly understand. It made no money at all."

Lori Singer said that in a scene where she wore a skintight

gown—"cut so low that I felt naked"—she felt so exposed, she got giddy. "Tom picked up on that and off-camera made suggestive lewd faces at me," she said. Singer laughed so hard, she fell over. She remembered that Hanks also kept things loose on the set by dressing up the boom microphone as a harlequin or as Mickey Mouse.

When they were shooting in the Washington, DC, subway system, Singer and Hanks took their lunch break in an isolated patch of the tunnel. Singer said, "He opened up about his life and described a side of himself diametrically opposed to his on-set antics and ebullience. I never forgot his sensitivity and trust."

For a scene where Hanks' character rode a bicycle down a flight of stairs, he agreed to attempt the stunt once on a trick bicycle. "Tom nailed the stunt in one take," she said, "and then rode off down the street, wobbling as if he was drunk."

Halfway through the shoot, Singer went to a party thrown by Carrie Fisher and Penny Marshall, attended by seemingly everyone in Hollywood. She said, "I spent the whole night raving to Penny and Jack Nicholson, in particular, about how brilliant Tom was." They were taken aback by her exuberance, but Singer insisted that Hanks was "unquestionably brilliant."

Marshall rolled her eyes. "Congratulations," she told Singer. "You've just fallen in love with your costar."

Singer conceded, "Well, maybe there was a bit of that too."

Volunteers

(1985, Lawrence Bourne III)

"I'm obviously not of Peace Corps fiber. It's not that I can't help these people—it's just that I don't want to."

A fundamental comedy decision: whether characters will remain in the confines of the story's architecture or break the fourth wall. It's Aristotelian drama versus Brechtian drama, it's Hope & Crosby versus Laurel & Hardy, it's *The Colbert Report* versus *The Daily Show*. In the case of *Volunteers,* it's a scene toward the end of the movie, when Tom Hanks and one other actor can't understand the accented English of a Thai bodyguard named Lucille. So they lean forward and crane their necks to read the subtitles on the screen.

This gag provoked a huge argument among the movie's creative principals: screenwriters Ken Levine and David Isaacs thought that it eviscerated the movie's internal logic and removed any sense of drama—with the climax looming, the audience is reminded that it's just a movie. Director Nicholas Meyer's logic was straightforward: the moment got a huge laugh. "The lesson is never sacrifice the integrity of your piece for the sake of a joke, no matter how funny the joke is," Levine said decades later, still angry.

While Levine had a point, he would have had more of one if *Volunteers* wasn't already a mish-mash of styles, encompassing social satire, screwball rom-com, and broad physical gags. (Also, unfortunately, some stereotyped ethnic humor: that character with the accented English is a dragon lady with lethally spiked fingernails. The name "Lucille" was chosen so she could show off her difficulty distinguishing L sounds from R sounds.)

Hanks plays Lawrence Bourne III: shallow, spoiled, a recent graduate of Yale (the movie is set in the year 1962). Our hero joins the Peace Corps and flees to Thailand, wearing a formal white dinner jacket, so he can duck out on twenty-eight thousand dollars in gambling debts. Hanks adopts a patrician clenched-jaw New England accent but is recognizably his insouciant comedic self, with an air of being vaguely amused that he's stumbled into this movie.

Although the whole enterprise feels like a discount-rack *Stripes,* Hanks pulls off the performance, gets laughs from lines like "Do I look like I'm associated with this hootenanny?" and mostly throws himself into the Bourne identity.

The movie marks the reunion of Hanks with John Candy (playing an eager-beaver engineer trying to build a bridge in rural Thailand—until he gets brainwashed by the Communists) but they never really get into a comedic groove together. Much better is the dynamic between Hanks and Rita Wilson, who plays Beth, an idealistic young Jewish woman from Long Island. Off camera, Hanks and Wilson were falling in love, even though they were both in other relationships; that balance of desire and denial fuels their on-screen dynamic.

Hanks and Wilson go toe to toe with quick-paced badinage, Lawrence's condescension matched by Beth's contempt, and inevitably love blooms. There's a sweet scene when Lawrence kits out a jungle hut as a fully stocked bar, invites Beth on a date where they dance to "As Time Goes By," and then declines her invitation to come into her own hut, saying, "If I go in there, I'm going to be tempted to make a pass at you, and that's not what you want."

Wilson gets the topper: "It isn't?"

The *Volunteers* script was written back in 1980—Levine and Isaacs were fans of Hanks' work on *Bosom Buddies* and got him a copy of the screenplay. "He loved it, but of course Tom Hanks couldn't get a movie made in 1980," Levine said. Four years later, after the success of *Splash,* Hanks said to his agent, "There was a script I read four or five years ago about a guy in the Peace Corps, what ever happened to that?" The agent said he would try to track it down, but knew it would be like finding a grain of sand on Zuma Beach.

As it happened, the movie had languished for years, but had finally been set up at TriStar/HBO. The producer called Hanks' agent soon after that conversation, saying, "Would Tom read this script about a guy in the Peace Corps?" The agent told him to messenger it over, and passed it on to Hanks. The actor flipped through the script, found a joke about Margaret Dumont he remembered liking, and immediately committed to the movie.

"Here's what he brought to it," Levine said. "The character had some flaws. He was an asshole, and he was condescending, and he was a coward—it would be so easy to hate that guy. But Tom brought a twinkle. There was something likeable about him. It was fun to watch him. That's not an easy thing. Once the audience makes up their minds—'Why am I sitting here for an hour and a half watching this asshole?'—then you're dead. Tom is one of the few actors who was able to pull that off. And he went in and out of the Cary Grant accent, but he got every joke."

The Money Pit
(1986, Walter Fielding)

"Did you hear about that guy up in the Bronx—went crazy, thought he was a pigeon? They found him in the park throwing breadcrumbs at himself. He was just putting in a guest bathroom."

The Money Pit, allegedly a movie about a couple enduring a disastrous home renovation, is basically an excuse for slapstick and Rube Goldberg sight gags. Tom Hanks pulls his front door off the hinges, sets his kitchen on fire, and gets catapulted into wet cement so he can blindly blunder around, toppling a work crew's scaffolding before he ends up in a decorative fountain.

Although Hanks plays a Yale-educated lawyer (his second Yalie in a row!), the movie has no particular interest in social satire, or even geography: most of the action happens in a generic New York City suburb, a territory familiar as Sitcomland. The stars, Hanks and Shelley Long, perfectly fit that aesthetic—journeyman director Richard Benjamin at least had the good sense to cast two extremely talented sitcom veterans. The movie follows in the footsteps of the 1948 comedy *Mr. Blandings Builds His Dream House*—but the stars of *that* restoration comedy were Cary Grant and Myrna Loy, which is a high standard to live up to.

Hanks said that he and Long bonded to an unusual degree on the movie: "We had miniature adventures, great philosophical discussions. We were playing two people who were very much in love, and that requires a certain kind of communication you're not going to invest in anybody else." Even when the movie throws in a particularly capricious third-act complication (Long's character mistakenly believes she drunkenly slept with her ex-husband, played with a perpetual glower by ballet dancer Alexander Godunov), Hanks and Long sail through their scenes together.

Also jammed into this movie: a pointless subplot about Hanks' father absconding to Brazil with his clients' funds; a cameo from the hair-metal band White Lion (who had not yet had a hit with "When the Children Cry"); and an appearance by a young, skinny Joe Mantegna, portraying a sexually harassing carpenter in a scene that plays very differently three decades later.

Hanks accurately summed up the whole rickety *Money Pit* enterprise: "Some parts of that are absolutely hilarious, but for the most part, it just doesn't cut it."

Nothing in Common
(1986, David Basner)

"Tomorrow I'm doing a commercial about a family that cares for each other, loves each other. I'm faking it."

You might remember *Nothing in Common* for the final performance by the legendary Jackie Gleason, for a scene-stealing turn by Barry Corbin as a gruff airline owner, or for the ludicrous sequence where Tom Hanks and Sela Ward make eyes at each other while watching a breeding stallion preparing to mount a mare.

Hanks, however, remembers the movie as one of the turning points of his career. "I learned an awful lot about acting in that one, stuff that kind of whacked me across the head," he said. "That was the first movie where the specific thrust was to be very funny and very emotional at the same time. I think we came very close to achieving that."

Not as close as he thought, alas. Director Garry Marshall (most famous as the creator of *Happy Days*) wanted to blend hilarity and pathos, but couldn't figure out the balance. The resulting film is vaguely amusing and mildly dramatic.

Hanks is a hotshot advertising man in Chicago, the type of guy who can seduce a flight attendant in midair. But when his elderly parents split up, he's forced to pay attention to the parts of his life he's been ignoring. His father is played by Gleason (*The Honeymooners*), blustery but effective. Unfortunately, Eva Marie Saint

(*On the Waterfront*), cast as the newly independent mother, gives a summer-stock performance. Hector Elizondo plays the vain boss at the advertising agency; for some reason, he does his big emotional scene while wearing a cap adorned with a button protesting night baseball at Wrigley Field.

Hanks had to play both a glib adman and a young man overwhelmed by his family, and mostly did a good job making them seem like aspects of the same person, rather than an actor on a manic-depressive jag. He made the funny stuff look easy, of course: for a long tracking shot where Hanks walks through the agency, bantering with everyone he sees, he and Marshall concocted all his dialogue on the day of the shoot. ("Davenport, Iowa—that's one of the Quad Cities, isn't it? I hear that's twice as good as the Twin Cities.")

His best scene, however, comes when he finally snaps on the job. When a commercial he's supervising isn't going well—the actress playing the doting grandmother showed up drunk—he goes on an unhinged rant. At the end, he's exhausted and silent, but he swallows hard, wrestling with his emotions. We can see Hanks growing as an actor before our very eyes, discovering how much he can express without saying a word.

Every Time We Say Goodbye

(1986, David)

"I was hoping like crazy you were going to come today, but I was half hoping that you wouldn't, because I knew that if I saw you again, I would want to go on seeing you, again and again, again and again and again."

The first time Tom Hanks played a World War II soldier was not *Saving Private Ryan,* but this romantic drama set in 1942 Jerusalem. Hanks is David Bradley, an American pilot who enlisted with Britain's Royal Air Force before Pearl Harbor but is now recuperating from injuries. He falls in love with the beautiful local girl Sarah (Cristina Marsillach), part of a Sephardic Jewish family (meaning their roots centuries earlier were in Spain and there's a lot of subtitled Ladino dialogue); he attends their Sabbath dinner and asks questions such as "What's it like being part of a tribe?" Her family disapproves of the relationship (for religious reasons, when the objection should be that it's severely underwritten) and does what they can to keep them apart, but naturally, true love triumphs.

The studio (TriStar) knew they had a flop on their hands, and kept changing the title before release: it was provisionally titled *Love Is Ever Young* and *Love Hurts,* and ultimately grossed just $278,623 in the United States, by far the least of any Hanks vehicle.

A few years later, Hanks said this was "probably the most visually beautiful movie I've ever made." The scenery is indeed sumptuous, both in the desert and in historic Jerusalem. The cast is also attractive and top-notch—mostly Israeli actors, with the notable exceptions of one American (Hanks) and one Brit playing his RAF chum (Benedict Taylor). The actors labor mightily to make their scenes compelling, but they can't overcome the cardboard characterization or the unbelievably slow pacing: the overall vibe is a Merchant-Ivory film where everybody drank too much wine at a story-meeting lunch and took a nap instead of finishing the screenplay.

So in his first purely dramatic role, Hanks is required to look dashing, to dial down his comic energy, and to sell lines like "D. H. Lawrence said that all love has to offer us is pain." Although he's top-billed, this goy-meets-girl movie is really Sarah's story.

"I saw Tom Hanks in *Splash* and felt as if I'd known him before," said director Moshe Mizrahi. "When I see such an actor I ask myself whether he could play a king as well as a clown." Deciding the answer was yes, he cast him. After working with Hanks, Mizrahi raved about his ability to make his performance look effortless, plus "his sincerity, his sensibility, his curiosity, and above all his being a *mensch*."

Taylor said that he didn't realize Mizrahi was shooting two movies simultaneously: "a film from the Tom Hanks point of view, which we all thought we were working on and the producers had invested in, and he was shooting a film from her point of view in Sephardic which no one knew about except him. His loyalties were split. I remember talking to Moshe and he said, 'You have to understand about making films, Ben—you need to know how to tell a story. First you tell a story to the producers and they give you money. And then you go and make whatever you like.'"

Taylor and Hanks both traveled with drumsticks, so between takes, they would hang out, playing backgammon together and burning off excess energy by drumming on their kneecaps. Taylor said, "I could see the level of commitment and the amount of homework Tom put into things. He'd never stay up late carousing with the crew. He was always very friendly and very warm, but he'd separate himself at the right time of the evening and get on with some work. I took a lot from seeing someone of my generation taking it seriously, making sure they did their best work."

Dragnet

(Streebek, 1987)

"You know, Friday, we're allowed to go fifty-five. On some occasions, even faster."

Dragnet exemplifies many of the problems of Hollywood comedy, in 1987 and today. It's a remake of a familiar TV property rather than an original idea. With the filmmakers trying to raise the stakes for the movie, the plot wanders into the ridiculous: the L.A. police detectives, instead of investigating a stolen jade collection or phony magazine subscriptions, have to figure out the nefarious election-rigging scheme of a shadowy group called P.A.G.A.N. (which, it turns out, stands for "People Against Goodness and Normalcy"). The film has plenty of full-tilt action sequences, which don't do much except keep stuntmen fully employed. And although it's got a first-rate cast, the jokes aren't as funny as they should be.

Dan Aykroyd anchors the movie as Sergeant Joe Friday, nephew of the identically named character played by Jack Webb in the TV show that ran for twelve seasons in the '50s and '60s. Henry Morgan, who was Friday's partner on the show, got a promotion to captain for the movie and is the younger Friday's boss. Hanks plays Friday's junior partner, Pep Streebek—an improbable name that looks like an anagram but when shuffled doesn't yield anything more exciting than "kept beepers."

The movie's core gimmick is Aykroyd deploying his deadpan just-the-facts straight-arrow impression of Webb, but in 1987 Los Angeles, not 1951. Typical setup: the detectives visit the mansion of a lisping porn magnate (Dabney Coleman), and although

Friday is surrounded by scantily clad women, he is oblivious to the sexual innuendo. (Ironic production note: the *Bait* mansion scenes were actually filmed at a Los Angeles convent.)

Hanks, on the other hand, is portraying a recognizably modern guy: for a scene where he's in bed with a female police officer played by D. D. Howard, he gropes for a condom box only to find it empty, a moment that was muddled but in a small way groundbreaking in its advocacy of safe sex. Hanks plays the straight man to Aykroyd, which is a double bank shot of a role, since Aykroyd's Friday is the straightest man imaginable. Hanks has to be the sidekick, the audience's "is this guy for real?" proxy, and the movie's designated wisenheimer. (His best line comes when he mimics Friday's cadences: "My name's Streebek. I'm a cop. I overslept.") Hanks mostly pulls it off.

The bottom line according to Hanks: *Dragnet* "made a lot of money but probably not nearly as much as anticipated. It's convoluted. There are problems with it. It should be funnier."

Twenty-six years after the movie's release, a British journalist tentatively mentioned "City of Crime," the dreadful rap song Hanks and Aykroyd performed in character over the closing credits. (Aykroyd had a surprisingly successful music career of his own, as half of the Blues Brothers and as a participant in USA for Africa—which made the passing dialogue reference to "We Are the World" in *Dragnet* play oddly.) Hanks barked with laughter and launched into the opening verse from memory: "They got the girl all frightened and that's not nice / I think she is the subject of a sacrifice!" It turned out that the "City of Crime" music video was the first clip he ever watched on YouTube; Hanks described his reaction to watching it as "repulsed and fascinated at the same time."

<u>Big</u>

(Josh, 1988)

"I'm going to be thirty years old for the rest of my life."

Big wasn't the only age-changing movie of 1987–88: preceding it were *Like Father Like Son* (Dudley Moore trades bodies with Kirk Cameron, via Native American potion), *Vice Versa* (Judge Reinhold switches bodies with Fred Savage, via Tibetan skull), and *18 Again!* (George Burns swaps bodies with Kirk Cameron, via birthday wish)—and that's not even considering the Italian movie *Da Grande*. Elizabeth Perkins, who played the love interest Susan in *Big*, said that on the set, knowing of all the competing projects that were coming out before their movie, she and Hanks "looked at each other at one point like 'Ugh, this is going straight to video.'"

However, *Big* proved to be the best and the most popular of the bunch: a perfectly executed crowd-pleasing comedy that also felt emotionally honest. Watching most high-concept Hollywood comedies, you have to not just suspend your disbelief but suspend your eye-rolling when characters do something implausible because the plot mandates it. But the characters in *Big* seem like actual people—Perkins, for example, gives a nuanced portrayal of a hard-driving professional woman who isn't an oblivious ditz, but who does has enough personal issues that she falls in love with a guy who has the maturity level of a twelve-year-old.

The script had a top-notch pedigree: for a time, Steven

Spielberg was planning to direct it (it was written by his sister, Anne Spielberg, and Gary Ross) and the movie shows his usual care, where every story beat counts. Penny Marshall, who actually did direct it, did a wonderful job, fully committing to the joy and the weirdness of the premise.

None of that would have mattered if not for Hanks, who gave a moving, hilarious, pitch-perfect performance as Josh, completely believable as a twelve-year-old thrust into an adult body. Humiliated at a carnival when he can't go on the "Super Loops" ride with the girl he has a crush on, Josh wishes to be big, and a mystical Zoltar arcade machine grants his wish. Stuck in Tom Hanks' body, Josh goes to New York City and gets a job with a toy company.

Hanks walks with floppy limbs in a ducklike stance (he was mimicking the gait of David Moscow, who played the juvenile version of Josh), he encounters baby corn for the first time and nibbles on it like it was corn on the cob, and he quivers with fear and indignation when New York City proves to be too much for a tween.

Big isn't really a kids' movie, and not just because it acknowledges the existence of sex. (It lightly glides by the fact that Susan is unwittingly committing statutory rape, or something like it, when she's intimate with Josh—although when she says goodbye to him, finally knowing the truth, Marshall made sure that she kisses him on the forehead, not the lips.) The movie is only superficially about the wish-fulfillment of getting to do cool stuff when you grow up; it's really aimed at adults who dream of regaining their lost innocence.

Other people who were approached for the role of Josh included

Harrison Ford, Kevin Costner, Randy Quaid, Sean Penn (who was deemed too young), and Robert De Niro—who was up for it, but couldn't agree with producer James Brooks on money. It's hard to imagine any of them doing better than Hanks, who was nominated for an Oscar for his work here (losing to Dustin Hoffman in *Rain Man*). Hanks modestly said, "I was good in an excellent, excellent movie that worked on all twenty-two cylinders."

Punchline

(Steven Gold, 1988)

"All of our lives are funny, babe. We're God's animated cartoons."

In the decades since *Punchline* was released, the United States has achieved Total Stand-up Comedy Saturation, with scads of sitcoms, blogs, and podcasts all devoted to the trials and tribulations of these lonely comedy warriors. But in 1988, the topic was still somewhat novel—even *Seinfeld* wouldn't debut for another year.

So this Sally Field vehicle—she plays Lilah Krytsick, a New Jersey housewife who keeps coming into New York City to live her dream of doing stand-up, failing miserably until she meets the brilliant but damaged young comic portrayed by Tom Hanks—could have felt fresh. Unfortunately, it saddled that housewife with a disapproving husband (John Goodman) and a neglected family, in a setup that felt like a discarded episode from *I Love Lucy*. The housewife-breaking-her-shackles plotline probably would have worked better as a period piece like *The Marvelous Mrs. Maisel* (made in the twenty-first century, but set in 1958) or even a bio-pic about Joan Rivers. (Field developed the movie herself, via her production company; the writer-director was David Seltzer, more famous for the horror movie *The Omen*.)

The movie also doesn't have the courage to commit to its own material. The climactic stand-up contest at the Gas Station nightclub (televised on a nationwide broadcast because it's that kind of movie) not only edits monologues like montages, it drowns out jokes with pointless soundtrack music. Damon Wayans is allegedly in the movie as a rival comic, but he barely gets any screen time—you will be forgiven if you suspect that's because as an experienced stand-up, he would be funny enough to blow both Field and Hanks off the screen.

Hanks plays the foil to Field: Steven Gold, a comic who's on his way to stardom but who gets locked out of his apartment because he can't pay the rent. Gold is a talented misanthrope man-child who flunks out of med school and doesn't have the courage to tell his physician father. "The guy in *Punchline* probably has the worst aspects of my worst aspects," Hanks said. "He is extremely competitive, for one thing. Competitive to a fault. He is unable to balance his daily existence so that real life and what he does for a living have an equal weight. I've certainly had those problems; I think any actor has. The only time you really feel alive is when you're working."

Hanks went to stand-up boot camp for his role, developing a routine and bombing at nightclubs until he developed some onstage chops, and the hard work shows: Steven Gold comes off as a guy who's rightfully confident onstage and a mess everywhere else. When Steven and Lilah bond over comedy, it feels unlikely and delightful. But when Steven falls hard for her and suddenly declares his burning desire to marry Lilah and be the father of her children, that seems not just erratic but actively out of character. (Although it is satisfying on a political level—there's an overabundance of movies where younger women have thinly motivated passion for older men.)

The awkward scene where Steven declares his love for Lilah does lead to Hanks' best sequence in the movie: spurned, he steps onto a rainy New York City street, spinning around a lamppost like Gene Kelly and doing a soft-shoe dance in the middle of the street. As cars zoom by and honk at him, he stomps in the puddles, a man who wants to turn his anger and pain into comedy, but can't quite remember how.

The 'Burbs

(Ray Peterson, 1989)

"We're the ones who are vaulting over the fences and peeking in through people's windows. We're the ones who are throwing garbage in the street and lighting fires. We're the ones who are acting suspicious and paranoid, Art. We're the lunatics! Us! It's not them. It's us."

On a cul-de-sac in a Midwestern suburban town, Ray (Tom Hanks) has the week off, but resists the entreaties of his wife Carol (Carrie Fisher) to pack the car and head out to their lake house. He plans to spend his vacation puttering around the house—an agenda that gets derailed when his pal Art (Rick Ducommun) becomes convinced that the new neighbors aren't just creepy, but actual murderers. Checking out their trash cans escalates into breaking and entering and digging in the basement; mayhem ensues and a house blows up.

Superficially, *The 'Burbs* is a suburban satire: everyone in the neighborhood is spying on each other. But despite the suspected murder, director Joe Dante ends up with a tone that's more antic than dark—there's lots of physical comedy and sight gags. When somebody falls through the roof of a garden shed, he leaves a recognizable outline, like Wile E. Coyote running through a wall.

In this ensemble comedy, Hanks is meant to be the regular guy who gets swept up in the whirlwind of all the insane characters around him. It's the type of part he can roll out of bed and do—and here he basically does. He gets a couple of good bits—sliding down a staircase, eating a sardine on a pretzel—but he's basically the straight man. The rest of the actors, unfortunately, are miscast or subpar. If the overbearing neighbor who prods Hanks into action were played by John Candy instead of Rick Ducommun, the scenes would probably be funny enough that we could skate past the thin plot. Bruce Dern works hard as the ex-military neighbor, in a role that calls out for Christopher Walken or Christopher Lloyd. Carrie Fisher is a kick-ass goddess, but she can't find anything funny to do with the role of the pestering wife.

Hanks called *The 'Burbs* an "interesting little suburban nightmare," and remembered it fondly just because he had fun making it—director Joe Dante filmed it on the suburban backlot of Universal Studios (a location that later became famous as Wisteria Lane on *Desperate Housewives*). The movie had a split schedule, where they'd show up around noon, do a half-day of work in the light, take a break while the sun set, and then work until midnight. Hanks loved that timetable: "You get enough sleep. You see your family." And the two-hour twilight break provided a lot of downtime for the cast to hang out and make each other laugh. Hanks said of the shooting schedule, "It's the absolute best way."

Some of the best off-camera time came with Fisher, who had also appeared in *The Man with One Red Shoe* with Hanks. She remembered when the two of them first figured out that they clicked. "Could we have a *conversation*?" Hanks asked her.

She said, "He said the word as if it were an exotic fruit, and that's exactly what it is in Hollywood. We decided that conversation is a kiwi."

Turner & Hooch
(Scott Turner, 1989)

"This is why man will prevail and your kind will never dominate the earth. This is what you can do if you've got thumbs!"

This overcooked piece of Hollywood product is credited to five different screenwriters, each of whom apparently thought he was working on a different movie. It's a slapstick comedy about a neatnik cop (Hanks) who has to look after a large, uncontrollable dog called Hooch—but for inexplicable reasons, it's also a crime drama, a murder mystery, and a heartwarming romance. And it has a tragic ending (in the tradition of *Old Yeller*) that's totally unearned. The movie came out just months after *K-9*, where Jim Belushi played a police detective with a new canine partner, so it didn't even have the advantage of novelty.

The big-dog sequences basically work, especially if you think a shoe covered in canine drool is the height of comedy. Hanks commits to the physical bits, letting the dog pull him around, slamming his body against doors, and even mimicking how the dog shakes water off his body. Hanks pulls out every bit of shtick in his repertoire, showing off a variety of flabbergasted expressions. He also has a couple of long scenes in tight black bikini briefs; if that fulfills your fantasies, this is the movie for you.

Mare Winningham is winsome as the local veterinarian who

treats Hooch and has a sweet romance with Turner. The crime story—about money laundering in a sleepy California coastal town—would be weak in any movie, but feels particularly off-key here: stabbings don't mesh well with dog-fart jokes.

Part of the reason for the discordant tone may be that the original director Henry Winkler (famous for playing the Fonz on *Happy Days*) was fired after thirteen days and replaced by Roger Spottiswoode. There were reports that Winkler and Hanks were arguing on the set. "Let's just say I got along better with Hooch than I did with Turner," Winkler said.

The best scene comes late: Turner has brought Hooch on a late-night stakeout and jabbers affectionately at the dog about old TV: the spy show *The Man from U.N.C.L.E.* and the parody-spy show cast with chimpanzees, *Lancelot Link, Secret Chimp*. It feels loose and real (and improvised by Hanks)—especially in contrast to the rest of the movie, which is a dog's breakfast of clichés.

It's a Hollywood truism that a bad movie is as much work as a good one. Despite its fifty-nine shooting days, *Turner & Hooch* puts the lie to that saying—watching it, you can't help but notice how sloppy and unimaginative it is and wish that everyone involved had worked a little harder. In the years since its release, however, the movie has become a reliable punchline—especially for people who have never seen it—both because of the goofiness of an Oscar winner starring opposite a slobbery dog, and because the title is inherently funny. On the brilliant comedy TV series *Party Down*, J. K. Simmons played a sleazy Hollywood producer who complained that Hanks hadn't spoken to him since he put him in *Turner & Hooch*. And when the hospital sitcom *Scrubs* featured one doctor named Turner and another named Hooch, the main characters successfully maneuvered to have the two physicians scheduled to work the same surgery. Which was amusing by itself—but the meta-joke was that Turner was played by Tom Hanks' younger brother, Jim Hanks.

Joe Versus the Volcano
(Joe, 1990)

"I've been doing some soul-searching lately, been asking myself some pretty tough questions—you know what I found out? I have no interest in myself. I start thinking about myself, I get bored out of my mind."

At the time of its release, this movie confused and even enraged audiences. It's a fable about a man with a miserable job in the advertising department for a medical-supply company ("Home of the Rectal Probe") who, told that he has six months to live, accepts a lucrative offer to go to a South Pacific island and jump into a volcano. It's an extremely stylized, theatrical film—the islanders have a mania for orange soda and their chieftain is played by Abe Vigoda. Although it was a moderate box-office success, it's become a footnote in Tom Hanks' career, usually remembered only because it marks the beginning of the on-screen partnership between Hanks and Meg Ryan.

The movie doesn't totally work, but it has plenty of virtues. Writer-director John Patrick Shanley, primarily a playwright, proved to have a strong visual sense, liking to frame memorable set design in wide-angle tableaus. The movie has an over-the-top sense of whimsy, nostalgia for a Manhattan that never was, and title cards. Which means that twenty-first-century audiences have a new lens to watch *Joe Versus the Volcano* through: it plays like the proto-version of a Wes Anderson film.

How did this unusual movie get made? Steven Spielberg took a liking to the script, encouraged Shanley to direct it, and made sure that the studio didn't interfere. According to Shanley, Hanks was trying to get out of a professional rut. "He'd leveled down to mediocre comedies they could make quick money on," Shanley said. "But he suddenly had a hunger for doing something of higher quality, and he was also, in addition to Spielberg, another great defender of the film. When the forces that be came down on me, Tom also very much stood up for me and the film, and helped me to get them to back down."

"Shanley can tear you a new asshole if you don't know what you're doing," Hanks said. "He gives you the goods and expects them right back from you. A lot of people in this town would call that ego. I think it's honesty." Hanks remembered the appeal of the screenplay being Joe learning he had six months to live because of a "brain cloud." "I thought, 'That's the most glamorous thing in the world! Imagine the freedom he must feel. All the rules are off. I can do everything I want and do it now!' I reacted to that and ended up lunging at it in order to do it."

The movie was an acting showcase for Ryan—she played three different characters so effectively that Hanks didn't recognize her the first day she showed up as DeDe, a coworker at Joe's hellish medical-supply job. "I didn't know it was Meg," Hanks said. "I thought I was talking to some goofy chick at the coffee table." Hanks didn't fare so well in his single role; although he played Joe capably, the movie's mannered aesthetic didn't cater to his comedic or dramatic strengths.

Hanks and Ryan have a lot of seafaring scenes in the movie, some where they're on a boat and some where they're drifting on a raft made of lashed-together steamer trunks. Those sequences were filmed in the water tanks at the old MGM studio where Esther Williams used to make her aquamusical movies. Ryan's predominant memory of those days was that Hanks kept immersing himself in the tank between takes. "He's just a nut for water," she said. "He loved diving in and out of that ocean water—to the point where he got a big ear infection."

The Bonfire of the Vanities

(Sherman McCoy, 1990)

"I'm going to jail, aren't I?"

Tom Hanks looks overwhelmed. His eyes flicker and dilate, expressing the fear and indignation that are roiling underneath the spackled mask of his own face. His character, bond trader Sherman McCoy, has been steamrolled by the movie's plot and thrust into a New York City tabloid nightmare. He spends much of *The Bonfire of the Vanities* with a big phony smile, an unsuccessful attempt to conceal his own despair. Hanks also looks like he's expressing his own plight: he's trapped in a cinematic bomb of historic proportions.

Hanks, like most of the movie's leads, was miscast—McCoy was supposed to be a patrician WASP. But producer Peter Guber insisted on Hanks, eventually convincing director Brian De Palma, on the logic that Hanks would make the central character of McCoy likable. That impulse was understandable for a Hollywood executive trying to maximize box-office grosses—the movie was an adaptation of Tom Wolfe's bestselling novel, a black-hearted satire of money, race, and power in New York City. But when the characters were made more palatable and the material was softened, *Bonfire* lost its comic punch, leaving only a movie-shaped lump of cynicism.

De Palma gives *Bonfire* visual pop and some bravura tracking shots, making it a movie best seen on an airplane with the sound off. Bruce Willis narrates and wanders through the action in a stupor. Although Morgan Freeman annoyed the filmmakers by showing up for his scenes without his lines memorized, he has the best performance in the movie. (However, even he can't pull off a final monologue advocating for decency and justice, which feels patently phony after a two-hour pageant of greed and jaundiced race relations.)

While Sherman McCoy spends most of the movie moping and whining after he and his mistress (Melanie Griffith) hit a young man in the Bronx with his Mercedes, he gets one great scene, where he breaks up a party at his own ritzy Park Avenue home by firing a shotgun into the ceiling. His fellow plutocrats run for the exits while Hanks shouts with unhinged delight, finally cutting loose—until he's knocked out by a chunk of plaster falling from the ceiling.

Radio Flyer

(Adult Mike [uncredited], 1992)

"No other kids in the history of the world ever had a better idea. And if they did, they never built it."

Radio Flyer, following in the footsteps of *Stand by Me* and *The Wonder Years,* is a nostalgic look back at kids whiling away the hours in the 1960s, fending for themselves, and growing up to the accompaniment of classic-rock songs and wry adult narration. What sets it apart is there's a lot more child abuse.

The story: Lorraine Bracco plays the single mom of two boys (one of them a young Elijah Wood) who relocates to California and marries a man who likes to be called "The King" (cue flashing red warning lights and air-raid siren), who regularly gets drunk and beats her younger son, Bobby (played by Joseph Mazzello). Bracco is good and the kid actors are fine (if a bit stoic), but the movie takes a bizarre turn at the end when the two kids build a flying machine out of the titular little red wagon and various spare parts; Bobby rolls it down a steep hill and off a ramp, soars into the sky, and flies away, never to be seen again.

The most plausible reading of this ending is that Bobby's escape is an unsettling metaphor for suicide, but apparently that's not what the filmmakers intended. The original script by David Mickey Evans set up the climax by weaving in a lot more magical realism— the idea being that until you hit puberty, animals really do talk and you can safely jump off a roof with an umbrella—but it all got stripped out except for the flying machine, which then felt like a random cut-and-paste from *E.T. the Extraterrestrial*.

The film had an unusual production history: although there was no track record of big box-office grosses for nostalgic fantasies about child abuse, there was nevertheless a bidding war for the screenplay. It was won by the profligate heads of Columbia Pictures, Peter Guber and Jon Peters, who paid $1.25 million and gave Evans the right to direct the movie—but Evans got fired after ten days of principal photography. The movie was rebooted, recast, and directed by Richard Donner (most famous for the *Lethal Weapon* series), who had no particular aptitude for the tricky material. (The best blending of surrealism and childhood horrors was probably in a movie that came years later: Guillermo del Toro's *Pan's Labyrinth*.)

Tom Hanks plays the adult version of Elijah Wood, the older son. Most of his work is in voiceover, telling the audience superfluous information and providing a reassuring adult presence.

Hanks was not yet an avatar of American decency, but his performance here—mostly measured and calm, a beacon of hope in a bleak situation—helps explain why he became one.

Hanks also appears in two brief scenes bookending the movie, at an airfield where he tells his own sons the tale of his childhood. They were done during a one-day reshoot after test audiences were baffled by the original ending. In that version, the two adult brothers reunite at the Smithsonian Air and Space Museum, where the Radio Flyer is on display, magically hovering in the air.

A League of Their Own
(Jimmy Dugan, 1992)

"Rogers Hornsby was my manager, and he called me a talking pile of pig shit, and that was when my parents drove all the way down from Michigan to see me play the game, and did I cry? No! No! And you know why? Because there's no crying in baseball."

A stand-up triple of a movie, inspired by the real-world exploits of the All-American Girls Professional Baseball League, which had its first pitch in 1943 when most of the USA's healthy young men were fighting in World War II, and kept going until 1954. Director Penny Marshall made that piece of history into a sparkling comedy, funny, inspiring, and just a touch sentimental.

To cast the movie, Marshall tested basically every young woman in Hollywood to find out who could actually play baseball. Demi Moore, cast as the lead, dropped out when she got pregnant ("She literally got fucked out of the part," Marshall joked), and her replacement Debra Winger quit when Madonna joined the cast; Geena Davis stepped in and starred as catcher Dottie Hinson. The other Rockford Peaches included Lori Petty and Rosie O'Donnell (making her screen debut, she was paid just $42,500). Jon Lovitz played the sarcastic talent scout ("See, how it works is the train moves, not the station"); Garry Marshall portrayed club owner Walter Harvey when Christopher Walken proved too expensive (it's always cheaper to cast your brother). And joining the ensemble as Jimmy Dugan, washed-up alcoholic manager of the Peaches, was America's sweetheart, Tom Hanks.

For most of the film's characters, their dramatic arcs are straightforward: joining the league gives these women a chance to have an adventure and see the world, and they become better versions of themselves as a result. But Geena Davis' Dottie and Hanks' Jimmy have a somewhat more complicated journey: initially reluctant to admit that the league means anything to them, by the end of the movie they embrace the fellowship of "dirt in the skirt."

Hanks introduces himself to his team by stumbling drunkenly into the clubhouse, ripping up a vintage baseball card of himself, and then taking a fifty-second piss, during which his face is an epic poem of exhaustion and ecstasy. Hanks makes the most of every moment, whether he's muttering "you can all kiss my ass" as he waves to a crowd, comparing an umpire to a penis with a little hat, or quietly talking about the war with Davis on a long bus ride.

According to Marshall, "Tom had done a handful of not-so-hot pictures, which happens when you work as often as he did, and he was reading scripts, looking for a movie that would get him back on track. He wanted a part where he wasn't the lead, but audiences would be happy every time he came on screen. *League* was perfect. 'Can I have it?' he asked. I thought he was wrong for the part. But he's a great guy and gets along with everyone."

"I specifically wanted to do it because this was a man who'd experienced bitter compromise in his life," Hanks said. "The script described the character as a fifty-two-year-old broken-down alcoholic. I said [to Marshall], 'Look, I don't want to play a fifty-two-year-old broken-down alcoholic. I want to play a thirty-six-year-old broken-down alcoholic.' That ended up changing the whole dynamic of the character. I said, 'Look, if he's thirty-six, how come he's not still playing ball? How come he's not serving in the war? This way, I just have to show up with a limp, and the entire character is explained.'" (The movie ultimately included an explanatory line about Dugan falling out of a hotel window, escaping a fire—that he had started.)

Marshall was still worried. If Hanks looked too cute, she reasoned, the audience would be wondering why there was no love connection between him and the Peaches. "So I tried him in glasses, messed with his hair, and finally said, 'Eat! You've got to eat! Get fat.'"

Liberated from the responsibility of carrying the movie, Tom threw himself into his physical transformation and his character. "I didn't have my skinny little wrists and pipe-cleaner neck," he recalled gleefully. "I had rolls of fat on my neck!" Hanks put on twenty pounds and looks sweaty and fleshy in the finished film: his neck bulges over his collar as he blearily rages against the unfairness of a universe where he has to manage girls.

Having thrown himself into a character role, Hanks wanted to go all the way. He regretted that the movie's epilogue established that Dugan lived until 1987: "I would say, kill him in 1962, have him completely succumb to his depression and alcoholism. Have him die in some bad cold-water walk-up in Truckee, California." How come? "Because I never get to play guys like that."

Sleepless in Seattle
(Sam Baldwin, 1993)

"It was a million tiny little things that when you added them all up they just meant that we were supposed to be together."

Men are from Seattle; women are from Baltimore. The extremely unusual structure of the rom-com *Sleepless in Seattle*—Tom Hanks and Meg Ryan don't meet, or talk, until the movie's closing minutes—not only teases out the tension between two people who might be long-distance soul mates, it provides director Nora Ephron with an ideal platform to explore her favorite theme of the differences between men and women. Ryan and Rosie O'Donnell bond over the 1957 romance *An Affair to Remember,* while Hanks and Victor Garber have great fun bringing a similar level of weepy intensity to a conversation about the 1967 war escapade *The Dirty Dozen.*

Although Hanks entered shooting somewhat uncertain about starring in a romance aimed at women, he became more upbeat as shooting progressed. That was partially because he learned to trust the genius of Ephron, and partially because of the magic of caffeine: at a point before Starbucks had blanketed the United States in a thin layer of cappuccino foam, he discovered why Seattle had a reputation for great coffee. "I drank *way* too much coffee," he said. "I drank so much coffee that they started sneaking me decaf without me knowing it. Because I was coming home so amped up because the stuff was just so delicious. This was the first time that I had been exposed—and anybody really had been exposed—to something other than drip coffee from a Bunn coffeemaker or something like that. With the hot milk in it? It was sensational. I drank it like hot chocolate. And I was coming home, wired on six or seven lattes in the course of the day."

Ephron did a brilliant job finding ways to connect Hanks and Ryan when their characters are on opposite sides of the country—one particularly elegant touch is Ryan opening a door in Baltimore, with a quick cut to Hanks walking through the same door in Seattle. (The production took the door off its hinges and shipped it across the country.)

Ryan is the protagonist, who embarks on a quixotic chase for true love after she hears Hanks' voice on the radio, but what gives the movie texture is that Hanks isn't asked to play Prince Charming of the Pacific Northwest. He's Sam, a man shattered after his wife died young, who's trying to navigate through his own grief and care for his eight-year-old son Jonah. (Jonah puts the plot in motion when he calls up a therapist's radio show looking for a new wife for his dad.)

Hanks has a few good scenes with adults—a lunch with Rob Reiner where Hanks is baffled by the word "tiramisu" is particularly fine—but most of Sam's character is established by how he interacts with Jonah. It's easy enough to establish a father-son rapport when they're playing football on the beach; more impressive is the genuine connection that comes when they're brushing their teeth together and discussing the sex scenes that Jonah has managed to see on cable TV. Fielding questions about the role of back-scratching in lovemaking, Hanks hits just the right note of nonplussed but tolerant.

What makes that rapport more remarkable is that Ross Malinger, who played Jonah, was not the first actor in the role.

Eight-year-old Nathan Watt was overwhelmed by the shoot; adorable off-camera, he had trouble remembering his lines or saying them in a natural fashion. Hanks didn't give the producers a him-or-me ultimatum, but everybody knew he wasn't happy working with Watt. When you're a movie star, you don't always have to express your desires as demands: after a few days of filming, Ephron fired young Watt and recast the role. (To facilitate the switch, they flipped the movie's schedule around—Ryan filmed her half first instead of Hanks.)

Hanks was impressed that Ephron had the guts to make the painful decision, saying, "I thought it was the bravest thing I'd ever heard. There was no doubt that it was not working.... That's all you can say about it. It was not going to be natural. And for Nora, on the first weekend of shooting to have to make that sort of change...well, then you're into the reason why most people don't want to direct movies. Or end up directing movies that have big, fat, gaping holes in the middle of them—because they don't want to fire somebody like that. They don't want to be the mercenary who has to do a very, very extreme and devilish deed in order to make the movie live the way they see it in their head." For all his bonhomie, Hanks knew it was show business, not show friends.

And if Ephron hadn't made the tough choice? Hanks shrugged; he would have survived. "I've worked with dogs, you know."

Philadelphia

(Andrew Beckett, 1993)

"I'll tell you what I'm going to do—I'm going to start planning my memorial service."

Antonio Banderas had just auditioned to play Tom Hanks'

boyfriend in *Philadelphia,* and he had a question, one based on his own experiences acting in the antic, libidinous films of Pedro Almodóvar in his native Spain: "So, Tom, you have played homosexual before in movies?"

Hanks was amused that Banderas didn't know just how heteronormative Hollywood was. "Well, Antonio," he replied, "I've actually been turning down all those great homosexual roles they keep offering me."

Philadelphia is the story of a gay lawyer, Andy Beckett (Hanks), who gets fired by his law firm when they discover he has AIDS and then sues them for discrimination. The movie was a political football from the moment it was announced: on one side, conservative commentators complained that it was pushing the "homosexual agenda" and Hollywood financiers worried that gay characters would alienate cineplex audiences, while on the other side, gay activists wanted to make up for decades of marginalization by including a wide spectrum of the homosexual experience and being bolder in the portrayal of man-on-man romance.

With all these pressures, it wouldn't have been surprising if director Jonathan Demme presided over a well-meaning but inert period piece. In fact, *Philadelphia* is, for the most part, thrilling and moving. Demme made sure that the action feels like it's happening in a real city—a crowded, living Philadelphia—but the reason the movie endures is the on-screen interaction between Hanks and Denzel Washington (playing Joe Miller, the bigoted lawyer who takes on his case and overcomes his own prejudices). Watching them on-screen together is like watching two championship tennis players in an extended volley, feeling out each other's rhythms, attuned to the nuances of every half-step.

During the courtroom scenes, Hanks didn't have much to do other than sit behind a table and watch Washington work. "The greatest acting lessons I have ever received was from those days," he said. "I steal from him every day, in every performance."

Andy Beckett's story is grounded in the mundane worlds of law offices and hospitals, but there's one scene where his spirit flies unfettered (a scene that the filmmakers had to fight for). When he's supposed to be rehearsing his testimony, Andy instead listens to Maria Callas sing "La mamma morta" and describes the meaning of the aria to Joe. Walking around with his IV drip, Andy lets the music take him out of his own fallible flesh. "I am divine; I am oblivion," he translates, his eyes closed and his palm on his forehead, and for a moment, Hanks makes it the truth.

The soul of the movie, however, is a simpler moment: leaving Joe's office after an early scene where Joe has declined to take his case, Andy stands on a busy Philadelphia sidewalk. Pedestrians walk by, but he is utterly alone. As a Bruce Springsteen song plays on the soundtrack, Hanks purses his lips and his eyes dart around. In that moment, he is utterly vulnerable, utterly heartbreaking, utterly human.

Forrest Gump

(Forrest Gump, 1994)

"Hello. My name's Forrest, Forrest Gump. Do you want a chocolate? I could eat about a million and a half of these. My mama always said life was like a box of chocolates—you never know what you gonna get."

Forrest Gump is a profoundly strange movie. It's a comedy, alternately deadpan and broad, that periodically erupts with scenes of shameless sentiment, which work because the principal actors, especially Hanks, commit so fully to their performances. If you've never seen the movie, you may have trouble believing this is an accurate summary: Forrest Gump tells his life story while sitting on a bus-stop bench. Despite an IQ of seventy-five, he has been a football star at the University of Alabama, a soldier in Vietnam, a Ping-Pong champion, a millionaire owner of shrimp boats, and a national inspiration for running across the United States seven times. He never fell out of love with his childhood sweetheart Jenny (Robin Wright), who went on her own, less fulfilling, exploration of America. Along the way, Gump met three U.S. presidents, taught Elvis Presley to dance, and invented the phrase "Shit happens."

The studio, baffled by the script's meandering structure, was reluctant to greenlight the movie, but agreed when Hanks and director Robert Zemeckis agreed to forgo their salaries in favor of percentages of the gross (an extremely lucrative trade, as it turned out—Hanks reportedly pocketed around $65 million). As they were making the movie, Hanks and Zemeckis were never sure whether it was working. "We didn't know if people would care about this man's life," Hanks said. "We didn't know if they'd be willing to sit with him on the bench long enough to ramble on and on about everything that happened to him."

People cared. The movie was the top box-office hit of 1994. It won six Oscars (including Best Actor for Hanks) and left behind a successful restaurant chain (the Bubba Gump Shrimp Company), a handful of catchphrases seared into popular culture ("stupid is as stupid does"), and a vast array of magazine thinkpieces trying to figure out what it all meant. Was the movie conservative? Anti-intellectual? A well-meaning but empty spectacle?

It was an ambitious movie, using computer graphics to blend Gump in with historical footage and to remove the legs of Lieutenant Dan (Gary Sinise) after an injury in Vietnam—standard procedure now, but jaw-dropping then. The film's a widescreen spectacle of big-budget excess. For example, it's not content to pull out a couple of vintage rock hits to set the scene in Vietnam: roughly every twenty seconds, it switches from Creedence to the Four Tops to Aretha Franklin, like a hyperactive child with a complete box set of the Time-Life *Sounds of the Sixties* collection.

The movie's central metaphor holds up: the history of the United States is the story of an enthusiastic dimwit, hurtling forward at maximum speed, with good intentions but no real understanding of the consequences of his actions. The movie has lots of comments from Gump on the famous folks he met, like John F. Kennedy and John Lennon, that feel pat until you realize how many of them end up getting shot.

Before filming started, Hanks spent some time in a home for developmentally delayed adults, but quickly realized that his character was not going to be a realistic portrayal of their lives. "It was like creating an alien," he said—although, as in *Big,* he drew crucial elements from the actor playing the young version of himself (Michael Conner Humphreys). The boundaries of his character: an austere haircut, an intense stare, rigid posture (even when running), and a thick, slow Alabama drawl. Within those strictures, Hanks displayed perfect comic timing and delivered one of the most deeply emotional performances of his career.

The centerpiece of his openhearted performance was the narration. For three straight days, Zemeckis filmed him sitting on a bench, on location in Savannah, Georgia. Zemeckis wanted the voiceover to sound like a performance rather than a reading, and he wanted to be able to cut to Gump whenever he needed to. Hanks said sitting on that bench was one of the most grueling experiences of his acting career: "You have to stay stock-still, but the engine inside is still fully stoked; it's just going. It's harder almost to stay completely reined in than it is to come in and just chat, chat, chat, chat. Like, there's a scene in *Sleepless in Seattle* where I'm getting ready for a first date, and I'm moving all over the place and forgetting my keys. You can rattle that stuff off ten, twenty, thirty, forty, fifty times without any difficulty. But at the end of three days of just sitting on a park bench and telling Forrest Gump's life story, I was exhausted."

Apollo 13
(Jim Lovell, 1995)

"Gentlemen, what are your intentions? I'd like to go home."

The most exciting scene in *Apollo 13* comes when a group of engineers have to cobble together a replacement air filter. That's not the stuff blockbuster movies are usually made of, but it's as engrossing as the sequence in *Rififi* where we watch a group of French burglars methodically drill through the ceiling of a jewelry store to gain access to the safe. *Apollo 13*, director Ron Howard's best movie, applies the same unblinking documentary rhythm to the 1970 lunar mission that, after a technical failure, aborted plans to land on the moon and barely made it back to Earth with its three astronauts alive.

Hanks plays the commander of that mission, Jim Lovell, with square-jawed commitment to the job. His one moment of duplicity comes when, ordered to drop his pilot (Gary Sinise) from the mission because he's been exposed to measles, he tells the pilot that he made the decision himself, not the upper brass—and even that comes off as adhering to the chain of command. Hanks said, "What has Jim Lovell in that space capsule is only his desire to be there. There is no other superstructure. He wanted to be there, he wanted to be an astronaut. He applied himself and he made that possible. My challenge is I have to explain to the audience why he's there. I don't get it done for me via the script or via the narrative."

Hanks' performance isn't flashy, or designed to be a star turn; he commits to the NASA mind-set, says his terse lines without emotional hyperbole, and trusts the story to carry him. Howard does an excellent job balancing life in the claustrophobic command module with mission control in Houston, populated by intense crew-cut nerds in shirtsleeves and led by Ed Harris, and the harrowing homefront experience of Marilyn Lovell (Kathleen Quinlan).

Producer Brian Grazer said, "Tom was at least 50 percent of the driving force of this movie. Because of his understanding of what actually happened on that mission, he was the truth meter of the movie. He paid attention to how astronauts are, how they should say things, and he made sure that we adhered to what really went on and portrayed things with an honesty. Astronauts go into space and rely on both their physical and mental capacities to survive. Tom made it very clear how the tone should be, and he helped police it. This is completely unusual for a star actor of his caliber."

Howard cast his three astronaut leads on temperament as much as acting ability or box-office clout: the three actors had to spend long days in the cramped quarters of the module, on a set that was cooled to thirty-two degrees Fahrenheit so you could see their breath condensing. (Between takes, they gulped down hot soup.) They found ways to relieve the tension of being packed into a small metal box; Hanks said that a phrase coined by Kevin Bacon stayed in his own vocabulary for decades after the film wrapped.

One day, when Howard was figuring out how to frame a difficult shot, Bacon walked up to the director and said, "I don't want to boss you around, Ron, but I really think the shot should be a B.F.C.U.K.B. right here."

Howard, confused, asked what that meant.

Bacon explained that it stood for a "big fucking close-up of Kevin Bacon."

Toy Story

(Woody, 1995)

"The word I'm searching for, I can't say, because there's preschool toys present."

The idea was simple and brilliant: toys have full lives and adventures when their owners leave the room. (Which makes one wonder why they want to hang around the owners at all, but let's move on.) However, it took the *Toy Story* creators (including director John Lasseter before he ran all of Disney animation and writer

Joss Whedon before he created the *Buffy the Vampire Slayer* TV show and directed *The Avengers*) some work to get it right.

As originally conceived, Woody the cowboy doll (voiced by Tom Hanks) was a jerk, belittling all the other toys in Andy's bedroom. Some of that personality remains in the finished film—Woody is often snarly and sour, not the icon of can-do enthusiasm and loyalty he became. But script revisions pushed him toward being an exemplary toy—when he's not feeling threatened by the arrival of the shiny new astronaut toy Buzz Lightyear (voiced by Tim Allen). Some of the computer animation, mind-blowing in 1995, looks a bit primitive three decades later, but the movie endures because it's unrelentingly smart and funny, and because it's the emotional origin story of a hard-won friendship.

While Hanks was recording the voice work for *Toy Story*, he had no idea it would be a massive hit—probably the role he'll be best remembered for fifty years from now. "We thought we were making a goofy cartoon!" he said. "You record your dialogue track, essentially in a room by yourself. You face the directors' booth, where this panel—they look like East German judges from the Olympics—are sitting in there, and they hear every word you say. You perform the script, there's a video camera, you record the scene, and you go back and rerecord some other parts of the scene, and you go back and do it almost line by line." That means taking dialogue like "Get down, you dope, you're going to get hit!" and doing it over and over: fast, casual, agitated, and every other line reading he could imagine.

"You just keep going and going and going and going and going and that's one line and it takes up half an hour," Hanks said. At the end, he'll look to the directors, like an ice skater waiting for the judges' scores. "And you've done it thirty-two different ways and they have found the thirty-third way, and so you perform it like that. It's fun, but it's tough work."

That Thing You Do!
(Mr. White, 1996)

"If the crowd doesn't go wild for you, don't worry—they will tomorrow."

The primary pleasure of *That Thing You Do!* is bathing nostalgically in the rock 'n' roll waters of 1964, so take a moment to appreciate how the movie gets the names of its fictional musical acts just right for the period: Johnny & the Walkers. The Hollyhocks. The Chantrellines. The Heardsmen. Saturn 5. And our stars, the Wonders, who start life as the homonymic Oneders but have to change the spelling because everybody keeps calling them the "Oh-Needers."

Tom Hanks made his feature-film debut as both a writer and a director with this movie; he proved to be a better director. (Before he started, he solicited advice from his successful friends; Garry Marshall advised him to change his shoes at lunch.) *That Thing You Do!* pops visually and has the snappy energy of its title song, while the writing is often just competent, and sometimes not even that—a running joke about Spartacus falls completely flat, for example. The story is simple: four young men from Erie, Pennsylvania, cut a single and unexpectedly ride it all the way into the top ten, ascending from talent shows to state fairs to nationwide TV broadcasts, and then promptly break up.

As Hanks said, "It's a show business story without any of the standard show business clichés. Nobody has problems with fame, nobody does drugs, it doesn't have bad guys, nobody slaps anybody. Of course, if the movie went into 1965 or 1966, it would probably happen, but because it ends in 1964, it doesn't."

Hanks cast himself in the movie in a supporting role, as the band's A&R man at Play-Tone Records, smoothly grooming them and guiding them through the shoals of show business. The record-company suit is usually portrayed as a stock villain with an insincere smile, but although Mr. White signs the band to a bad contract and plays hardball with them, he's also the movie's most charismatic figure and ultimately its greatest source of wisdom. The young musicians are the stars, but the movie's on the record company's side—and in real life, Hanks did become an executive at his own Playtone production company.

The lead singer of the Wonders, Jimmy (Johnathon Schaech), is a prima donna who's a jerk to his girlfriend, but he's also right to be wary of the contracts the other band members are so eager to sign. (On the other hand, those exploitative contracts got them out of Erie—our protagonist Guy [Tom Everett Scott] ends up with the glamorous life of a Hollywood session drummer instead of toiling at his dad's appliance store.)

Most of the characters are male, but Hanks makes a point of letting his female characters shine. Liv Tyler, playing Jimmy's girlfriend Faye, isn't asked to do much more than look beautiful and cough, like a consumptive heroine in a Victorian novel (at least she has a cold, not tuberculosis), but she gets a poetic breakup speech: "I have wasted thousands and thousands of kisses on you…shame on me for kissing you with my eyes closed so tight." And Hanks saves his sharpest writing for the small role of Margueritte, the cocktail waitress played by his wife, Rita

Wilson: "I left Vancouver for Tacoma, Tacoma for Portland—oh, I got married in Portland. Yeah. Then I left Portland for Reno, and I got divorced in Reno, then wised up and faced the inevitable— you know, move to L.A." She makes a pass at the younger Guy but realizes with amused resignation that he only has eyes for his jazz heroes.

If the movie's accomplishments are minor, that doesn't make them any less endearing. Directing presented a thousand new challenges for Hanks; surprisingly, the achievement he said he was proudest of was finding a way to include the song "That Thing You Do!" in the movie ten different times. "We don't have a movie if that song's not catchy," he said. "If we did anything that was truly artistically brilliant, is we figured out a way to hear this one hit song enough times for it to register as we're tired of hearing it, but we still like the song. Finding that balance was the hardest conceptual aspect of the movie."

Saving Private Ryan

(Captain Miller, 1998)

"This Ryan better be worth it. He better go home and cure some disease or invent the longer-lasting light bulb or something."

"What is the great national consciousness we have participated in?" Hanks asked about the baby boomers, the generational tranche shared by director Steven Spielberg and himself. "The rock and roll culture. Not hugely demanding of us from the point of view of sacrifice."

Saving Private Ryan is a masterpiece about the meaning of sacrifice—an easy enough concept to endorse, when considered as the general idea that made winning World War II possible, but a heavy, bloody weight in practice. The movie proper begins with twenty-four minutes of the Normandy invasion, a visceral sequence full of blood, severed limbs, and dead fish lying on the sand next to dead human beings. It's an intense piece of film-making that might have earned any director other than Spielberg an NC-17 rating, but it's not there as a bravura aria of violence—every explosion and every bullet through the head underlines the horrible human cost of righteous wartime bravery.

The plot: after three brothers from a single family die in combat, the army wants to send the fourth Ryan brother (Matt Damon) home to Iowa. Captain John Miller (Hanks) leads a squad through France to find Ryan, even though he and his soldiers are uncertain of the sense in risking eight men to save one. When they find Ryan in Ramelle, he doesn't want to leave his unit; Miller and his men stay with him in a desperate effort to defend a strategically crucial bridge.

Hanks wears the mantle of command naturally, an officer who treats his soldiers with respect and inspires their devotion. "I don't gripe to you, Reiben," he tells one of his men (played by Ed Burns). "I'm a captain. There's a chain of command. Gripes go up, not down. Always up. You gripe to me, I gripe to my superior officer, and so on, and so on, and so on. I don't gripe to you. I don't gripe in front of you. You should know that."

Captain Miller is under such stress that his right hand visibly shakes. He is a Pennsylvania schoolteacher in an unimaginable world, performing acts of awesome bravery despite constant overwhelming fear. But his concern isn't principally for his own safety—it's for the lives of the men he commands. He knows exactly how many have died because of his orders (ninety-four) and his only comfort is the moral algebra that gives him hope that he may have saved the lives of ten times as many.

The France of *Saving Private Ryan* is beautiful and devastated, populated by terrified civilians and an array of Hollywood stars (the two most surprising: Ted Danson and Vin Diesel). Acts of war can have a terrible cost in this movie: taking out a Nazi machine gunner at a radar station results in the death of Wade, the squad's medic (Giovanni Ribisi). Acts of mercy can have a price just as high: when Miller lets a Nazi soldier go free, that man ends up shooting him in Ramelle. Hanks plays Miller, the fulcrum of all these decisions and consequences, with good humor and a modesty that only hints at the guilt and confusion churning within.

To prepare to play G.I.s, the eight principal actors of *Saving Private Ryan* went through a boot camp with the film's military advisor, Captain Dale Dye, a retired twenty-one-year veteran of the United States Marine Corps. Dye said, "Actors—who are like dry sponges until you pour on the water—need to be immersed in the rigorous lifestyle, in the horrors facing infantrymen and combat people all over the world. So to the extent that insurance and lifestyles will allow, I immerse those actors in that lifestyle. I take them to the field, I make them eat rations, I shoot at them with blank ammunition, I beat them up, I beat on them, I make them crawl and sleep in the mud and the cold and the dirt."

This military crash course was scheduled for only six days instead of the thirteen weeks that a real-life boot camp would last, but halfway through, the actors decided that they had spent enough time being called turds, doing calisthenics in the rain, and sleeping in tents so small their feet stuck out the end. They held a meeting on whether to continue boot camp, and decided to cut it short. The vote was unanimous—except for Hanks, the actor Dye had dubbed "Turd No. 1." He convinced the other actors that they needed to stick it out, that the palpable knowledge of being tired and cold and wet would translate on-screen. They voted again, and this time decided to stay—cementing not just their commitment but Hanks' role as their leader on-screen and off. Hanks wouldn't confuse a week away from hotel beds and room service from the actual sacrifices made by American soldiers, but he also knew that you don't honor sacrifice, or even represent it meaningfully, by taking shortcuts.

You've Got Mail

(Joe Fox, 1998)

"Oh, right, yeah—a snap to find the one single person in the world who fills your heart with joy."

For *Sleepless in Seattle 2: Electric Boogaloo,* writer/director Nora Ephron not only reunited Tom Hanks and Meg Ryan, she once again made a movie that kept her two stars away from each other as long as possible. *You've Got Mail* is an update of the 1940 movie *The Shop Around the Corner* (itself based on the 1937 play *Parfumerie*), where two coworkers at a leather-goods store in Budapest fall in love via pseudonymous letters, each unaware that their beloved correspondent is standing right next to them—now the epistolary medium is email and the setting is New York City's Upper West Side. Hanks is running the chain bookstore Fox & Sons (a thinly disguised Barnes & Noble) that's going to put Ryan's children's bookstore (called The Shop Around the Corner, naturally) out of business. High stakes—if not as life-and-death as in the original, where the unspoken shadow of the Holocaust loomed over all the characters.

When Joe Fox (Hanks) and Kathleen Kelly (Ryan) cross paths in person, they trade acidic insults, not realizing that they are also "NY152" and "Shopgirl" online. After Delia Ephron, Nora Ephron's sister and collaborator, came up with this approach to the source material, the director said she wanted "to do it in the next five minutes, or there won't be email anymore." As it turned out, email lasted decades longer than she expected.

When both leads in a rom-com are already in relationships, their on-screen partners need to be wrong enough that viewers don't lament the inevitable breakup, but not so off that you doubt the heroes' sanity. Kathleen is paired with Frank Navasky (Greg Kinnear), a preening public intellectual, while Joe is matched with Patricia (Parker Posey), a book editor so high-strung that she provokes the movie's best one-liner: "Patricia makes coffee nervous."

It's a tough-minded, uncompromising movie in many ways—Kathleen has to accept that her soul mate is the man who put her cherished family bookstore out of business. And when Joe figures out that Kathleen is also Shopgirl, he embarks on a campaign to win her over that is both ardent and cruelly manipulative. He approaches matters of the heart with the same winner-take-all ethos he brings to business—and since the movie finds a tearfully happy ending in a sunny garden, all is forgiven.

"The thing I liked about working in these movies with Nora is that they were about grown-ups," Tom said. "They're about adults who had already witnessed bitter compromise, some degree of pain, varying degrees of loss, and they weren't the kind of people

who were hoping aliens will make their lives happy. They had gone through something and knew what it was like to be alone. They also knew what it was like to be with someone they were not meant to be with. And that's grown-up stuff. I gotta tell you, we were billed for a while as America's Sweethearts, which was something that made our stomachs turn. Inside that there is a forceful presence. A very, very forceful presence."

To help stay in the groove of their characters, Hanks and Ryan kept up their own email correspondence off-screen. (Sample email from Hanks to Ryan: "In the Park, on one of the Ballfields, completely by himself, a saxophone player is standing on the pitcher's mound wailing some practice solos, giving his chops a workout without disturbing any neighbors but the trees—a musical score perfect for a movie scene in the city today.")

Costarring in their third movie together, the stars had a real camaraderie—but when it came time to film the final scene, they felt awkward about having to kiss each other. Hanks defused the tension by chattering about the least sexy topic possible: the United States government suing Microsoft for antitrust violations. "I knew just what he was doing," Ryan said. "It was so generous."

Toy Story 2
(Woody, 1999)

"I can't stop Andy from growing up. But I wouldn't miss it for the world."

Toy Story smashed everyone's expectations, including the toy stores that didn't order enough Buzz Lightyear action figures and the toy companies that hadn't granted permission to have their intellectual property appear in it. (Barbie was notably absent from the first *Toy Story* installment, but made a great cameo in the sequel.) Even the people who made the movie were taken aback by how well it turned out: "It kinda blew me outta my hut," Hanks said.

Similarly, this sequel was intended to be a straight-to-video quickie done by Pixar's video game division, but at some point everyone involved figured out that it was an instant classic, maybe even better than the original. *Toy Story 2* features Woody discovering his heritage as a 1950s collectible who starred in his own TV show: he has to choose between being celebrated for those glories in a Japanese museum and sticking around for the more meaningful pleasures of Andy's room. (Why doesn't Woody remember anything about his life before Andy, by the way?) It also extends the Woody's Roundup gang with a new set of characters: Bullseye the horse, Stinky Pete the Prospector (a great villain turn by Kelsey Grammer), and best of all, the exuberant cowgirl Jessie (voiced by Joan Cusack).

One of the best early decisions by the *Toy Story* creators was to make Woody three inches taller than Buzz, reflecting the eras in which they were manufactured. That attention to detail was then multiplied a thousand times over when the characters became real-world toys. Hanks accepted that on the nation's playgrounds, Buzz Lightyear was more popular than Sheriff Woody. "Nothing wrong with that," he said. "I've had my time. He's bendable and poseable and that's what it comes down to. Woody is far too pliant. There's a lot of give in him. You gotta work at him just to have him sit up, otherwise he just lies there like a rag doll because, son of a gun, he *is* a rag doll. But Buzz has notches and ears and things like that. So I can understand that. I'm gonna give the man his due."

But given Hanks' affinity for astronauts, did it rankle that he was cast as a cowboy while Tim Allen got to be the outer-space traveler? Hanks was unconcerned. "The astronaut's not that smart," he said.

The Green Mile

(Paul Edgecomb, 1999)

"On the day of my judgment, when I stand before God, and He asks me why did I kill one of His true miracles, what am I going to say? That it was my job?"

Before he became famous as the first showrunner of *The Walking Dead* TV series, Frank Darabont occupied one of the oddest cinematic niches in Hollywood, writing and directing adaptations of two different Stephen King stories set in prison. *The Green Mile* was the second; the first, *The Shawshank Redemption,* stiffed at the box office, but within months, was recognized as a stone classic. It was nominated for seven Academy Awards in 1994—Darabont and Hanks met at the annual lunch for Oscar nominees, an encounter that led to this collaboration.

The production values of *The Green Mile* are high and the cast is excellent (alongside Hanks are Michael Clarke Duncan, James Cromwell, Sam Rockwell, Paul Morse, Bonnie Hunt, and once again, Gary Sinise). Unfortunately, the movie feels like reheated *Shawshank* casserole. With languorous pacing, plus a prologue and an epilogue at a retirement home, the movie clocks in at 3:09, Hanks' longest movie—and it's weighed down throughout with self-importance.

Hanks' character, Paul Edgecombe, works at a Louisiana penitentiary in 1935, where he runs death row and treats the doomed prisoners with respect. He is forced to confront the limits of that approach when he has to execute John Coffey: humongous, dark-skinned, simple-minded, innocent, a bona-fide miracle worker. But if an executioner has a crisis of conscience only when he's face-to-face with a man with the initials of "J.C." who can heal the sick and resurrect the dead, then that's somebody who needs to be whacked in the forehead with the Crowbar of Morality before getting the point.

Although Coffey proves to be an instrument of justice, not purely mercy, he is definitely an example of the "Magical Negro"—the term Spike Lee used to describe the cinematic archetype of the African American with otherworldly powers serving primarily for the improvement of a Caucasian lead character. Ironically, the actual magic makes this movie less magical. It also limits Hanks' performance: he's mostly asked to embody human decency and to look awestruck in the face of according-to-Hoyle miracles.

"There's a great dichotomy to this man who kills people for a living," Hanks said. "It's as gruesome and as horrifying a paycheck as you'll ever earn, and yet he's been asked to rationalize it." You may not need a dark soul to play a killer, but you at least need shadowy corners of the interior, Hanks acknowledged: "I understand his motivation."

Cast Away

(Chuck Noland, 2000)

"Time rules over us without mercy, not caring if we're healthy or ill, hungry or drunk, Russians, Americans, beings from Mars.

It's like a fire. It could either destroy us or it could keep us warm. That's why every FedEx office has a clock. Because we live or we die by the clock. We never turn our back on it. And we never, ever allow ourselves the sin of losing track of time!"

At the center of *Cast Away* is a seventy-seven-minute tour-de-force performance by just one actor: Tom Hanks, playing a FedEx efficiency expert who survives a plane crash and washes up on a Pacific island. The tropical paradise becomes his prison, where he has to survive for four years. The turning point on the uncharted desert isle comes when he opens most of the packages that wash up on the beach, letting him fashion tools out of unlikely materials such as ice skates and video cassettes. Hanks doesn't say a word as he rips open the cardboard, but from the stricken expression on his face, the audience can see that he's come to terms with the grim realization that he's not getting rescued anytime soon—he needs to abandon his previous imperative of getting the packages to their intended recipients as soon as possible. (He leaves one box sealed, and it becomes a symbol of his hope that he can find his way back to who he used to be.)

On the island, Chuck Noland (or "C. Noland"—"see no land") discovers that he can no longer live in his previous state of hyper-stimulation, where he could micromanage his schedule down to the minute but was incapable of confronting the impending death of a coworker's wife. Now he has control over only death and life: he can decide when and whether he commits suicide, and he can make himself a companion (the volleyball Wilson, a surprisingly affecting invention).

What makes *Cast Away* a great movie, though, is what comes before and after that tropical sojourn. The twenty-minute sequence before Noland gets on the airplane deftly shows his devotion to his woman (Helen Hunt) and his corporation (Federal Express). And the final act, after Noland returns to the United States, is devastating. That's not because he's readjusting to the small daily miracles of ice and dentistry and background music, but because he suffers real heartbreak, and no longer has the carapace of modern Western civilization that will let him ignore it.

"It's almost like making a silent movie," Hanks said. "You have to tell every aspect of the story physically, being totally alone." Hanks gave a magnificent performance as Noland, even losing fifty-five pounds and growing a monstrosity of a beard to show what a man would look like after years of living on a deserted island. (The production shut down for a year so he could transform himself—the only way to make that unusual schedule work financially was for the director Robert Zemeckis to make an entirely different movie with the same crew during the hiatus: *What Lies Beneath*, starring Harrison Ford and Michelle Pfeiffer.) Beyond Hanks' physical and emotional commitment to the role came the years he put into it before Zemeckis came on board. Inspired by a true story Louis L'Amour told about being shipwrecked in the Gulf of Mexico—and how people had trouble understanding that it wasn't a grand adventure—Hanks worked with screenwriter William Broyles to turn a goofy concept originally titled *Chuck of the Jungle* into something more profound.

The shoot proved to be punishing—and not just because the crew couldn't walk on the beach (they'd leave footprints) and all the filmmakers had to take a boat from base camp in Fiji to the chosen island of Monu-riki every day (one hour each way). An insect bite resulted in such a nasty staph infection that Hanks needed to have what he described as "a big chunk" of his leg surgically removed: he was hospitalized for three days and then production shut down for three weeks so he could recuperate. It all would have been simpler if Noland had opened that last FedEx package and it had contained, as Zemeckis once joked it did, a waterproof, solar-powered satellite phone.

Road to Perdition

(Michael Sullivan, 2002)

"This house is not our home anymore. It's just an empty building."

In 1999, Sam Mendes directed his first feature film, *American Beauty,* which was so well received (five Oscars, including Best Picture) that people thought he might be a major film auteur, not just the solid pro that he turned out to be. So for his second movie, the gangster drama *Road to Perdition* (set in the Midwest in 1931), he was able to assemble an absolutely bonkers all-star cast: Tom Hanks, Jude Law, Daniel Craig, Jennifer Jason Leigh, and in his last on-screen film role, a seventy-seven-year-old Paul Newman.

Hanks is stoic but compelling in the central role of the Irish mobster Michael Sullivan, seeking revenge against the man who murdered his wife and son—although the protagonist is actually his other son (Tyler Hoechlin), along for the ride on a bloody road trip. Previously a remote father, Sullivan is suddenly forced to be a parent. He takes some steps in that direction, but is undone by his need for vengeance—another Hanks character who objectively does terrible things but somehow seems fundamentally decent.

Even though the movie proves to be less than the sum of its parts, it's full of fine performances and scenes. None are better than the interactions between Newman and Hanks. Newman plays a mob boss who took in the orphaned Sullivan as a child and raised him—but when his own biological son (Craig) rubs out Sullivan's family, the patriarch remains loyal to his bloodline. In their scenes together, Newman and Hanks savor every pause, letting their characters' complicated history together fill the silences. The movie shoehorns in a couple of extra scenes featuring the two of them; they're extraneous, but nobody watching is complaining. Newman described their working relationship thus: "We respected each other's territory. He pissed on his tree, and I pissed on my tree, and then someone yelled 'action.'"

Hanks said he was in awe of Newman: "If he wants to call me 'kid' and never learn my name, fine. If he wants to do one take and walk away, fine. If he wants to come in with two little lapdogs and talk to them all day long, he could have done that too."

Hanks' friend and collaborator Peter Scolari nominated *Road to Perdition* as Hanks' finest work. "I called him and said, 'I've known you more than twenty years, and I cannot quite get my mind around how you do this.' It was a brave performance— America's nice guy is a mercenary, a gun for hire, a dark soul. But that's the minimal compliment," Scolari said.

"There's a scene in which Tom's character comes home and sees his son traumatized in an alcove at home and realizes, when the kid can't speak and is in shock, that his wife has been murdered. And the filmmaker demonstrates this gigantic show of faith. He runs Tom's character up the stairs to the bedroom where he's about to find his wife with her chest blown out. And he keeps the camera on the boy. All you hear is the sound, and you know."

Scolari is all too aware of the circumstances in which Hanks had to produce his howl of grief. "Any actor will tell you that was achieved over by the craft-services table, where there were sliced bagels, grapes, and coffee to a greater and lesser degree of heat and age. And a sound guy with a boom standing over Tom and saying, 'Sound is rolling, quiet on the set, please. Alright, Tom, go ahead.' No dead body, no three hours of makeup to achieve a gunshot wound, just Tom hanging out by the craft-services table. And that sound is as disturbing a thing as you will hear in a motion picture. That's how good it is."

Catch Me If You Can

(Carl Hanratty, 2002)

"I can't stop. It's my job."

There's a great scene early in *Catch Me If You Can*, where the teenager Frank Abnagale Jr. (Leonardo DiCaprio), eager to show off how well he's done since he ran away from home, takes his father, Frank Abnagale Sr. (Christopher Walken), out for a fancy lunch. The son coaches the father on the etiquette of chilled salad forks, and the two of them catch each other up on what they've been doing, both of them telling one lie after another. They're not swapping stories to entertain each other—each desperately wants the other to believe him, and to believe in him—but they know each other too well to buy the bullshit.

The movie is based on the real-world exploits of the younger Abnagale: he posed as an airline pilot, passed millions of dollars in bad checks, and bluffed his way into jobs as an assistant district attorney and a chief resident pediatrician. Directed by Steven Spielberg, the movie crackles and snaps—DiCaprio looks great in pilot uniforms and mod orange sweaters—but there's a melancholy tone to the story. Abnagale is always running away: from the law, from his lies, from his own past.

Hanks plays Carl Hanratty, the FBI agent tracking Frank down, through several years and across multiple continents. While Frank is scamming his way into rooms at luxury hotels, Carl is washing his white shirts at public laundromats (and turning them pink when somebody leaves a red sweater in the washer). Carl is square, relentless, and humorless. When two other agents badger him to lighten up and tell a joke, this is what he comes up with:

"Knock, knock."

"Who's there?"

"Go fuck yourselves."

Although Hanks plays these moments perfectly deadpan, there's some warmth to Carl: he proves to be the movie's good father figure. The actual father played by Walken is dashing and a great dancer, but also a tax cheat who doesn't even have the moral force to ask his son to stop committing felonies. Carl puts Frank in jail—but he also recognizes his wasted potential and helps him make a new life.

Hanks read the script when Spielberg and DiCaprio were developing the movie, and basically invited himself onto the project (politely calling both of them, of course). He pointed out that if the movie was called *Catch Me If You Can,* the Javert in hot pursuit of the star needed to have some heft.

For Hanks, the appeal of the role was that it was something

he hadn't played before: an antagonist who felt like a protagonist. And there was another perk to playing a buttoned-down FBI agent: "Not a lot of costume changes."

The Ladykillers

(Professor G. H. Dorr, 2004)

"Madam, we must have waffles! We must all have waffles forthwith."

The title for *The Ladykillers* shimmers onto the screen over a huge pile of garbage—but it's really not as bad as that. The movie, written and directed by Joel and Ethan Coen, is a modernization of the 1955 British black comedy that starred Alec Guinness and Peter Sellers. It was originally written for their former cinematographer Barry Sonnenfeld to direct; when he took on another project, the brothers decided to do it themselves. The story: a gang of thieves disguise themselves as classical musicians so they can gain access to the basement belonging to an elderly, God-fearing widow and from there tunnel into the vault of a nearby casino. They succeed, but the widow discovers them and tells them they have to give the money back and go to church, or she'll report them to the police. The gang decides to bump her off—which proves trickier than expected.

The plot is thin for a caper, and despite strenuous efforts, the movie's not especially funny. (Along with the previous year's *Intolerable Cruelty,* this was probably the nadir of the Coens' career.) Nevertheless, the movie has its pleasures. Every frame is composed beautifully by the Coens and cinematographer Roger Deakins, and a few of the characters perfectly match the actor with the Coens' verbal inventions: Irma P. Hall as the widow, J. K.

Simmons as an overconfident demolitions expert, and best of all, Tom Hanks as the criminal scheme's mastermind, Goldthwaite Higginson Dorr, PhD.

Dorr is a remarkable invention, a preening Southern gentleman who loves to quote Edgar Allan Poe and claims to be on sabbatical from his post as a university professor. (It's unclear whether this is the truth, part of his con-man patter, or an insane delusion.) Hanks is magnetic in the Faulknerian role, capturing Dorr's vanity and desperation and letting dialogue such as "Gentlemen, I'm sure you're all aware that the solons of the state of Mississippi—to wit, its legislature—have decreed that no gaming establishment shall be erected within its borders upon dry land" roll trippingly off his tongue.

When Dorr laughs at one of his own jokes, it's an asthmatic gasp, as if he were briefly so overcome by his own cleverness that he forgot to breathe. Hanks said, "I had this vision that he's a college professor of a very, very boring subject, and every now and again he would make these witticisms that he'd be the only one laughing at, up at the lectern. And it made Ethan laugh, so I just tried to make him laugh again and again over by the monitor."

Joel added, "We called it 'the rat quiver laugh.' And the question was 'How many times can you go to that well? How many times is too many for the rat quiver laugh?'"

Ethan concluded, "There's no formula, unfortunately."

Some years after *The Ladykillers'* release, Hanks was in Paris, doing interviews for a different movie. A French journalist said, "Mr. Hanks, you've made so many films playing the nice guy. Why do you not ever, say, make a film for the Coen brothers?"

Hanks answered, "I made a film for the Coen brothers. It was a remake of Alec Guinness' *The Ladykillers*. I made a film with the Coen brothers. They came to me. The Coen brothers themselves asked me to be in their film. It was my opportunity to be that artist that I always wanted to be and you always wanted me to be. I made a film with the Coen brothers. And from then on I've always felt like hot shit because I made a film with the Coen brothers."

The journalist replied, "Yes, but a good Coen brothers film."

The Terminal

(Viktor Navorski, 2004)

"He waits for you to answer, at Sbarro."

"I wanted to do another movie that could make us laugh and cry and feel good about the world," Steven Spielberg said of *The Terminal,* the third collaboration between the director and Tom Hanks. Mawkish-comedy Spielberg is the worst version of Spielberg, but he nevertheless turns on his heartlight here.

Hanks plays Viktor Navorski, a traveler from the fictional Eastern European country of Krakozhia who comes to New York City but spends months trapped in the international lounge of JFK Airport; there was a revolution in Krakozhia while he was in the air and his passport is no longer valid. He hunkers down, gets a job doing airport construction, befriends a motley collection of airport workers, and inspires almost everyone he meets to become their best selves. Catherine Zeta-Jones plays the flight-attendant love interest, with an underwritten role but great soft lighting, while Stanley Tucci is the officious border-control bureaucrat antagonist. In a clunky but insistent metaphor, the terminal itself stands in for the USA.

Hanks has fun with his broken English and thick accent (Krakozhian is based on Bulgarian, which let him borrow from the mannerisms of his father-in-law) and gets to do some solid physical comedy, like when he tries to fold up his body so he can sleep on airport furniture. For all its good intentions, the movie feels like a feature-length adventure of Latka (Andy Kaufman's eccentric foreign character on *Taxi*), made with an extremely high level of craft and professionalism.

In one funny scene, Navorski keeps watch at a pay phone, unwilling to miss an important phone call, even though he desperately needs to go to the bathroom. This was just one more entry on a long list of Hanks movies where urination plays an important part: consider Forrest Gump announcing he needs to pee at the White House, or the urinary tract infection in *The Green Mile*, or the fifty-second whiz in *A League of Their Own*. There's many more examples, including *Captain Phillips*, *Apollo 13*, *The Money Pit*, and *Saving Private Ryan*—weirdly, piss is a Hanks motif.

The Terminal came out three years after the 9/11 terrorist attacks made airport security more overtly stressful and ideological, something the movie studiously ignores. In different hands, this project might have been darker or more explicitly political—but the movie Spielberg and Hanks wanted to make was an optimistic American fable.

The Polar Express

(Hero Boy, Father, Conductor, Hobo, Scrooge, Santa Claus, 2004)

"Sometimes seeing is believing. And sometimes the most real things in the world are the things we can't see."

Some of the scenic design in *The Polar Express* is beautiful, capturing the wonder of Chris Van Allsburg's picture book, where Christmas seems like a steampunk fever dream. The story, about kids who doubt Santa's existence making a train trip to the North Pole, is wistful and evocative. The cast, featuring the Tom Hanks one-man repertory company, does admirable work. But none of that matters, because every single human (and elf) character in this movie looks creepy and unsettling.

In animation, the human eye will accept stylized cartoons (like Fred Flintstone) or hyperrealism (like Gollum). But in between lies "the uncanny valley," where faces look like sweaty Halloween costumes. *The Polar Express* doesn't just venture into the uncanny valley, it pitches a tent and takes up residence for a hundred minutes.

Hanks can't overcome the limitations of computer animation circa 2004, where the whole movie looks like the cutscenes in a video game, but he does a fine job with six different characters—providing not just their voices, but their movements via motion capture. (Hanks performed with 150 reflective "jewels" glued onto his face, so every expression and twitch could be captured by the computers.) Some of Hanks' roles are small—a scary turn as a Scrooge marionette, a few lines of voiceover narration—but he also has the key roles of Santa Claus, the brusque but caring conductor of the train bound for the North Pole, and the nameless "hero boy" at the center of the story. (In the case of the "hero boy," Hanks did all the movements, but not the voice.) Now and then, there are three-way scenes where Hanks played all the roles—Tom after Tom.

It turned out that this movie wasn't the first time Hanks played

Santa Claus: when he was twenty-one years old, he had a gig impersonating Kris Kringle at a shopping center in Sacramento. "I was rail thin, so it's not like I was a traditional Santa Claus," he said. "I had a square stomach that was the shape of the sofa cushion that I had stuffed into my pants. That was my first pass at the role and I was let go after two weeks, as there just weren't that many visitors to Santa's little gingerbread house."

Elvis Has Left the Building

(Mailbox Elvis, 2005)

Kim Basinger stars in this comedy as a cosmetics saleswoman with an unusual quality: when she's around Elvis impersonators, their lifespan is extremely limited. Through no fault of her own, they stand underneath falling billboards or above exploding radiators. The movie is professional (meaning it stars some recognizable faces and the camera's in focus) but dull, and it barely got a theatrical release: the movie never made it to American theaters, but appears to have played on a few screens in Spain, Italy, Taiwan, and the United Arab Emirates.

Tom Hanks has the most fleeting of cameos: in a scene where Basinger's character is forced off the road, she swerves her pink Cadillac into some mailboxes, one of which flies through the air and lands on the head of an Elvis impersonator riding a motorcycle, killing him immediately. When John Corbett (he's the love interest) comes along later and opens the mailbox, we see a split second of Tom Hanks, an insert shot of his face contorted into a deathly grimace.

Hanks had long believed that his fame precluded him from taking on supporting roles—not because he needed to protect his identity as a leading man, but because in many movies he would be a distraction rather than an asset. "That type of visibility usually precludes going off for a couple weeks in a zippy picture to do a cool part," he said. "I envy guys who have artistic ability. For me, in many cases, it would come off like stunt casting. Guys like Harvey Keitel and Gary Oldman—guys who are somewhat mysterious to the public—they can do that. I'd be like a big honking cinder block in a small part in the kinds of movies they do."

In this case, he made the appearance as a favor to director Joel Zwick, who helmed many episodes of *Bosom Buddies* and the extremely lucrative Hanks-produced *My Big Fat Greek Wedding*. As Zwick told the story, "He said that's the only time in his life he ever got to play a head in a mailbox, so he wants to put that on his résumé."

The Da Vinci Code
(Robert Langdon, 2006)

"I have to get to a library—fast."

In the very selective cinematic category of "characters solving elaborate puzzles that will lead them to the Holy Grail," the analysis of *The Last Supper* in *The Da Vinci Code* comes up well short of the medallion and the shaft of light in *Raiders of the Lost Ark*. An international thriller with a corpse at the Louvre and a crazed albino S&M assassin on the trail of our heroes should be a witty, slightly nutty caper, but somehow *The Da Vinci Code* is nearly three hours of self-important tedium; director Ron Howard treats the source material way too reverentially, probably because Dan Brown's novel had sold about eighty million copies worldwide.

The supporting characters get to camp it up a bit, at least—Ian

McKellen and Alfred Molina both seem aware of how ludicrous this endeavor is, and dive into the absurdity with gusto. Not Tom Hanks—as Robert Langdon, a Harvard professor of "religious symbology," Hanks gets to unscramble an anagram now and then, but mostly he gets guns pointed at him. He's a passive hero buffeted by insane events; his main job is to deliver crackpot explanations of art history in calm, measured tones, like his graduate degree was actually in expository dialogue.

For some reason, the public decided that the problem with this charmless movie was Hanks' hair, a thick wavy do that looked like something fished out of the back of John Travolta's closet. "I loved the media reaction," Hanks said, of his experience at the center of a meaningless scandal. "I literally had someone jam a microphone in my face and ask, 'What do you *mean* by the hair?'"

Cars

(Woody Car, 2006)

"You are a toy car!"

On its release, *Cars* was the worst of the Pixar feature films—it felt like it ran long on potential merchandising tie-ins and short on actual inspiration. But after a spate of cash-in Pixar sequels like *Finding Dory,* it's easier to take pleasure in what's good about this movie: the vocal performances of Owen Wilson, Paul Newman, and Bonnie Hunt; some beautiful southwestern scenery; the way the movie commits to the freaky premise of a world run by cars but utterly lacking people, taking the horror movie *Maximum Overdrive* and flipping it into children's entertainment.

During the closing credits, the characters gather at a drive-in, watching this universe's version of other Pixar films, where characters from *Monsters Inc.* and *A Bug's Life* are rendered as cars. (This lets them point out how John Ratzenberger has a role in every Pixar movie.) Hanks makes an extremely quick appearance in "Toy Car Story," playing Woody as a station wagon.

Hanks' work as Woody has also led him to a slew of spinoff *Toy Story* projects, including shorts such as "Small Fry" and "Partysaurus Rex." When Hanks is too busy to do Woody's voice—like in a multitude of Disney video games or the interstitial spots called "Toy Story Treats" that ran on ABC channels in 1996—he hands the work off to his brother Jim Hanks. (Jim, the youngest child in the Hanks family, stayed with their mom when the family split up. Jim and Tom became closer as adults when Jim moved to L.A. as an aspiring actor; he's also worked as Tom's body double, most notably in some of the long-distance running shots in *Forrest Gump*.) At least nobody from the Hanks family has to wear the Woody costume for theme-park appearances.

The Simpsons Movie
(Himself, 2007)

"Hello, I'm Tom Hanks. The U.S. government has lost its credibility so it's borrowing some of mine."

The Simpsons family, having fled their hometown of Springfield for Alaska, watches TV and sees a government-funded PSA featuring Tom Hanks at his most avuncular. "Tousle my hair, Mr. Hanks," says a cute kid; Hanks complies, and then announces the opening of the New Grand Canyon, which will be at the location of Springfield. (D'oh!) Hanks is a convincing enough pitchman that it's easy to imagine an alternate universe where he made his living in commercials. He asks, "If you're going to pick a government to trust, why not pick this one?"

The Simpsons Movie was just as funny and smart as the early years of the show, which felt like a miracle—it was the big-screen version of a TV program that, at the time, had been on the air for eighteen seasons. Although Hanks never did voice work for the weekly *Simpsons,* the show referred to him in one episode (the thirteenth season's "Jaws Wired Shut"), where Lisa is doing the "Movie Star Scramble" word puzzle while waiting for a movie and is contemptuous of the trivially easy "Mot Hanks." The answer, it turns out, is not Tom Hanks but Otm Shank—who, we learn from Apu, is India's answer to Brian Dennehy.

Charlie Wilson's War

(Charlie Wilson, 2007)

"If anyone asks what the hell I'm doing on the ethics committee, we'll just tell them I like chasing women and drinking whiskey and the Speaker felt we were underrepresented."

Charlie Wilson's War is about the congressman who arranged for a half-billion dollars of off-the-books financing for the mujahideen rebels in Afghanistan, bogging down the Soviet military through the 1980s. While the script by Aaron Sorkin is clever, that's still a big bite of a public-affairs biscuit. Director Mike Nichols makes it digestible by casting big names and letting them have movie-star moments.

Julia Roberts, playing a sassy Texas right-wing socialite, gets to browbeat people and to emerge from a swimming pool looking stunning in a bikini. Philip Seymour Hoffman reams out his boss at the CIA with an epic rant and then shatters a plate-glass window. And Tom Hanks, portraying the party-boy congressman of the title (a hawkish Democrat), has the time of his life. Whether he's cavorting with strippers in hot tubs, summoning his team of nubile aides by barking "Jailbait!" or trampling over diplomatic protocol by asking for whiskey at the Pakistani presidential palace, he looks at the world through a drunken squint and a bleary grin, concealing his considerable intelligence.

The movie breezes by when Hanks and Roberts are having a fling, or when they're engaged in byzantine negotiations involving an Israeli arms dealer and a belly dancer. It falls apart somewhat toward the end, when it fast-forwards through years of the war through a montage and a quick barrage of subtitles. But that clunky third act is necessary to get to the movie's conclusion: the United States successfully foiled the Soviet Union's military efforts in Central Asia, but unwilling to help rebuild Afghanistan, "fucked up the endgame."

As delightful a rascal as the on-screen Charlie Wilson is, his war might actually have been a terrible idea, leading directly to the formation of a well-armed Al Qaeda—a contradiction that the movie ultimately embraces. "You don't know the consequences of any act," Nichols said. "You don't know good things from bad things when they're coming at you, and sometimes [you don't know] for ten or twenty years, or ever—because good and bad things keep turning into one another."

The Great Buck Howard
(Mr. Gable, 2008)

"You think I danced out the front door every morning in my adult life happy about where I was going to be spending my day?"

John Malkovich is goofy and magnetic as Buck Howard, an aging stage magician who was once a regular guest on Johnny Carson's *Tonight Show* but now does shows in half-empty theaters in towns like Akron, Ohio, and Bakersfield, California. It's a gloriously outsized performance, based on the real-life mentalist The Amazing Kreskin. The lead role of Buck Howard's road manager Troy Gable, a regular guy who dropped out of law school to follow his dreams, is the sort of part Tom Hanks would have jumped at in the 1980s; here it's played by Colin Hanks, his eldest child.

The movie is eager to please, if a bit lacking in the bite that one might expect from a behind-the-scenes show-biz story. It's packed full of stars, including Emily Blunt, Adam Scott, and Tom Hanks—who is cast, sensibly enough, as Troy's father. Tom has two scenes with Colin, embodying the voice of pinstriped authority, expressing his stern disapproval of his son's frivolous choices and encouraging him to return to law school. (It would have all felt more Oedipal if real-life Colin were not following real-life Tom's career path.) It was a single day's work for Tom, but he had to do it twice—the first time, one of his scenes was in a room with a too-low ceiling, and despite the best efforts of cinematographer Tak Fujimoto, the actors were literally overshadowed.

Because of the family connections, Playtone also produced the movie. At first director Sean McGinly was surprised by Hanks sitting in on meetings and casting sessions—"I've taken a lot of meetings over the years at other production companies where there's a star, and you never see them"—but he grew accustomed to it. "He watched the film four or five times—he came into the editing room with a yellow legal pad and gave his notes to me," McGinly remembered. "Some of the notes were amazing and wonderful; some weren't so good." He laughed: Hanks was astute and smart, not super-powered. "He's a human being. And he never presented himself in an authoritarian way."

Angels & Demons
(Robert Langdon, 2009)

"Look, I don't study symbols because I consider them unimportant."

Operating on the principle "if audiences liked hand-waving art-historical argle-bargle about Catholicism, they'll love hand-waving pseudo-scientific argle-bargle about antimatter, so long as we throw in some Catholicism," this sequel to *The Da Vinci Code* is generally superior to the original. Unity of time and place make the movie zippier and more engaging: most of the action happens in one night in Rome and Vatican City (meaning the secret title is *Before Vespers*).

Although it improves on the first installment, it's still not an especially good movie. It seems less intent on being taken seriously, which helps because the plot centers on superstar Harvard symbologist Robert Langdon deciphering clues to track down the Illuminati, a secret society who have kidnapped four cardinals from a papal enclave and are threatening to blow up Vatican City with antimatter. (For some reason, the Church has flown Langdon in from Boston because they need an expert on Catholic history—a classic example of Vaticansplaining.) This time, the beautiful but chaste European sidekick (here, an Italian scientist played by the European actress Ayelet Zurer) is not just one of the world's greatest nuclear physicists; she's also fluent in Latin and conveniently expert on the symptoms of Tinzaparin poisoning.

The plot twists will be predictable to anyone who has seen more than three movies before. And a sequence with a severed eyeball activating an optical scanner is a retread of a memorable bit from *Minority Report,* seven years earlier.

For his second adaptation of a Dan Brown novel, Tom Hanks reunited with director Ron Howard, screenwriter Akiva Goldsman, and composer Hans Zimmer (doing fake Orff); the cast is rounded out with high-quality European actors, of whom the best is Ewan McGregor. Returning to the role of Langdon, Hanks has a bit more urgency in his performance and a bit less bouffant in his hairdo. To say the character is paper-thin does a disservice to paper—however, it is nice to see a movie hero who takes murder and mayhem in stride, but gets really excited when he enters a library.

Toy Story 3

(Woody, 2010)

"Through every yard sale, every spring-cleaning, Andy held on to us! He must care about us or we wouldn't be here."

The *Toy Story* movies were always wide-ranging delights, capable of shifting from sight gags to self-aware commentary to heartbreaking tales of betrayal and abandonment. But the third movie—not just the crowning accomplishment of this series, but one of the best final chapters of a film trilogy ever—had an amazing one-two emotional punch in its final half hour. The gang of toys first come close to death at the garbage dump and find solace only in the knowledge that they're together. Then they bid farewell to their beloved Andy as he plays with them one last time before passing them on to a new home with the younger Bonnie.

The trilogy ends so perfectly that it's hard to imagine any reason to make *Toy Story 4*. Maturity and mortality are always intertwined in life, but they hold hands especially tightly here.

The movie also has Michael Keaton excelling as Ken, the inevitable love interest for Barbie; Buzz's previously undisclosed Spanish-language mode; and the best villain in the trilogy. Lotso, the strawberry-scented teddy bear, has turned the toys' paradise of the Sunnyside Daycare center into a totalitarian state that he rules with a plush fist. Barbie gets the best criticism of Sunnyside: "Authority should derive from the consent of the governed, not from the threat of force!"

As ever, Hanks recorded his dialogue in a room with a team of Pixar directors, who had learned over the years how to get the most out of their star. Pixar honcho John Lasseter said, "We found out that if we gave him props, he would just come up with ideas." An improvisation involving a severed arm, for example, led to a sequence in the first *Toy Story* movie where Woody uses Buzz's arm like a puppet. Hanks gave the Pixar people so much material, they're still working through the backlog. In fact, *Toy Story 3* incorporated ad-libs and outtakes from vocal sessions Hanks did for the original *Toy Story*, back in 1994.

Larry Crowne

(Larry Crowne, 2011)

"My presentation will be on the very particular subject of how to prepare restaurant-quality French toast—but don't worry, I'll speak in English."

Fifteen years after directing his first feature film, Tom Hanks went behind the camera again. "You have to be infected with a certain kind of E.coli," he said of the urge to direct a movie. "You have to be like, 'The only thing I can do now is direct this film. I've got to see it all the way through!' Because it's about two years of your life. And quite frankly, being a movie star is a much better gig. Pay's better. Less is expected of you."

That sensible perspective makes it all the more puzzling that Hanks got obsessed with this toothless project. Hanks cast himself in the lead role this time: Larry Crowne, eight-time employee of the month at the big-box retailer "UMart," gets fired because he has no college education (he's a navy veteran) and hence no chance of promotion. In short order, he goes back to school, makes new friends, gets a new wardrobe, and falls in love with his speech teacher (Julia Roberts). It all comes pretty easy—Larry's smarter than Forrest Gump, but like him, he has a simple moral code, an upbeat attitude, and an open heart. The movie feels like Hanks is exploring the notion of what it would mean for a regular guy to live a Gumpier life.

Hanks opined, "Larry Crowne can maybe look back and say, 'The best thing that ever happened to me was losing my job. Otherwise, I wouldn't have gone to college, I wouldn't have got a scooter, I wouldn't have met this magnificent woman.'" He conceded, "That's the fantasy of a movie about it, as opposed to the reality."

The cast is rounded out by Gugu Mbatha-Raw (a manic pixie dream girl who leads a motor scooter gang and gives Larry a makeover), Bryan Cranston (the jerk who's married to Julia Roberts' character), Cedric the Entertainer (a cantankerous neighbor), and cowriter Nia Vardalos (the voice of the satellite-navigation system). To ensure domestic tranquility, Hanks wrote another great small role for Rita Wilson, as the brassy loan officer at the bank holding Larry's underwater mortgage, magnificently named Wilma Q. Gammelgaard.

The whole thing is amiable, professional, and completely forgettable. (Except in the Hanks household: his son Truman said that "we constantly quote *Larry Crowne* and *That Thing You Do!*"—which makes sense, since the scripts written by Hanks tap directly into his own sense of humor.) Five years later, when Terry Gross interviewed Hanks on the *Fresh Air* public-radio program, she told him how much she loved *That Thing You Do!* and wondered why he had never directed another movie. That moment must have stung, but Hanks quickly mentioned *Larry Crowne* and moved on.

Funnier than anything on-screen in *Larry Crowne* was a prank Hanks organized with his costar Roberts as the target. Roberts, who like Hanks has spent a large percentage of her life on movie sets, has developed a strategy for killing time between scenes. While Hanks plays cards, Roberts likes to knit. As soon as the camera stops rolling, she'll pick up her knitting, and clack away with her needles, even as a director gives her notes.

So one day Hanks made sure that the entire crew had knitting needles and skeins of yarn and then summoned Roberts to the set—"Hey, kiddo, come on in," he called. "We need some help." When Roberts saw dozens of crew members knitting and purling, she dissolved into laughter.

"That is the funniest thing," she said as she hung on to Hanks' arm. Then she considered the implications of the prank and asked, "Are we this far ahead of schedule?"

Extremely Loud & Incredibly Close

(Thomas Schell, 2011)

"As with anything, if you want to believe, you can find reasons to."

Meet Oskar: a precocious nine-year-old boy (played by Thomas Horn) who may or may not have Asperger's but who definitely is not neurotypical. Shattered after the death of his father in the collapse of the World Trade Center, Oskar ventures around New York City, avoiding the subway and rattling a tambourine to calm himself. He's carrying a key he found in his dad's closet, searching for the lock it will open. On his quest for any possible connection to his father, Oskar discovers that the people he meets have loss and pain of their own. Even in mass tragedies, grief is individual, like a fingerprint.

The film, directed by Stephen Daldry and based on a novel by Jonathan Safran Foer, got mixed reviews—while it was well-regarded enough to earn an Oscar nomination for Best Picture (plus another for Max von Sydow in a silent supporting role), it was also dismissed as "kitsch," "colossally misguided," and "extremely loud and incredibly manipulative." Your relationship to tragedy and the events of September 11, 2001, is your own: all I can tell you is that this author, who lived one block away from the World Trade Center on that day and has a son about the same age as Oskar, wept profusely while watching this movie, in a way that both transcended and precluded critical nitpicking.

Speaking for my (admittedly narrow) demographic, I think this movie is an honest attempt to make art out of trauma, not a cynical effort to exploit it. It's helped by an unbelievably strong supporting cast that includes not just von Sydow, but Viola Davis, Jeffrey Wright, and John Goodman. As Oskar's mother, Sandra Bullock has to radiate maternal love and earth-shattering grief simultaneously (she mostly pulls it off). Playing Oskar's dad, Hanks has an easier role—as he observed, the meat of his performance was in the mode of "September 9." He didn't need to foreshadow tragedy: he could be an individual father who loved science, had a distinctive shrug, and captivated his son with tall tales about the missing sixth borough of New York City. That quirky but devoted father was just one victim among thousands. But by making him feel like a real-life individual, Hanks (and this movie) showed that although grief is like a fingerprint, love is too.

Cloud Atlas

(Dr. Henry Goose, Hotel Manager, Isaac Sachs, Dermot Hoggins, Cavendish Look-a-Like Actor, Zachry, 2012)

"There is only one rule that binds all people. One governing principle that defines every relationship on God's green earth: the weak are meat and the strong do eat."

Cloud Atlas is a mess. An ambitious, inspiring, sometimes beautiful mess, but a mess nonetheless. It's an adaptation of a brilliant 2004 novel by David Mitchell, which has six narratives about man's inhumanity to man nested within each other like Russian matryoshka dolls, sometimes switching styles and decades in the middle of a sentence; Mitchell himself assumed it was unfilmable.

However, after the inconceivably huge success of the *Matrix* trilogy, the writer-director Wachowski siblings were looking for a challenge—and wow, did they get one. They tore down the structure of *Cloud Atlas* and built something new from the rubble, hopscotching among the six different stories. To do it, they partnered with their friend Tom Tykwer (the man behind *Run Lola Run*): the three co-directors simultaneously filmed on multiple sets on a German soundstage.

The logistics were mind-boggling, as was the cost, reportedly over one hundred million dollars, making it the most expensive independent film of all time. When the finances were looking rocky before shooting started, Hanks was the one who made sure that the cast—which also included Susan Sarandon, Jim Sturgess, and Hugo Weaving—didn't bolt. Lana Wachowski said that even when agents were advising actors not to fly to Berlin, Hanks declared that he was getting on the plane: "And then once he said he was getting on the plane, basically everyone said, 'Well, Tom's on the plane, we're on the plane.'"

The reason the project was so appealing to Hanks, beyond its artistic ambition: it was a way for him to return to repertory theater for a few months, trying on different voices and hairstyles and motivations. With six different stories, actors might star in one sequence, play a supporting role of a different ethnicity in another, and make a gender-flipped cameo in another. Nobody seemed to be having more fun than Halle Berry, who got to sink her teeth into period roles for the first time, but Hanks ran a close second.

Hanks plays a murderous doctor on a nineteenth-century sailing ship, a balding hotel manager in Edinburgh, a Cockney gangster-turned-author, a whistleblower with a terrible 1970s haircut at a nuclear power plant, an actor in a TV melodrama, and a goat herder in postapocalyptic Hawaii. The postapocalyptic character, Zachry, is the most good-hearted of the bunch, even if he does have to slit the throat of the invading Kona cannibal played by Hugh Grant. (*Cloud Atlas* didn't do well at the box office; perhaps it would have sold more tickets if the posters had just blared "TOM HANKS CUTS HUGH GRANT'S THROAT.")

For decades, Hanks shied away from roles with too much sex or violence—although those are the twin motors for lots of movies, his interests lay elsewhere. But it turned out that murder unlocked something in his acting: Hanks was never so gleeful as when he got to portray the thug Dermot Hoggins, who throws a condescending critic at a London book party off the roof. "I don't give a fuck what happens when I'm dead," Hoggins says. "I want people to buy me book now." Hanks might not have wanted to be Hoggins for a whole movie, but he loved the role as a short vacation from his usual sunny self: "How often do you get to be filled with that much violence and anger?"

Captain Phillips
(Captain Richard Phillips, 2013)

"We all got bosses."

To keep the tension high on both sides, director Paul Greengrass kept the two factions of the movie *Captain Phillips* away from each other as long as possible. So Tom Hanks (in the title role) and the rest of the actors playing his merchant marine crew had never met Barkhad Abdi and the other neophyte actors playing a band of Somali pirates—until they filmed the scene where the pirates board a container-laden freighter ship and storm the bridge, pointing AK-47s in the faces of the crew.

"I'm the captain now," Abdi tells Hanks, in a high-pressure confrontation.

To achieve his choppy documentary style, Greengrass likes to film extremely long takes with multiple cameras—but finally he called "cut." When Greengrass paused for a break, Hanks crowed with delight and said, "Welcome to the movie, guys. It's a pleasure to finally be working with you!"

Actor Corey Johnson was a little surprised as Hanks worked the room, shaking hands with the newcomers. "I thought we were going to keep this tense," he said to himself, and then shrugged, accepting Hanks' open-armed approach. "Okay, we're making a movie—let's make it fun."

Abdi told Hanks that he couldn't believe he was working with the Forrest Gump guy.

Through its tale of piracy, the movie opens a window on the trillion-dollar business of international naval shipping, and explores the economic imperatives for both crews, not to mention the asymmetric warfare that ends up with the USA deploying a destroyer and a team of Navy SEALs to take care of a single bobbing lifeboat that contains the pirates and their hostage, Captain Phillips. When Greengrass first met with Hanks, he talked about the thematic terrain he thought the story covered. Hanks shrugged. "Yeah, I guess so," the actor said. "But it kind of seems like it's the story of a guy who's in peril on the sea."

They were both right: while Greengrass brilliantly lays out those larger themes in the movie, he couldn't do it without Hanks' riveting performance at the center. Hanks plays somebody human in scale, a flesh-and-blood middle-aged captain with a paunch. He doesn't suddenly build a flamethrower to fight off the pirates or otherwise engage in the heroics we'd expect in, say, a Bruce Willis movie. As rendered by Hanks, Phillips is efficient and competent, but also brusque and not especially beloved by his crew.

The movie ends with Phillips rescued and brought on board a U.S. Navy ship. He's promptly attended to by a medical officer: after days of crisis and stress, Phillips finally allows himself to collapse. The intense scene was unscripted and unplanned— Hanks said, "I understood what the scene was about but I didn't know what was going to happen." When the filmmakers were shooting on an actual navy destroyer and found out the real-life Phillips had been taken to the infirmary immediately after his rescue, they quickly improvised the climactic scene in the ship's clinic.

The medic is played by the woman who happened to be on duty the day the movie crew showed up: Danielle Albert, petty officer second class. She had no advance warning that she was going to be acting in a movie, let alone opposite Tom Hanks— her only previous acting experience was blowing bubbles as the Caterpillar in a fifth-grade production of *Alice in Wonderland*. Understandably, she got flustered and tongue-tied on the first take. "Hey, Doc," Hanks said. "Do you need medical attention? Do you need to sit down?" Too overwhelmed to speak, she sat down with the star. "Look, it's okay," he told her. "We all go through moments like this at one time or another in our acting careers. You're fine. I just want you to react to how I'm acting. You do this every day. Just react."

Albert nodded; on the next take, she snapped into her professional role and treated the man in front of her like a traumatized patient, not a Hollywood star. They did the scene twice after that and her work was done. At the end, she approached Greengrass for a private word; taking Hanks' vital signs, she had noticed something. Albert whispered to the director, "Tom's blood pressure is really, really high."

Saving Mr. Banks
(Walt Disney, 2013)

"I love Mary Poppins and you, you've got to share her with me."

Pamela Lyndon Travers, the author of *Mary Poppins*, didn't want to sell her book's film rights to Walt Disney or his eponymous studio, although the movie producer pursued her for twenty years—she worried that he would make her beloved nanny benign and whimsical. *Saving Mr. Banks* tells the fascinating story of P. L. Travers in 1961, a British grande dame in need of money, finally succumbing to Disney's entreaties and flying out to California to work on the movie—and as a young girl in Australia with a devoted but alcoholic father (Colin Farrell). It leaves out some fascinating middle bits of her life (moving to London to become an actress, her decade-long relationship with another woman) but the heart of the movie is the battle of wills, and the culture clash, between Travers (an exceptional performance by Emma Thompson) and Disney (a very fine Tom Hanks).

Playing the founder and namesake of a multi-billion-dollar corporation can be a delicate affair—especially in a movie financed and released by that same corporation. Hanks, however, had enough freedom to make Walt feel like an actual human being—savvy, exasperated, manipulative—not just the smiling TV host Hanks grew up watching. The biggest limitation was on his smoking: although the real Disney sucked down three packs a day, the studio wouldn't allow Hanks to smoke on-screen. We do catch a glimpse of him stubbing out a cigarette, and Walt's cough lingers in the movie like a premonition of the lung cancer that killed him.

"I don't look too much like him, but there is an angular figure you can get from the boxiness of the suits and playing around with various pieces of hair," Hanks said. "He had the most discussed, photographed, analyzed, diagrammed, tested mustache on the planet. I think documents actually went to the United States government to discuss the angle of the shave and how much mustache was going to be there."

In 1961, having succeeded as a filmmaker, a studio head, and a theme-park impresario, Walt Disney had mastered the art of playing "Walt Disney." Hanks puts on that identity like a well-tailored suit, but he also shows the savvy operator behind that public persona. Hanks insisted on getting the details as right as possible, not just out of a sense of journalistic ethics, but because adhering to the truth is what liberates him to do his job. "You can't just go in and make stuff up," he said. "I mean, people do, but I don't."

Once Hanks knows he's playing somebody as authentically as he can, he's happy to roll with necessary dramatic compressions and inventions. For example, *Saving Mr. Banks* climaxes with a scene in London: Travers has gone home without granting Disney the rights to *Mary Poppins*, and so he follows on the next flight, knocks on her door, and persuades her to sign the deal. Hanks said that the meeting actually happened, and he would have loved to have been a witness, since nobody's sure what the author and the studio chief said to each other. In the film, it's an emotional scene where Disney tells Travers about his own hard-driving father, but Hanks said he could easily imagine a crasser version, where Disney told Travers, "Honey, you're gonna make a shitload of money."

Bridge of Spies

(James B. Donovan, 2015)

"What makes us both Americans? Just one thing. One, one, one. The rulebook. We call it the Constitution. And we agree to the rules and that's what makes us Americans. It's all that makes us Americans, so don't tell me there's no rulebook. And don't nod at me like that, you son of a bitch."

"When you play somebody real, you have to have meetings with them if they're alive and you have to say, 'Look, I'm going to say things you never said and I'm going to do things you never did, and I'm going to be in places you never were. Despite that, how do we do this as authentically as possible?'" Tom Hanks explained.

In the case of James Donovan, the man himself was dead, but Hanks was able to read his book and even search online for news footage of him. Donovan was a fascinating character, an insurance lawyer with zero diplomatic experience who ended up brokering a prisoner exchange between the United States and the Soviet Union in 1962—you can see why Hanks described himself as a selfish actor for lunging at the opportunity to play him.

The movie was Hanks' fourth collaboration with Steven Spielberg (and his second with the Coen brothers, who wrote the screenplay). It shows Donovan's legal defense of the captured

Soviet spy Rudolf Abel (a brilliantly understated performance by Mark Rylance)—at first reluctant, when his firm agrees to take Abel on to prove that the American judicial system works, and then fervent, when Donovan appeals his case all the way to the Supreme Court. Donovan is willing to weaponize decency—when everyone around him is telling him to ease up, for the security of his nation and his family, he insists that American values and jurisprudence are meaningful only if we adhere to them in times of difficulty.

That bullheaded determination carries him through a baroque negotiation in East Berlin, where he's faced with Russians and East Germans working at cross-purposes and impersonating each other. Donovan's supposed to swap Abel for Gary Powers, an American pilot who got shot down over Soviet airspace, but he stubbornly insists on including Frederic Pryor, an American student who got stuck on the wrong side of the Berlin Wall, in the deal.

Through most of *Bridge of Spies,* Hanks plays Donovan as a man in low-grade misery: he's freezing (he gets mugged for his coat), he's hungry, he's got a cold, even the U.S. government isn't being straight with him. He responds not with fury or self-pity, but with mild astonishment, filling his face with a look of wonder: how can a world capacious enough to include the United States of America also contain such indignities?

Spielberg keeps the movie as taut and forceful as the Coens' script. Particularly striking is a pair of scenes Donovan witnesses from trains: in East Berlin, some young people trying to scale the Wall are shot down by guards. In New York City, some young people running through a backyard, clambering over a wall, are just kids at play.

Scott Shepherd, who played the CIA agent trying to manage Donovan's swap of intelligence assets, particularly remembered one scene he did with Hanks. It's nothing viewers of the movie would focus on: just a shot with four people crammed into a car, pulling up to the run-down lodgings where Donovan is staying in Berlin. "The car had to park, and we'd get our stuff out and go into the building," Shepherd recalled. The guy driving the car was a German extra, and he was nervous—maybe because he had Tom Hanks in his car and Steven Spielberg telling him what to do. Shepherd said, "I don't think he was a stunt driver or any kind of car expert. Every time something would go wrong with the car, it would lurch and stall out." Shepherd said that Hanks was normally the soul of graciousness to his fellow actors: "being interested in us, taking us out for dinner, just being the greatest regular guy to everyone around him." Which is why Shepherd treasured moments where Hanks would make hay of his higher status. When the actors started joking that the car was going to explode, Hanks informed them that if it did, the resulting head-line would be "Hanks, Others, Die in Car Explosion."

Ithaca

(Matthew Macauley, 2015)

"*Katey.*"

Ithaca is a World War II movie where the soldiers don't smoke or swear but do earnestly confide, "Even though I wish there were no war, I'm happy to be serving my country." The story centers on

Homer Macauley, a fourteen-year-old boy who takes a job with a telegraph office in his town; he has to grow up quickly when he delivers messages to local mothers about their sons being killed in combat.

There's a lot of fine actors in this movie, doing their best to make vaguely ennobling dialogue sound human—the only one who really pulls it off is Sam Shepard (in one of his final performances), as the aging drunkard manning the wire at the Postal Telegraph office. In her directorial debut, Meg Ryan reaches for poetry but mostly ends up with homilies and sluggish sentimentality.

Tom Hanks and his Playtone partner Gary Goetzman served as executive producers. Hanks knew that Ryan was a fan of William Saroyan's 1943 novel *The Human Comedy* (based on his script for the movie of the same name starring Mickey Rooney—Saroyan got fired from the movie, but won an Oscar for it anyway), so when he discovered that *Band of Brothers* cocreator Erik Jendresen also loved the book, he introduced them to each other and helped shepherd the project along.

Hanks has a cameo as a ghost, appearing as Homer's recently deceased father, visible only to Ryan (who plays Homer's mother), and saying no dialogue other than her character's name. Hanks and Ryan look a bit long in the tooth to be the parents of a four-year-old, but their on-screen history imbues their brief scenes with significance. In their fourth movie together, Hanks and Ryan aren't overcoming obstacles so they can fall in love—the casting implies that every love story with a happy ending has another ending, maybe years later, where somebody dies.

A Hologram for the King

(Alan Clay, 2016)

    "I've lost direction, I think."

The first forty-five seconds of _A Hologram for the King_ are an overcaffeinated blast: Tom Hanks performs a version of Talking Heads' "Once in a Lifetime," reciting "You may find yourself living in your garden shack" as his cushy suburban life disappears in clouds of purple smoke. It's an unusual bit of exposition that doesn't feel much like the rest of the movie, except as an exploration of dislocation.

A Hologram for the King is built on a hoary comedy trope: it's a movie where a hot-shot lead character gets stranded outside the big city until he discovers the virtues he's been missing. Examples include _Groundhog Day, Doc Hollywood,_ and _Cars._ The best example from Hanks' career came when he was punching the clock on the 1980s comedy assembly line; in _Volunteers,_ the environment for his spiritual transformation was rural Thailand. Here, it's an empty city in the desert of Saudi Arabia.

The movie, written and directed by Tom Tykwer (based on a novel by Dave Eggers), is witty and weird, but what sets it apart from the genre is that it stars a sixty-year-old, which gives extra weight to the question of whether his future can outweigh his past. Hanks stars as Alan Clay, a former executive at the Schwinn Bicycle Company who presided over the corporation's decline by moving its manufacturing plants to China and now finds himself working for a tech firm hoping to sell a holographic communications network to the monarch of Saudi Arabia for his new model city, the King's Metropolis of Economy and Trade.

Alan—divorced, broke, and jetlagged—spends day after day in

a tent without air-conditioning on the edge of the empty city. He's hoping the King will show up, or even the King's representative—like *Waiting for Godot,* if Vladimir and Estragon had regular phone calls from a younger boss demanding to know why they hadn't closed the deal with Godot yet. Hanks finds the comedy of the aggravated American but also the uncertainty of somebody who, after a lifetime of optimism, is questioning whether his belief that he would always end up on top was merited. "It was printed all over the pages, vividly, that Alan Clay had to be played by Tom Hanks," Tykwer said. "Alan Clay, an American, that iconic ideal of someone full of thoughts and hopes running into this wall in no-man's-land—there was nobody else."

As the genre demands, there's a comic sidekick (a local cabdriver played by Alexander Black) and a love interest. Although Alan is pursued by a foxy Danish expatriate (Sidse Babett Knudsen), he falls for a Saudi Arabian professional woman—a doctor (Sarita Choudhury) who treats the grotesque cyst on his back but who, by law, can't drive a car. They have a formal courtship by email, and at the end of the movie, Alan stays in Saudi Arabia to pursue their secret romance.

Hanks had long resisted doing love scenes on-screen—in movies where he ends up in bed with somebody, the camera discreetly pans away before anything explicit happens (or the scene gets cut entirely, as happened in both *Philadelphia* and *A League of Their Own*). "It's not going to convince me that these two people love each other more or want each other more by this simulated fucking," he said in 1993. "I don't need to see it to get the story." But Hanks got over his cinematic prudery around the same time he qualified for the senior-citizen discount at Applebee's.

Hanks and Choudhury make love at the movie's end—they're not hard-bodied, but they are attractive, and the scene has real emotion and intimacy to it. We're witnessing a moment of connection that could get them both killed if the authorities find out about it. (Her character is separated but not divorced, and in Saudi Arabia, adultery can be punished by stoning.) "Not everybody looks like a layout in a lingerie ad," Hanks said. "But we weren't worried about it. We embraced the fact that, when it gets down to it, you're all sweaty and damp. So we end up being fleshy, but it's about the tactile pleasures of it as opposed to the purely visual ones. You can almost smell the pleasure."

Sully

(Chesley "Sully" Sullenberger, 2016)

"Mayday, mayday."

The story of Chesley "Sully" Sullenberger, the airline captain who handled a catastrophic engine failure en route from New York City to Charlotte by landing his plane in the Hudson River, saving the lives of everyone on board, is inherently dramatic. The problem with converting it into a feature film is that the flight lasted only five minutes from runway to river, so director Clint Eastwood does a lot of vamping and stretching to fill out this movie: flashbacks to Sullenberger's youth, phone calls with his worried wife (Laura Linney in a thankless role), repeated computer simulations of alternate versions of the flight.

And because Sullenberger's water landing was a story without an antagonist, the movie concocts one, turning the routine investigation by the National Transportation Safety Board (which lauded the captain's decision-making) into a belligerent inquisition hell-bent on finding fault. Directors push reality into movie-shaped boxes all the time, but in this case the cheap theatrics don't add any real suspense. Just as we know from the full-blast news coverage of "The Miracle on the Hudson" that Sullenberger successfully landed the plane in the water, we also know that he was not later pilloried as an incompetent flyboy who should have just turned back to LaGuardia Airport instead.

The core of the story is powerful enough that the movie basically works anyway: it's inspirational to watch the plane's crew, led by Sullenberger, get everybody off the plane alive, and then to see New York City's ferryboats and emergency vehicles fish everyone out of the freezing-cold water. Tom Hanks loves stories of national institutions working as designed and hard-earned competence triumphing over obstacles without showboating, so he's a natural fit for Sullenberger, both in the cockpit (alongside a mustachioed Aaron Eckhart) and outside it, trying to maintain his dignity in a media cyclone even as he suffers from PTSD flashbacks of how everything might have gone wrong.

The role of Sullenberger is probably the one in Hanks' career that makes the least use of his comedic instincts. Hanks had played the straight man before, but the upright Sully seems to live on a planet that hasn't discovered humor. To prepare for the part, Hanks spent a half-day visiting the real-world Sullenberger, impressing the pilot by showing up at 12:58 for a 1:00 p.m. meeting. Since Eastwood famously likes to shoot scenes in one take, Hanks had to make sure he was ready from the word go. But there were advantages to collaborating with Eastwood, Hanks said: "The pleasure of working with somebody who's an actor is they don't waste time with stuff that doesn't matter. There is a shorthand...I don't have to explain anything, I just have to do it."

One unexpected obstacle on the movie was Hanks' transformation to silver fox. He discovered that it was chemically difficult to replicate white hair: "I spent a lot of time in hair and makeup while experts stood behind me and talked about the problems with my scalp. It turns out there's no reverse Grecian Formula."

Inferno

(Robert Langdon, 2016)

"During the Black Deaths, the Venetians made all the ships anchor in the harbor for forty days before they would allow the crews into the city, making sure that they were not carrying the plague. The word 'quarantine' comes from the Italian quaranta: forty."

Robert Langdon has always felt more like a Wikipedia page on two legs than an actual person, although Tom Hanks has worked hard to turn him into something resembling a human being on-screen. In his third adaptation of a Dan Brown novel, Hanks gets to play something beyond academic expertise: he wakes up in a hospital room with a head injury and partial amnesia. The famed "symbologist" can't even remember the word for coffee: "Can I ask you for a cup of...it's, it's, it's, um, well, it's brown and it's hot and people drink it in the morning for energy." And there's an assassin coming down the hall, shooting people.

The Dante-themed plot for *Inferno* is particularly incoherent—there's even less reason than usual for Langdon to be solving elaborate anagrams and religious riddles. But it's got a great villain, scary because he's plausible: a bio-tech billionaire (Ben Foster) who's read Malthus and convincingly diagnoses our planet's fundamental problem as overpopulation. Unfortunately, his Thanos-like solution is a virus that will cause a pandemic, killing half the world's people. Art history versus cellular biology is an incongruous matchup, and so director Ron Howard keeps his finger on the fast-forward button, making sure audiences don't have enough time to think about the plot holes, sending Langdon and the British doctor Sienna Brooks (Felicity Jones) racing through the museums and gardens of Florence, Venice, and Istanbul. There's no time to take even a single selfie, because they are perpetually climbing walls, dodging bullets, and running, running, running.

"I'm always running in these movies," Hanks said. "These movies keep me fit and relatively healthy, I like to think. We're running to save the world—that's the best kind of running there is. But at least with all my running, I'm in a dreadful pair of Hush Puppy-type shoes. Thank God for that because the cobblestones and gravel steps of Florence and Venice are a hodgepodge of hidden death, but at least I'm running in flats. Felicity is running in high heels."

The movie's not great, but it has visual panache, satisfying twists, and as usual with the *Da Vinci* franchise, a talented supporting cast of international actors. Sidse Babett Knudsen, a sexually voracious Dane in *A Hologram for the King,* appears here as an old flame of Langdon's who's now running the World Health Organization—which apparently she's transformed from a dull collective of doctors and bureaucrats into an international paramilitary force. *Inferno* is the best of the *Da Vinci* films—one can question the wisdom of Howard and Hanks making these movies at all, but on this installment, they didn't give a half-assed effort: they went straight to Hell.

The Circle

(Eamon Bailey, 2017)

> *"I am a believer in the perfectibility of human beings. When we are our best selves, the possibilities are endless."*

In consecutive years, Tom Hanks starred in movies adapted from Dave Eggers novels, two tales of people taking jobs at technology firms and discovering the limitations of their new workplaces. This one is the story of Mae Holland (Emma Watson), who gets a dream job at a social-networking tech company called The Circle. The perk-filled corporate culture verges on the cultish, but more problematic are its efforts to wipe out privacy through cheap, omnipresent cameras. While it wasn't especially prescient to identify Facebook as a pernicious cultural force, it was at least accurate. But this movie had too many problems to make it out of beta-testing: a clunky plot, a lack of sharp satire or genuine tension, and risible dialogue like "We used to go on adventures and have fun and see things, and you were brave and exciting."

The biggest trouble ticket belongs to Watson, who is asked to execute several sharp turns for thinly motivated reasons; she is delightful in smaller doses but isn't able to carry this film. The standout performances belong to Patton Oswalt and Tom Hanks, playing the executives who run The Circle. Hanks is particularly good as CEO Eamon Bailey, capturing the tech-billionaire affect where a patina of unbuttoned surfer casualness doesn't hide the hard-driving capitalist underneath. Bailey's avuncular concern for his employees (and the world outside his corporate campus) plays elegantly off Hanks' own public image—can the average citizen, this movie reminds us, be sure that Hanks' good-guy reputation isn't just an elaborate façade?

At the end of the movie, Mae leads a rebellion, possibly a self-destructive Jacobin revolution that doesn't actually change The Circle's fundamentals. It starts with her signing the corporation's leaders up for the radical transparency they've advocated for everyone else. Hanks murmurs an epitaph for an entire era of human civilization: "We're so fucked."

The David S. Pumpkins Halloween Special
(David S. Pumpkins, 2017)

"Any questions?"

The original "Haunted Elevator" sketch on *Saturday Night Live* in October 2016 featured a young couple (Beck Bennett and Kate McKinnon) on a "100 Floors of Frights" amusement-park ride where a ghoulish bride and a waiter serving a severed head give way to David S. Pumpkins: Tom Hanks playing a crazy dude in a suit decorated with pumpkins, accompanied by two dancing B-boy skeletons. The utterly confused couple try to figure out whether he's a character they should know somehow. "I'm David Pumpkins, man," he tells them.

A desperate McKinnon asks, "And David Pumpkins is?"

"His own thing," he informs them, with a flourish of his hands.

The sketch was something writers Mikey Day, Streeter Seidell, and Bobby Moynihan cooked up when Hanks kiboshed their first idea, about a breakdancing SWAT agent, telling them, "Fellas, I don't breakdance."

"I don't know why we assumed Tom Hanks would know how to breakdance," Seidell said. The replacement sketch about David Pumpkins evolved as the show grew closer: the skeletons' names

("Tommy Lee Bones" and "Oprah") got dropped, as did an elaborate rap. In between the dress rehearsal and the actual show, Hanks came up to the writers and told them, "I don't quite know who this guy is yet, but I'm gonna get it. Gentlemen, I swear I will figure out who this David Pumpkins is by the time it's on television."

What Hanks came up with was a gaspy, raspy voice, doing a lot of pointing with two fingers on each hand, and pulling some insane faces. Hanks hadn't hosted *SNL* in a decade, but he happily threw himself back into the show's madcap pace. After the sketch, Hanks changed out of the black-and-orange suit and said he wanted to take it home. "That is how much he loved it," said Tom Broecker of the wardrobe department.

Then the character took off: reporters asked Hanks about it on the red carpet for *Inferno,* Bill Gates dressed up as David S. Pumpkins, lots of other people wore Pumpkins costumes for Halloween, and Madame Tussaud's exhibited a wax statue of Hanks as David S. Pumpkins. The world's confusion as to how David Pumpkins had gotten to be such a big deal mirrored the bewilderment of Bennett and McKinnon in the elevator: Should we know who this guy is?

Day thought at least part of the reason for the sketch's success was that it was nonpolitical at a point where everyone had reached Trump overload: "It's this weird alchemy of Halloween, the best host ever, the time of the country, and just a silly song. It all kind of came together."

The following year, NBC commissioned an animated special about the David Pumpkins character, narrated by Peter Dinklage. Unfortunately, the giddy randomness that was delightful for four and a half minutes was painfully unfunny when stretched out into a half hour. Perhaps they should have gone straight to a feature film. Hanks had an idea for it: "The first movie should be called *David Pumpkins 2*."

"Just making the world go, 'Was there a first David Pumpkins movie?'" Seidell said admiringly. "I think he knows David Pumpkins better than we do at this point."

The Post

(Ben Bradlee, 2018)

"Is anybody else tired of reading the news instead of reporting it?"

The Post is in love with the mechanics of putting out a newspaper circa 1971: the pneumatic tubes to transmit marked-up articles, the handfuls of loose change for pay phones, the printing presses that make a whole building shake. It's an old-fashioned social thriller that, with its constant valorization of newspaper work, could be subtitled "Why a Free Press Is Important."

Although the movie is the fifth collaboration between Tom Hanks and Steven Spielberg, the star is Meryl Streep, playing the publisher of *The Washington Post*. She gives a lovely, measured performance as Katharine Graham, the socialite who had the responsibility of running the family business thrust on her after the suicide of her husband. At first more comfortable hosting cocktail parties for the DC elite than she is handling the business of the paper, by the end of *The Post* she has stopped deferring to her male advisors and has found the inner steel to authorize publication of material from the Pentagon Papers, in the face of potential legal jeopardy and the wrath of the vengeful Nixon White House.

Hanks plays the *Post*'s executive editor, Ben Bradlee, with gusto, disappearing into the role of a jovial ink-stained preppy pirate. The delight Bradlee takes in breaking news echoes the joy Hanks takes in working in his chosen medium—it's just newsprint instead of celluloid. The editor was famously portrayed in the 1976 movie *All the President's Men* by Jason Robards, a daunting predecessor. Hanks considered himself fortunate that he had spent time with both Bradlee and Robards before they died: "I was going to find some other way into the character that had nothing to do with me doing an imitation of Jason or an imitation of Ben. It was a matter of finding some other way to walk into a room, barrel-chested, filled with a confidence that I do not have."

Robards was one of Hanks' earliest acting heroes, alongside Robert Duvall: "I was drawn toward the guys who didn't look like movie stars," he said. When Hanks was at community college, he used to visit the library and, over and over, would take out a record album of Robards performing the monologues of Eugene O'Neill. (Decades later, on the set of *Philadelphia*, Hanks told Robards about this, and says "he confessed to recording those monologues at ten in the morning after lots and lots of coffee.") Four decades later, Hanks could say that he had turned himself into the kind of actor that he had always wanted to be.

Acknowledgments

Fittingly, the name of Tom Hanks abbreviates to T. Hanks, or just "Thanks." That spirit of gratitude has suffused all my work on *The World According to Tom Hanks*—but this section is where I get to thank people by name.

It has been a delight working with my editor, Suzanne O'Neill: this book wouldn't have happened without her, and it was hugely improved by her wisdom and her diligence. My profound thanks to her and her colleagues at Grand Central Publishing, including Nidhi Pugalia, Claire Brown, Regina Castillo, Yasmin Mathew, Andy Dodds, Andrew Duncan, Karen Kosztolnyik, Ben Sevier, and Michael Pietsch.

Thank you to my agent, Daniel Greenberg, a wellspring of publishing knowledge and chilled-out wisdom. I am profoundly grateful to him and all his colleagues at the Levine-Greenberg Rostan Agency, especially Tim Wojcik, Mick Coccia, Kerry Sparks, Jim Levine, and Beth Fisher.

This is my second book illustrated by Robert Sikoryak; by now I should have grown accustomed to his astonishing talents and the inspiration he constantly brings to the page, no matter what style he's working in, but I am nevertheless perpetually gobsmacked by his art. In addition, he's a high-quality human being. My thanks to him; in turn, he would like to thank his wife, Kriota Willberg. If you like what he does here, check out his other books, most recently *The Unquotable Trump* and *Terms and Conditions* (a brilliant graphic-novel adaptation of the iTunes user agreement).

I interviewed (in person, on the phone, and via email) dozens of people who crossed paths with Tom Hanks—in some cases they met the man glancingly, in other cases they maintained a friendship across the decades. I thank them all for their time and their generosity: Lucy Bredeson-Smith, John Frankenheim, Stephen Fry, Holly Fulger, Mary Beidler Gearen, Richard Kaufman, Ken Levine, Joe Mantegna, Sean McGinly, Jeff Michalski, Moshe Mizrahi, Jane Morris, Doug Nichol, Whitney Pastorek, Clive Rosengren, Ksenia Roshchakovsky, Paul Rudnick, Adam Ryon, John Scalzi, Peter Scolari, Scott Shepherd, Lori Singer, Benedict Taylor, Michael Weithorn, and Nili Yelen.

Many people helped me with my research—by flagging stories, making introductions, or politely letting me know when I had wandered into a dead end. I am particularly grateful to Rabia Ahmad, Todd Alcott, Jennifer Keishin Armstrong, Erin Carlson, John Collins, Jo Crocker, Julie Farman, Karl Gajdusek, Jeff Giles, Andy Greene, David Handelman, Carson Kreitzer, Mara Mikialian, Josh Rottenberg, Alan Schwarz, Morgan Worth, and the librarians at the Margaret Herrick Library (of the Academy of Motion Picture Arts and Sciences) in Los Angeles, California, and the staff of VisArt Video in Charlotte, North Carolina. And an extra-special shoutout to Abby Royle, transcriber extraordinaire.

Bill Tipper provided invaluable feedback on early versions of some chapters in this book when they contained paragraphs that were wandering around like they had buckets on their heads. In addition, Bill is one of the best people on planet Earth. The mighty Rob Sheffield also generously offered perspicacious commentary on the manuscript, and made a strong case for the *Splash* poster as being an underappreciated turning point in Tom Hanks' career. Jeff Jackson and Rob Janezic both were wonderful company as I worked my way through Tom Hanks' movies (some of which are, you know, better than others). Steve Crystal, James Hannaham, and Robert Rossney all provided long-distance encouragement while I worked on the manuscript. I am lucky to have such excellent friends.

Many other people all around the world made life worth living while

I worked on this book, including Amy Bagwell, Chuck Barger, Shannon Barringer, Maggie Bean, Peter Bove, Hilary Burt, Nick Catucci, Theresa Claire, Michael Corressell, Scraps de Selby, Stephanie Dempsey, David Fear, Jeremy Fisher, Ted Friedman, Caryn Ganz, Joe Greene, Wendy Greene, Amy and David Grimes, Matthew Hawn, Molly Ker Hawn, Katie Hollander, Hannah Hundley, Erin Janezic, Holly and Andrew Kesin, Greg Lacour, Meg Leder, Kate Lewis, Colin Lingle, Philip and Jody Lomac, Caitlin McKenna, Moby, Chris Molanphy, Brendan Moroney, Tom Nawrocki, Emily Nussbaum, Alan Michael Parker, Lisa Rab, Jeff Schauble, Susan Schnur, Helen Schwab, Ally Sheffield, Massoud and Sherill Shiraz, Syd Sidner, Ben Smith, Brian and Sabrina Smith-Sweeney, Michael Solender, Tommy Tomlinson, Felicia van Bork, Melissa Vrana, Beth Troutman Whaley, and Craig Whaley. I raise a glass to each of them.

My brilliant, indefatigable wife, Jen Sudul Edwards, is the love of my life and a constant inspiration. All my love to her, our sons Strummer and Dashiell, and the rest of my family, especially my parents; Julian and Sharon; Nick, Will, and Miranda; Aunt Lis; Tim, James, and Chris; Megan, Trina, Zane, and Sage; and Alex and Cynthia and Big Al.

Thanks most of all to Tom Hanks himself. This is not an authorized biography, but when I first contacted him about this book, he sent back a delightful letter (typed, of course), saying, "Regarding the world according to me, I am not against the use of time and paper to record such for posterity." Although his busy schedule didn't allow him to sit for a one-on-one interview with me before my deadline, he was unflaggingly gracious about this book: when his friends and colleagues asked him directly whether it was okay for them to talk with me, he repeatedly gave them his blessing. I thank him for that generosity, and for having lived a life that's worthy of close study.

My hope in writing *The World According to Tom Hanks* was that it would nudge the world, even slightly, into being a Hanksier place—if after reading it, you find yourself emulating his example, in ways large or small, then I thank you as well.

Sources

If you want to know where I got my information or if you're looking for further Hanks-related reading, you've made it to the right part of the book. *The World According to Tom Hanks* wasn't intended as a scholarly tome—but if you're a professor assigning it to students as part of your "Introduction to Hanksology" syllabus, please drop me a line at gavin42@gmail.com or on Twitter at @mrgavinedwards.

PREFACE: THE NICE MANIFESTO

xiii "I suppose it's the sheer bloody Tom Hankness of Tom Hanks": author correspondence with Stephen Fry.

xiii "He is the most accomplished actor ever": Hillary Atkin, "Rave Reviews," *The Hollywood Reporter,* June 12, 2002.

xiv "The guy could be, should have been, a professional soldier": Richard Corliss and Cathy Booth, "Tom Terrific," *Time,* December 21, 1998.

xiv "Sometimes the mind-set of actors is fueled by neuroses or intense need": author interview with Holly Fulger.

xv "Another Actress Steps Forward Accusing Tom Hanks of Being Nice": bluerockpublicradio.com, November 9, 2017.

xv "World Doesn't Even Know Who to Admire Anymore After Tom Hanks Murders 5": theonion.com, February 20, 2013.

xv "Here's the deal": Ned Zeman, "No More Mr. Nice Guy," *Buzz,* September 1996.

SECTION ONE: A BRIEF HISTORY OF TOM

2 "Basically he ran the kitchen": Richard Corliss and Cathy Booth, "Tom Terrific," *Time,* December 21, 1998.

2 "My parents pioneered": Dolores Barclay, "Tom Hanks: From Forrest to Apollo 13, an Everyman for All Seasons," *Entertainment Today,* June 29, 1995.

3 "I was only five": Gerri Hirshey, "Tom Hanks Lights It Up," *GQ,* June 1995.

3 "We were total strangers": David Sheff, "Tom Hanks: The *Playboy* Interview," *Playboy,* March 1989.

3 "I don't know if they actually drew blood": Joe Rhodes, "Tom Hanks," *US,* September 1996.

4 "When he and she split up": Sheff.

4 "not much farther than half a tank of gas": David Thomson, "Huge," *The Independent on Sunday* (UK), September 18, 1994.

4 "If the house didn't have": Bart Mills, "The Shoe Fits Tom Hanks," *Movieline,* July 26–August 1, 1985.

4 "Here's what never happened": as told to Margy Rochlin, "When I Was Eight," *Life,* November 2004.

5 "I could entertain": Ibid.

5 "We never broke laws": Ibid.

5 "We'd hang plastic models": Ibid.

6 "We didn't know about sauces": David Gardner, *The Tom Hanks Enigma,* John Blake UK, 2007.

6 "I knew what time it was": Stephen Ambrose, "Man with a Mission," *Reader's Digest,* September 2001.

7 "They tried to have rules": Rochlin.

7 "We talked to the rest of the family": Sheff.

8 "It was a big urban public school": Ingrid Sischy, "Tom Hanks," *Interview,* March 1994.

8 "I was death with women": "Tom Hanks: Funny, frank and fancy-free," *Ladies' Home Journal,* April 1987.

8 "I'm not a child of the '60s": Peter Travers, "Tom Hanks," *Rolling Stone* 1039, November 15, 2007.

9 "The most influential": Sheff. (He didn't stop watching *2001* as he got older; as of 2014, Hanks said he had seen the movie over one hundred times in his life.)

10 "He was the polar opposite of me": Cal Fussman, "Confessions of an Average Man," *Esquire,* June 2006.

10 "Any knothead could be assistant manager": "It's All Relative," *People,* July 22, 2002.

11 "It was not a Holy Roller place": Kevin Sessums, "Tom Terrific," *Vanity Fair,* June 1994.

11 "He had a self-righteousness that goes along": Linda Lee, *People Profiles: Tom Hanks,* Time Inc., 1999.

11 "I mostly just wanted to get out of the house": Sischy.

12 "How come *I'm* not up there": Ibid.

12 "The class kind of rotated around him": Lee.

12 "My dad sat there": Jess Cagle, "Two for the Road," *Time,* July 8, 2002.

13 "Thom Hanks": Lee.

13 "Not much is expected of you": Gardner.

13 "You're bending the shafts!": *Late Night with David Letterman,* NBC, June 25, 1993. (Hanks was the featured guest on David Letterman's last show on NBC—the interview is very funny and worth checking out.)

13 "The curtains in Elvis's suite": Gardner.

13 "knowing such fine schools": Tom Hanks, "I Owe It All to Community College," *The New York Times,* January 14, 2015.

14 "Jeez, I should have got out of high school": Kurt Andersen, "The Tom Hanks Phenomenon," *The New Yorker,* December 7–14, 1998.

14 "My looks are not stunning": the letter, and George Roy Hill's response, can be found in the archives of the Margaret Herrick Library of the Academy of Motion Picture Arts and Sciences (in Los Angeles, California).

15 "veterans back from Vietnam": Hanks.

15 "such are the pleasures": Ibid.

15 "A public speaking class": Ibid.

16 "It didn't matter": Laurel Delp, "Hanging Loose," *US*, July 16, 1984.

16 "Shame on you!": Kim Williamson, "Tom's New Direction," *Boxoffice*, October 1996.

18 "I've found another Tony Curtis": Lee.

18 "You'd always see him moving about": Carol Troy, "It's a Cool Gig," *American Film*, April 1990.

18 "People, if they want to": Sheff.

20 "He was a golden retriever puppy": Author interview with Mary Beidler Gearen.

20 "I really knew how to entertain": Author interview with Ksenia Roshchakovsky.

20 "I had a terrible crush on him": Author interview with Lucy Bredeson-Smith.

20 "Razor-tipped": Gearen.

21 "And he was able to cut through the obtuseness": Bredeson-Smith.

22 "Boom, I had a card in my wallet": Corliss and Booth.

22 "I remember thinking: *what?*": Author interview with Holly Fulger.

22 "I tell people who are coming to Los Angeles": David Galligan, "Tom Hanks," *Drama-Logue*, April 5–11, 1984.

23 "He remembers you": Roshchakovsky.

23 "As far as TV, commercials, or soaps": Lee.

24 "We were young and impetuous": Gardner.

24 "He had no bad habits": Gardner.

24 "secret formula": Lee.

25 "He had long hair": Lee.

25 "Everybody then was making, essentially, slasher movies": Lynn Hirschberg, "The Actors," *The New York Times Magazine*, November 10, 1997.

26 "We showed it to our secretaries": Lee.

26 "Tom worked the Tony Curtis side of the street": Author interview with Peter Scolari.

27 "Everybody who's ever owned a Volkswagen": Hirshey.

27 "What? They can't strike now!": Susan Christian, "A Series of Setbacks for New Stars," *Los Angeles Herald-Examiner,* July 27, 1980.

27 "the one guy on *The Love Boat* who didn't get lucky": Cagle.

28 "It was like going to an airplane factory": "Tom Hanks," *Cable Guide,* August 1986.

28 "They cancelled us": Scolari.

29 "In the fall of 1982": Author interview with Michael Weithorn.

30 "Your job is not to get laughs": Jamie Etkin, "Tom Hanks Reveals the Movies That Have Meant the Most to Him," buzzfeed.com, October 14, 2015.

30 "It would have been nice": Jerry Roberts, "A Superstar Talks Business," *Variety,* March 9, 1995.

30 "He probably knew that if he had yelled": Barclay.

32 "If I have to wait": Galligan.

32 "The Guy in a Hole": Hirshey.

33 "I didn't really know what I was doing": Amy Wallace, "Average Joe Versus the Icons," *Los Angeles Times,* November 7, 1999.

33 "You'd be surprised": Fussman.

33 "I did not have a clue": Cagle.

34 "I got fired": "Rita Wilson," biography.com, April 15, 2015.

34 "that girl's cute": Maggie Parker, "Tom Hanks Recalls Watching Wife Rita Wilson on *The Brady Bunch*," people.com, March 16, 2016.

34 "I've forgotten how many times I've played the girl": Gardner.

35 "You'd see farmers": Fussman.

35 "Rita and I looked at each other": Grace Gavilanes, "Inside Tom Hanks & Rita Wilson's Long-lasting Love Story," people.com, January 18, 2018.

35 "It was a beautiful thing": Fussman.

36 "I told him that I was sincerely sorry": Garry Marshall, *My Happy Days in Hollywood,* Crown Archetype, 2012.

36 "I didn't talk to my dad": Fussman.

37 "My stepmother kept my dad alive": Sara Davidson, "Magnificent Obsession," *Reader's Digest,* August 2005.

37 "dead from the feet up": Kristine McKenna, "He's Serious About This One," *Los Angeles Times,* December 19, 1993.

38 "somehow, no matter what I'd do to combat it": Thomson.

38 "Food didn't taste good": Mark Morrison, "Tom Hanks: The US Interview," *US,* August 1994.

38 "official date": Ibid.

38 "the strangest thing they'd ever seen": Gardner.

38 "trial marriage love nest": David Wild, "Big Again," *Vogue,* July 1993.

38 "It's like Starsky and Hutch": Gardner.

39 "When I hit my thirtieth birthday": Morrison.

39 "I was an asshole for six months": Bruce Buschel, "Tom Hanks, Unpeeled," *GQ,* January 1989.

39 "There was a while there": Sischy.

39 "You never have to change anything": "Tom Hanks & Rita Wilson," *People,* February 12, 1996.

40 "You bet!": Sessums.

40 "We had a Greek band and a rock band": "Who's News," *USA Weekend,* August 16, 2002.

40 "I've grown to really love more people": Hirshey.

40 "Rita saved me": Hillary Atkin, "Road to Success," *The Hollywood Reporter,* June 12, 2002.

41 "Date Night U.S.A.": "Where Tom Takes Rita," *People,* August 9, 1993.

41 "Because of the love": Morrison.

41 "The best-case scenario": *Cable Guide.*

41 "I don't want you to play *cute*": Wild.

43 "No, those are for Eastern-bloc governments": Joe Logan, "Tom Hanks, working stiff," *Long Beach Press-Telegraph,* March 24, 1990.

43 "We just worked ourselves into the grave": Bill Zehme, "Tom Hanks Acts Like a Man," *Esquire,* September 2001.

43 "The idea of me playing Sherman McCoy": Julie Salamon, *The Devil's Candy,* Houghton Mifflin, 1991.

44 "I just can't act with Uma": Ibid.

44 "Some people will assume": Wild.

44 "There was a chance": Joe Rhodes, "Back from the Bonfire," *Los Angeles Times,* July 5, 1992.

45 "I made a particularly disappointing string of cheap comedies": Andersen.

45 Elliott Gould: Ibid.

45 "What do you want to do?": Ibid.

45 "Well, it's not like I know": Andersen.

45 "I don't want to play a pussy anymore": Wallace.

46 "And that was that": Andersen.

47 "It's truly great": Wild.

47 "'Likable' can be a terrible burden": Rhodes.

47 "There have been periods": Wallace.

48 "In some ways we've all been waiting": Jennet Conant, "Tom Hanks Wipes That Grin off His Face," *Esquire,* December 1993.

48 "It's not just playing a disease": Wild.

48 "There were times when I got hit on by guys": "Playing the Part," *Newsweek,* February 14, 1994.

48 "Look, you know, I can feel you": Conant.

48 "Without even knowing it": Ibid.

49 "the streets of Heaven": Academy Awards Acceptance Speech Database, http://aaspeechesdb.oscars.org/link/066-1/

49 "communicated more about what *Philadelphia* was saying": Sessums.

49 "It's an incredibly personal moment": Ima N. Seider, "Tom Hanks," *Blockbuster News & Previews,* May 1995.

49 "I didn't know exactly what he was going to say": *People* staff, "Be True to Your School," *People*, April 11, 1994.

50 "Tom Hanks' acceptance speech": author correspondence with Paul Rudnick.

50 "That's tremendous": Hirschberg.

50 "They didn't want to spend the money": Thomson.

51 "Look, *Forrest Gump* was fabulous": Joe Leydon, "Aboard the Star Ship," *Los Angeles Times,* June 27, 1985.

51 "goofy cartoon": *Inside the Actors Studio,* episode 185, Bravo, May 14, 2006.

53 "It seemed like it was Month 82": Patrick Goldstein, "Wonder of Wonders," *Los Angeles Times,* September 29, 1996.

53 "I am so friggin' tired": Rhodes.

53 "big honking movie star": Ned Zeman, "No More Mr. Nice Guy," *Buzz,* September 1996.

53 "Most actors I've come across": Wild.

54 "You should get together": Terry Gross, "Tom Hanks Says Self-Doubt Is 'A High-Wire Act That We All Walk'" (transcript of *Fresh Air* interview), April 26, 2016, npr.org.

55 "You've become this great actor": Wallace.

55 "Swinging!": David Ansen, "A Stand-Up Guy," *Newsweek,* September 26, 1988.

55 "I used to just show up": Wallace.

56 "One thing I find myself doing": Andersen.

56 "He basically rewrites": McKenna.

57 "Just keep those box-office grosses up": Sessums.

57 "You really have to go a lot of years here": Wild.

57 "Rita and I have been married": Davidson.

58 "I like to nap": Morrison.

58 "Don't you worry your pretty little head": Parker.

58 "It's always fun to watch him yell": "Party Lines," *New York,* May 11, 2009.

58 "Oh, any failure of technology": Ibid.

59 "I'm not as nutty a guy": Ambrose.

59 "Family always comes first": Jillian Michaels, "Jillian Michaels Interviews Rita Wilson on Her Career and Her Family," goodcleanhealth.com, 2011.

59 "If I play one more warm, understanding mother": Ibid.

60 "I like sitting up high": Zehme.

60 "I asked": Maureen Dowd, "Hollywood's Most Decent Fella on Weinstein, Trump, and History," *The New York Times,* October 11, 2017.

60 "impervious to perks": Ibid.

60 "Is this what's going on": *The Late Show with Stephen Colbert,* episode 341, CBS, April 28, 2017.

60 "How much better can I eat?": Hirschberg.

60 "If you're in debt": Emma Brockes, "Tom Hanks: 'I've made a lot of movies that didn't make sense—or money'," *The Guardian* (UK), October 14, 2017.

60 "fuck-you money": Ibid.

61 "I do wrestle with the amount of money": Chris Connelly, "Hollywood Survivor," *Talk,* November 2000.

61 "relatively modest": Brockes.

61 "They remember when life was normal": Ibid.

61 "Both Rita and I have communicated": Ibid.

61 "My dad is a goofy guy": Truman Hanks, "I am the youngest child of Tom Hanks. Would anyone be interested in an AMA?" AMA ("Ask Me Anything") on reddit.com, 2012.

62 "It's like living": Truman Hanks.

63 "You want your kids to follow their passion": Luis Gomez, "No punching Tom Hanks," *Chicago Tribune,* June 26, 2011.

63 "Let's go hit on some models": Amos Barshad, "242 Minutes with…Chet Hanks," *New York,* April 30, 2012.

63 "I AM A WALKING PR DISASTER": Soraya Nadia McDonald, "What the Heck Is Going on with Tom Hanks' Son, Chet Haze, and His Insistence on Using the N-word?", *The Washington Post,* June 2, 2015.

63 "You got to applaud the bravery": Alex Ungerman, "Tom Hanks Addresses His Son Chet's Sobriety: 'Love Your Kids Unconditionally'," etonline.com, October 5, 2015.

63 "I was a total idiot": "Tom Hanks on *A Hologram for the King,* the Challenges of Age and the Rise of Donald Trump," *Radio Times,* May 20, 2016.

64 "It wasn't like I was going to be": Rita Wilson, "Rita Wilson on Life After Breast Cancer," *Harper's Bazaar,* October 2017.

64 "You just clear the decks": Anna Lewis, "Tom Hanks Helped His Wife Get Through Breast Cancer in the Sweetest Way," cosmopolitan.com, February 21, 2017.

64 "I'm on the back nine": *Radio Times.*

64 "I have a book of my own to push": Author correspondence with Tom Hanks.

64 "I pray that evolution": Bill Higgins, "AFI Salutes Hanks," *Variety,* June 14, 2002.

SECTION TWO: THE TEN COMMANDMENTS OF TOM HANKS

67 "I'm a pessimist": Dan Yakir, "Why Tom Hanks Acts the Way He Does," *Family Weekly,* July 14, 1985.

67 "Shamelessly so": Stephen Ambrose, "Man with a Mission," *Reader's Digest,* September 2001.

67 hedonic adaptation: Melissa Dahl, "A Classic Psychological Study on Why Winning the Lottery Won't Make You Happier," thecut .com, January 13, 2016.

68 "It's a choice I make, yes.": *Entertainment Weekly* Tumblr interview with Hanks, http://entertainmentweekly.tumblr.com /post/130001528567/are-you-happy-my-mother-wants-to -know-this

68 "I apologize to my friends and family": Ambrose.

68 "I look at the United States of America": Ibid.

68 "Look, lady": Kim Williamson, "Tom's New Direction," *Boxoffice,* October 1996.

69 "We knew it was going to be one damn thing": Sara Davidson, "Magnificent Obsession," *Reader's Digest,* August 2005.

69 "something good jammed up": Williamson.

69 "It's still going to be": Ibid.

The First Commandment: Excel at your life's work.

72 "Hark, a mourning dove": Josh Eells, "A League of His Own," *Rolling Stone* 1169, November 8, 2012.

72 "Blindly": Beverly Walker, "Close Up," *Screen Actor,* Summer 1989.

73 "You can do a whole movie with Tom just by using those words": Garry Marshall, *Wake Me When It's Funny,* Adams Publishing, 1995. (Directing a whole movie using just those words seems like it should have been one of Lars von Trier's *Five Obstructions.*)

73 "I see this scene as chartreuse": Ibid.

74 "That was terrible": Duane Byrge, "Actor's Dialogue," *The Hollywood Reporter,* March 8, 1995.

74 "You attack and it's finally done": Joe Rhodes, "Tom Hanks," *US,* September 1996.

74 "I was basically an extra in that scene": Author interview with Scott Shepherd.

75 "Because if you don't get up from the desk": Chris Connelly, "Hollywood Survivor," *Talk,* November 2000.

76 "Call me by my character's name": Kurt Andersen, "The Tom Hanks Phenomenon," *The New Yorker,* December 7–14, 1998.

76 "You mean when I crossed my eyes": Rick Lyman, "At the Movies: Can Lightning Strike Thrice?" *The New York Times,* December 22, 2000.

76 "The older I get": Andersen.

76 "You know, underneath there's somebody else": Bill Zehme, "Tom Hanks Acts Like a Man," *Esquire,* September 2001.

76 "You can only mine these things": David Wild, "Big Again," *Vogue,* July 1993.

77 "If you're paying attention to the artificiality": Cal Fussman, "Confessions of an Average Man," *Esquire,* June 2006.

77 "I've worked on a set": Sara Davidson, "Magnificent Obsession," *Reader's Digest,* August 2005.

The Second Commandment: Honor the sacrifices your elders made in the service of a seemingly impossible goal.

79 "We had a painting commissioned": *Late Night with Conan O'Brien,* episode 9.147, NBC, July 9, 2002.

79 "Astronauts, test pilots": Douglas Brinkley, "The World According to Tom," *Time,* March 15, 2010.

79 "The fact is": Ibid.

80 "Two guys side by side": Sara Davidson, "Magnificent Obsession," *Reader's Digest,* August 2005.

80 "Then, of course": Ibid.

80 "Growing up, I always knew": Brinkley.

81 "When it came to understanding history": Ibid.

81 "convinced that things were harder": Stephen Ambrose, "Man with a Mission," *Reader's Digest,* September 2001.

82 "I walked where they died": Army Archerd, "Just for Variety," *Variety,* August 19, 1998.

82 "You can't find Sherman tanks": David Gritten, "To the Front Once More," *Los Angeles Times*, August 20, 2000.

82 "I feel like I've been working on my historical doctorate": Ted Johnson, *TV Guide,* September 22–28, 2001.

83 "You think, 'Well, I've been outside' ": Bill Zehme, "Tom Hanks Acts Like a Man," *Esquire,* September 2001.

83 "the meatball" and "the worm": *The Nerdist Podcast,* episode 267, nerdist.com, October 8, 2012.

83 "Wally Schirra was cranky": David Handelman, "To the Moon!" *TV Guide*, April 4–10, 1998.

84 "flight parabolas": Caroline Siede, "On Apollo 13's 20th Anniversary, a Look at How They Made the Film So Realistic": avclub.com, June 30, 2015.

84 "I remember talking about bringing in a mime": Linda Lee, *People Profiles: Tom Hanks,* Time Inc., 1999.

84 "How dare we have such faith": Tom Hanks, "Right Now," *The Hollywood Reporter,* April 3–5, 1998.

85 "it was a combination": Handelman.

85 "Made of flesh and sinew": Hanks.

Interlude: Peter Scolari, Bosom Buddy

Author interview with Peter Scolari.

The Third Commandment: Embrace your passions.
Star Trek

96 "My entire family worshipped": *The Graham Norton Show,* Season 9, episode 9, BBC, June 10, 2011.

97 "And there was the bridge of the Starship *Enterprise*": Andrew Husband, "Tom Hanks Once Snuck onto the Set of 'Star Trek II: The Wrath of Khan' While Filming 'Bosom Buddies,' uproxx.com, September 9, 2016.

97 "he told me he doesn't just watch the show": Cindy Pearlman, "Tom Hanks, 'Star Trek' junkie?", *Entertainment Weekly*, December 16, 1994.

97 "Let me play a peaceful Romulan": *The Graham Norton Show.*

Surfing

97 "There was a lot of really cool stuff": Johnny Dodd, "Talking With…Tom Hanks," *People,* December 9, 1996.

98 "I remember Tom sitting on the beach": Richard Corliss and Cathy Booth, "Tom Terrific," *Time,* December 21, 1998.

98 "You're out there and you get scared": Carol Troy, "It's a Cool Gig," *American Film,* April 1990.

98 "There's really a placidness to it": David Sheff, "Tom Hanks: The *Playboy* Interview," *Playboy,* March 1989.

99 "There he was": Ibid.

99 "A guy wrote about me surfing once": Joe Rhodes, "Back from the Bonfire," *Los Angeles Times,* July 5, 1992.

Randy Newman

99 "Through each illuminating track": Peter Travers, "Tom Hanks," *Rolling Stone* 1039, November 15, 2007.

Blasting Caps

100 "The Willie Mays Blasting Caps Spot": https://www.youtube .com/watch?v=skfZQ9fRpf4

100 "I'd never seen blasting caps": *The Nerdist Podcast*, episode 267, nerdist.com, October 8, 2012.

Reading

101 "Oh yeah, here we go": Alex Ben Block, "Hanks Ranks," *The Hollywood Reporter,* April 27, 2009.

102 "The most important thing ever pulled out of the ground is a potato": Josh Eells, "A League of His Own," *Rolling Stone* 1169, November 8, 2012.

102 "Some of the best vacations": Sara Davidson, "Magnificent Obsession," *Reader's Digest*, August 2005.

103 "But it made my editor": author correspondence with John Scalzi.

103 "A collection of stories": Douglas Brinkley, "The World According to Tom," *Time,* March 15, 2010.

103 "It's simply a novel": Ibid.

103 "He weaves a glamorous world": Kevin Sessums, "Tom Terrific," *Vanity Fair,* June 1994.

103 "You learn so much": Kate Samuelson, "How Tom Hanks the Movie Star Became Tom Hanks the Short Story Writer," time.com, November 3, 2017.

103 "That fellow connected": Hanks.

103 "I went on a reading rampage": Brinkley.

103 "And when someone tells me": Hanks.

Nudity

104 "That's as close": Cindy Adams, "Times Square's topless ladies aren't the only ones who go bare," pagesix.com, August 31, 2015.

The Beatles and the Dave Clark Five

104 "If I had my way": Ingrid Sischy, "Tom Hanks," *Interview,* March 1994.

105 "I was convinced": B. Love, "Tom Hanks: Jack of All," *University Reporter,* October 1996.

105 "blare from a speaker": "Induction of the Dave Clark Five," https://www.youtube.com/watch?v=KKTtGjYl5yU

The Godfather

106 "at probably the best time": Ingrid Sischy, "Tom Hanks,"
Interview, March 1994.

Television

106 "Bad TV was great in our day": David Handelman, "To the
Moon!" *TV Guide,* April 4–10, 1998.

106 "It's become cheap and profitable": Gerri Hirshey, "Tom Hanks
Lights It Up," *GQ,* June 1995.

107 "three fabulous reality TV shows": *The Nerdist Podcast,* Episode
267, nerdist.com, October 8, 2012.

Red Vines

107 "I've never actually tasted": Tom Hanks, "Tom Hanks'
Concession Speech: Confessions of a Red Vines Junkie,"
Boxoffice, May 1995.

The Fourth Commandment: Treat women with respect.

110 "I graduated from high school in 1974": Ingrid Sischy, "Tom
Hanks," *Interview,* March 1994.

110 "I never thought": Ibid.

110 "The ideas that were put forward": Ibid.

110 "I think I'm a gentleman": Ibid.

111 "There are a lot of writers": David Blum, "Tom Hanks's Real
Splash," *New York,* July 28, 1986.

111 "The wives are pretty much always treated": Robert Sullivan,
"It's a Wonderful Life," *Vogue,* December 1998.

111 "I didn't understand the question": Sischy.

111 "The most commercially successful": Ibid.

112 "Unfairly, I don't think there is one": Emma Brockes, "Tom
Hanks: 'I've made a lot of movies that didn't make sense—or
money'," *The Guardian* (UK), October 14, 2017.

112 "We all left town": *The Axe Files with David Axelrod*, episode 197, December 2, 2017.

112 "love hitting on": Maureen Dowd, "Hollywood's Most Decent Fella on Weinstein, Trump, and History," *The New York Times*, October 11, 2017.

113 "I know that I have participated": Cara Buckley, "Meryl Streep and Tom Hanks on the #MeToo Moment and 'The Post'," *The New York Times*, January 3, 2018.

113 "There's no reason": Ibid.

The Fifth Commandment: Worship in the church of baseball.

115 "I wish I'd had a little camera": Cal Fussman, "Confessions of an Average Man," *Esquire,* June 2006.

115 "Baseball is the perfect metaphor": Bruce Buschel, "Tom Hanks, Unpeeled," *GQ*, January 1988.

116 "a bitter guy sitting on a park bench": Louise Sweeney, "Film Star Tom Hanks: Having Fun Making Movies Filled with Mirth," *Christian Science Monitor*, September 17, 1984.

116 "that bastard Charlie Finley": Peter Hartlaub, "Tom Hanks Sounds Off on Raiders Moving to Las Vegas," *San Francisco Chronicle*, April 26, 2017.

116 "Cleveland has no built-in national affection factor": Stu Schrelberg, "There Is No Joy in Mudville—Mighty Hanks Has Been Rained Out," *USA Weekend,* June 5, 1988.

117 "Our friendship revolved around baseball": Author interview with Clive Rosengren.

117 "A Good Clean Christian Game": courtesy of Clive Rosengren.

118 "the little-boy fantasy": Lisa Birnbach, "Tom Hanks' Fantasy: If I Only Were a Cleveland Indian," *Parade Magazine*, November 8, 1987.

118 "I don't root for the home team": Birnbach.

118 "fatball": Fussman.

120 "Big Fat capital K": *The Late Show with Stephen Colbert,* episode 232, CBS, October 24, 2016.

120 "I know the entire world": Ibid.

120 "Armageddon": Ibid.

121 "You know, the sporting analogy": Fussman.

Interlude: Random Acts of Hilarity and Kindness

123 Scott Shepherd: Author interview with Scott Shepherd.

Lost gloves

124 "the absolute best use": Elizabeth Flock, "Why Tom Hanks Posts Photos of Lost Things on His Twitter Feed," pbs.org, October 27, 2017.

124 "Hold on to this!": Katie Kindelan, "Tom Hanks Returns Fordham Student's ID With Handwritten Note," abc.go.com, October 7, 2015.

124 "It's really kind of a visual haiku": Flock.

124 Ken Levine: Author interview with Ken Levine.

Awards shows

125 "are kind of like the door prizes": "Tom Hanks," *Cable Guide,* August 1986.

125 Santa Claus costumes: Liz Smith, "Liz Smith," *Los Angeles Times,* December 22, 1995.

125 "I was at the table": *The Ellen DeGeneres Show,* season 15, episode 78, January 9, 2018.

126 Hood ornament: Erik Hayden, "Tom Hanks Tapes Emmy Award to the Hood of a Towncar," hollywoodreporter.com, September 24, 2012.

Joe Mantegna

126 Author interview with Joe Mantegna.

Girl Scouts

127 "Tom Hanks surprises Girl Scouts," *Los Altos Town Crier,* March 11, 2015.

Israel desert

128 Author interview with Benedict Taylor.

Dead monkey

129 Army Archerd, "Just for Variety," *Variety,* April 13, 1993.

Backstage at Lucky Guy

130 Author interview with Adam Ryon.

Carly Rae Jepsen

130 "Don't hurt the bird!": Andrea Dresdale, "Why Tom Hanks Appears in Carly Rae Jepsen's Music Video," abcnews.go.com, March 9, 2015.

130 "We laughed about it": Ibid.

131 "Why didn't you guys ask me?": Shannon Carlin, "Carly Rae Jepsen On How You Get Tom Hanks To Star In Your Music Video," radio.com, March 6, 2015.

Violin

131 Author interview with Richard Kaufman.

Tim Meadows

133 David Wolinsky, "Tim Meadows: Random Roles," avclub.com, June 9, 2008.

Mr. Ferrari

134 Brandon Stanton, "Humans of New York" (website, Instagram, Twitter), October 27, 2014.

Amy Poehler feud

135 Julie Miller, "Tom Hanks Jokes About Six-Month Romance with Amy Poehler," vanityfair.com, September 28, 2015.

Winnebago

135 Garry Marshall, *Wake Me When It's Funny*, Adams Publishing, 1995.

Feeding the crew

136 "It's amazing": Amy Wallace, "Average Joe Versus the Icons," *Los Angeles Times*, November 7, 1999.

136 "It's made of paper": Author interview with Scott Shepherd.

Celebrity

137 "I don't usually do this": Mary Murphy, "Tom Hanks: One Hunk Who Refuses to Go Hollywood," *Cosmopolitan*, March 1987.

138 "Ninety-nine percent": Jeff Giles, "Catch Them If You Can," *Newsweek*, December 23, 2002.

138 "I've traveled with Tom": "Jim Hanks sounds just like his brother Tom," https://www.youtube.com/watch?v=yrPbt03-8lI, January 18, 2015.

138 "I often wonder what it must be like": Giles.

138 "One of the most surprising things": Author interview and correspondence with Sean McGinly.

140 "By and large": Giles.

140 "walk around with a phalanx": Ibid.

Weddings

140 "I think that anybody": Sierra Marquina, "Tom Hanks: I Studied the Ministry for $35 to Officiate Allison Williams' Wedding," usmagazine.com, September 28, 2015.

141 "I've got a film to make": Thomas Whitaker, "Real-Life Action Hero Tom Hanks Is an Angel in Rome as He Saves the Day for British Bride Natalia Moore," *Hello!* (UK), June 24, 2008.

141 "congratulations you kooky kids": Dave Paulson, "A Nashville Couple Sent Tom Hanks a Wedding Invitation. He Wrote Back," *The Tennesseean,* February 14, 2018.

141 "We can all see": Chris Baldwin, "Tom Hanks Helps a Texas Couple Fulfill Their Biggest Romantic Fantasy in Sweetest Way Possible," papercitymag.com, November 13, 2017.

141 "He leaned in close": "When Tom Hanks runs into your wedding photos," bbc.com, September 27, 2016.

141 "It was pretty surreal": Ibid.

142 "We just wanted": Meredith Lepore, "Tom Hanks Officiated Allison Williams's Wedding: 'He Should Marry Everyone'," instyle.com, March 24, 2016.

142 "If you want to call me": Marquina.

142 "He should marry everyone": Lepore.

142 "I'm for rent": Marquina.

142 "Both have beaten the odds": Devan Coggan, "Tom Hanks talks *Bridge of Spies,* Offers Love Advice in EW Tumblr Q&A," ew.com, September 27, 2015.

The Sixth Commandment: Use the right tool for the job.

144 letter from Tom Hanks: Author correspondence with Tom Hanks.

144 "There's something about the clean mechanics of the hammer striking": Robert Sullivan, "It's a Wonderful Life," *Vogue,* December 1998.

145 "I hate getting email thank-yous": *California Typewriter* (director Doug Nichol), American Buffalo Pictures, 2016.

146 "Just who do you think you are": Chris Hardwick, "The Tom Hanks Typewriter Saga," nerdist.com, October 9, 2012.

146 "I've tried to foster": *California Typewriter.*

146 "He said, 'If you give me your name and address' ": Author interview with Doug Nichol.

147 "let's call it a harmless vice": Mark Medley, "Tom Hanks on His New Book, Nora Ephron, and His 'Harmless Vice'—Typewriters," *The Globe and Mail,* October 13, 2017.

147 "My desire is to eventually": Ibid.

147 "There is a wonderful way to spend time": *California Typewriter.*

147 "a cadence and rhythm": "Hanx Writer" app, as accessed via iTunes, 2018.

147 "The truth is no good typewriters": *California Typewriter.*

148 "An old German man": Sullivan.

148 "Along with cuckoo clocks": Tom Hanks, *Uncommon Type,* Alfred A. Knopf, 2017.

149 "As an actor in movies": Medley.

150 "Christmas Eve 1953": For example, Stephen Ambrose, "Man with a Mission," *Reader's Digest,* September 2001.

150 "Being Anna's boyfriend": Hanks, *Uncommon Type.*

151 "He really gets into the female psyche": Author interview with Mary Beidler Gearen.

151 "That's not writing, that's typing": Or something close to that; the line may have been paraphrased and improved over the years. See https://quoteinvestigator.com/2015/09/18/typing/

151 "and if the idea": *California Typewriter.*

The Seventh Commandment: Don't dwell on the road not taken.

153 "I've read plenty of things": Chris Connelly, "Hollywood Survivor," *Talk,* November 2000.

154 *Nixon*: Pat H. Broeske, "Tom Hanks Considers What's Next," *Entertainment Weekly,* July 14, 1995.

154 *Dead Poets Society, Field of Dreams, The Postman*: Linda Lee, *People Profiles: Tom Hanks,* Time, Inc., 1999.

154 *Shall We Dance*: Jeff Vice, "Film Review: Shall We Dance," *Deseret News,* September 21, 2004.

154 *Night and the City*: EW Staff, "Entertainment News for August 16, 1991," ew.com, August 16, 1991.

154 *Benny & Joon*: "AFI Catalog of Feature Films," afi.com.

155 "Audiences would have been sitting there": John Hudson, "No, Tom Hanks Did Not Star in 'Groundhog Day,'" theatlantic.com, February 2, 2012.

155 "There's a style of talking": Lee.

155 *Primary Colors*: B. Love, "Tom Hanks: Jack of All," *University Reporter,* October 1996.

156 "Well, I will say without question": Connelly.

156 "It was one of those passes": Robert J. Emery, *The Directors— Take Four,* Allworth Press, 2003.

156 *Jungle Cruise*: John Young, "Disney pairing Tom Hanks and Tim Allen for 'Jungle Cruise'," ew.com, March 2, 2011.

156 *The Inns of New England*: Jeffrey Wells et alia, "Entertainment News for April 17, 1992," ew.com, April 17, 1992.

157 *Lonely Hearts of the Cosmos*: Broeske.

157 *Major Matt Mason*: Adam Chitwood, "Major Matt Mason Moves Forward with Tom Hanks and Robert Zemeckis," collider.com, October 15, 2012.

157 *Stranger in a Strange Land*: Broeske.

158 *Khe Sanh*: Beth Laski, "Zwick enlisted for 'Khe Sanh'; Hanks on team," *The Hollywood Reporter,* March 22, 2001.

158 *A Cold Case*: Stephen Saito, "Nine Great Unrealized Films from Scott, Nolan, Scorsese, and Other Notable Contemporary Filmmakers," moveablefest.com, June 6, 2012.

159 *Ikiru*: Michael Fleming and Nicole LaPorte, "Irish Eyes Smile on Dreamworks' 'Ikiru' Remake," *Variety,* September 9, 2004.

159 *How Starbucks Changed My Life*: Mike Fleming Jr., "'Starbucks' Percolating at Weinstein Co.," deadline.com, November 15, 2012.

160 "Nick Pileggi and I killed ourselves": Rebecca Murray, "Why Martin Scorsese Never Made His Planned Dean Martin Biopic," thoughtco.com, March 18, 2017.

160 "When somebody says": Broeske.

161 "a third-rate if not fourth-rate": Hilary Lewis, "Tribeca: 6 Revelations From Tom Hanks' Wide-Ranging Talk With John Oliver," *The Hollywood Reporter,* April 23, 2016.

161 "I never got a shot": Connelly.

Interlude: Steven Spielberg and the Bond of Brothers

163 "Mr. Smartypants": Chris Hewitt, "Empire Meets Tom Hanks: On *Bridge of Spies*, *Toy Story 4*, and *The 'Burbs*," empireonline .com, December 2, 2015.

163 "Tom is an Everyman": Richard Corliss and Cathy Booth, "Tom Terrific," *Time,* December 21, 1998.

164 "We had never really seen a movie": Daniel D'Addario, "Tom Hanks and Steven Spielberg on *Bridge of Spies,* Diversity in Hollywood and *Star Wars*," time.com, October 6, 2015.

164 "When I was watching dailies": Hillary Atkin, "Friends and Collaborators," *The Hollywood Reporter,* June 12, 2002.

164 "bestest friends": Kevin Sessums, "Tom Terrific," *Vanity Fair,* June 1994.

164 "So often": Ibid.

165 "The nice thing": Ibid.

165 "We were always reading biographies": D'Addario.

165 "car pools": Corliss and Booth.

165 "Captain Miller was a stock one-dimensional war hero": Kurt Andersen, "The Tom Hanks Phenomenon," *The New Yorker,* December 7–14, 1998.

166 "We decided our friendship came first": Atkin.

166 "We have a shorthand": Ibid.

166 "Hey, Boss": Jeff Giles, "Catch Them If You Can," *Newsweek,* December 23, 2002.

166 "It makes me self-conscious": Ibid.

167 "He only sees the honesty": Atkin.

167 "Steven will want them to come in with a great idea": Hewitt.

167 "sweat and anxiety": Ibid.

167 "You don't want to" (transcribed as "You don't wanna"): Ibid.

167 "Guys, this is what I know about the Boss": Ibid.

168 "Tom Hanks is a great person": Nathan Rabin, "Random Roles: Tom Sizemore on *Point Break, True Romance,* and Getting Yelled at By Pete Rose," avclub.com, March 6, 2013.

168 Berlin balcony: "The New Establishment," *Vanity Fair,* October 2004.

168 "They talk on a different level": Author interview with Scott Shepherd.

The Eighth Commandment: Remember that Shakespeare will tell you the truth.

170 "learning to play the violin on a Stradivarius": Robert Goldberg, "Hollywood's Hottest Comic Actor Is Branching Out," *Connoisseur,* September 1986.

170 "You know, 'Speak the speech, I pray you'": Tony Brown, "Tom Hanks Returns to Cleveland to Say Big 'Thanks' to Great Lakes Theater Festival," *The Cleveland Plain Dealer,* October 10, 2009.

171 "Look, I played a guy": Ibid.

171 "Hip": Adam Moss, "How to Look Like a Page Out of *Esquire,*" *Esquire,* March 1987.

171 Origins of Iago: Harold Bloom, *Shakespeare: The Invention of the Human,* Riverhead Books, 1998.

172 "lost out on a promotion": Maureen Dowd, "Hollywood's Most Decent Fella on Weinstein, Trump, and History," *The New York Times,* October 11, 2017.

173 "When I first heard that": Brendan Lemon, "Tom Hanks," *Interview,* December 1993.

173 The motivations of Iago: Nicholas Hytner, "With Shakespeare, the Play Is Just a Starting Point," *The Guardian* (U.K.), April 12, 2013. (I also particularly benefited here from conversation with Bill Tipper.)

173 Wilson as Celia: Libby Denkmann, "Tom Hanks will make his LA stage debut as Shakespeare's Falstaff at the West LA VA," www .scpr.org, February 12, 2018.

174 "The whole message is": Josh Eells, "A League of His Own," *Rolling Stone* 1169, November 8, 2012.

174 "Look, I'm asked to do this": Ibid.

174 "An error on my 2008 tax return": Author interview and correspondence with John Frankenheim.

The Ninth Commandment: Value your friends but accept your loneliness.

179 "All the great stories": James Poniewozik, "Saving Tom Hanks," Time, May 15, 2000.

179 "The cinema has the power": Ingrid Sischy, "Tom Hanks," *Interview,* March 1994.

179 "this desire to belong": "Tom Hanks on *A Hologram for the King*, the Challenges of Age and the Rise of Donald Trump," *Radio Times,* May 20, 2016.

179 "I have no best friend": Kurt Andersen, "The Tom Hanks Phenomenon," *The New Yorker,* December 7–14, 1998.

180 "The requirements": Kevin Sessums, "Tom Terrific," *Vanity Fair,* June 1994.

180 "I can pretend": Bill Zehme, "Tom Hanks Acts Like a Man," *Esquire,* September 2001.

181 "The next year": Sara Davidson, "Magnificent Obsession," *Reader's Digest,* August 2005.

181 "We better do this now": Author interview with Lucy
     Bredeson-Smith.

181 "We tooled all over town": Ibid.

182 "Hey, how you doing?": Andrea Simakis, "Tom Hanks gloried
     in his Great Lakes Theater days on a whirlwind Cleveland visit,"
     The Cleveland Plain Dealer, June 28, 2016.

182 "He would never say this": Author interview with Mary Beidler
     Gearen.

183 "People were reacquainting themselves": Ibid.

183 "Tom is just really in touch": Kevin Sessums, "Tom Terrific,"
     Vanity Fair, June 1994.

The Tenth Commandment: Stand up for what you believe.

185 "politicized me": "Playing the Part," *Newsweek,* February 14,
     1994.

185 "we're all kind of questioning ourselves": Deborah J. Kunk, "Tom
     Hanks' Star Quality: He's Impossible Not to Like," *Los Angeles
     Herald-Examiner,* June 29, 1987.

185 "I think we have no responsibility whatsoever": David Sheff,
     "Tom Hanks: The *Playboy* Interview," *Playboy,* March 1989.

185 "Having thought about AIDS": Kristine McKenna, "He's Serious
     About This One," *Los Angeles Times,* December 19, 1993.

186 "the promised land": Stephen Ambrose, "Man with a Mission,"
     Reader's Digest, September 2001.

186 "We examine our failures": Ibid.

187 "My image is a really good one": Kurt Andersen, "The Tom
     Hanks Phenomenon," *The New Yorker,* December 7–14, 1998.

187 "It's an asinine, ridiculous idea": David Eimer, "Nice? Me?" *The
     Sunday Times* (UK), January 23, 2000.

188 "I wouldn't want": Maureen Dowd, "Tom Hanks: Confirm or
     Deny," *The New York Times,* October 11, 2017.

188 "You can be the biggest policy geek": Marshall Sella,
     "Introducing the Next Tom Hanks," *GQ*, December 2007.

188 "un-American": "Tom Hanks Apologizes for Calling Mormon
     Support of Prop 8 'Un-American'," *People*, January 23, 2009.

188 "more division": Ibid.

189 "Well, you know what?": *The Axe Files with David Axelrod*,
     episode 197, December 2, 2017.

189 "doublespeak": Maureen Dowd, "Hollywood's Most Decent
     Fella on Weinstein, Trump, and History," *The New York Times*,
     October 11, 2017.

189 "Bush-Clinton continuum": Ibid.

190 "I hope this machine": Tamara Keith, "Tom Hanks Sends the
     White House Press Corps a Caffeine Infusion (Again)," npr.org,
     March 4, 2017.

190 "I can't promise favorable coverage": Ibid.

190 "Let me see what I can do for the poor slobs": Ibid.

191 "Keep up the good fight": Ibid.

191 "Is there some brand of Western intellect": Sella.

191 "Is the United States of America still on the cusp": Ibid.

191 "You'd be looking for folks": Peter Travers, "Tom Hanks,"
     Rolling Stone 1039, November 15, 2007.
     Sara Davidson, "Magnificent Obsession," *Reader's Digest*, August
     2005.

SECTION THREE: THE FILMS OF TOM HANKS

For those of you keeping score at home: This filmography
encompasses all of Tom Hanks' feature-film work as an actor
(including cameos), plus a few one-shot projects that happened to
be released on television. It doesn't cover a multitude of production
credits or his work on various TV miniseries, ongoing episodic TV
programs (for example, his appearance as a karate black belt on
Happy Days or a pothead college student on *Taxi*), web series such

as *Tom Hanks' Electric City*, or the various *Toy Story* specials and shorts. The names of Hanks' characters are rendered in this section as they appeared in the movie's credits; the dialogue quoted at the beginning of each entry was all spoken by Hanks.

He Knows You're Alone

196 $800 and SAG membership: Lee Pfeiffer and Michael Lewis, *The Films of Tom Hanks,* Citadel Press, 1996.

197 "we liked him too much": commentary track on *He Knows You're Alone* DVD, Warner Home Video, 2004.

Bachelor Party

200 "The movie is just a sloppy rock 'n' roll comedy": David Sheff, "Tom Hanks: The *Playboy* Interview," *Playboy,* March 1989.

201 "We had so many funny scenes": Mandi Bierly, "Adrian Zmed: PopWatch 'Teen Idol' Q&A," ew.com, December 30, 2008.

202 "You have to explore your past": "Tom Hanks Interviews" on *Bachelor Party* DVD, 20th Century Fox, 2001.

The Man with One Red Shoe

203 "Not a very good movie": David Sheff, "Tom Hanks: The *Playboy* Interview," *Playboy,* March 1989.

204 "cut so low that I felt naked": author correspondence with Lori Singer.

204 "Tom nailed the stunt": Ibid.

204 "I spent the whole night raving": Ibid.

Volunteers

205 "The lesson is never sacrifice the integrity of your piece": Ken Levine, "The scene That Ruined *Volunteers*," kenlevine.blogspot .com, July 8, 2007.

206 "He loved it": Author interview with Ken Levine.

207 "Here's what he brought to it": Ibid.

The Money Pit

208 "We had miniature adventures": Mary Murphy, "Tom Hanks: One Hunk Who Refuses to Go Hollywood," *Cosmopolitan,* March 1987.

209 "Some parts of that": David Sheff, "Tom Hanks: The *Playboy* Interview," *Playboy,* March 1989.

Nothing in Common

209 "I learned an awful lot": Joe Logan, "Tom Hanks, working stiff," *Long Beach Press-Telegraph,* March 24, 1990.

Every Time We Say Goodbye

211 "the most visually beautiful": David Sheff, "Tom Hanks: The *Playboy* Interview," *Playboy,* March 1989.

212 "I saw Tom Hanks in *Splash*": Author correspondence with Moshe Mizrahi.

212 "a film from the Tom Hanks point of view": Author interview with Benedict Taylor.

212 "I could see the level of commitment": Ibid.

Dragnet

214 convent: Tim Allis, "Chatter," *People,* July 20, 1987.

214 "made a lot of money": David Sheff, "Tom Hanks: The *Playboy* Interview," *Playboy,* March 1989.

215 "repulsed and fascinated": Hadley Freeman, "Tom Hanks on His Diabetes, Pirates and Rapping with Dan Aykroyd," *The Guardian* (UK), October 10, 2013.

Big

215 "looked at each other": Larry Getlen, "How Tom Hanks Got 'Big' 25 Years Ago," *New York Post,* December 7, 2013.

217 "I was good": Joe Logan, "Tom Hanks, Working Stiff," *Long Beach Press-Telegraph,* March 24, 1990.

Punchline

218 "The guy in *Punchline*": David Sheff, "Tom Hanks: The *Playboy* Interview," *Playboy*, March 1989.

The 'Burbs

220 "interesting little suburban nightmare": Chris Hewitt, "Empire Meets Tom Hanks: On *Bridge of Spies*, *Toy Story 4*, and *The 'Burbs*," empireonline.com, December 2, 2015.

220 "You get enough sleep": Ibid.

221 "Could we have *a conversation?*": Kevin Sessums, "Tom Terrific," *Vanity Fair*, June 1994.

221 "He said the word": Ibid.

Turner & Hooch

223 "Let's just say": Michael A. Lipton, "How Now, Mr. Fonzarelli?" *People*, April 12, 1993.

Joe Versus the Volcano

225 "He'd leveled down": Matt Zoller Seitz and Scout Tafoya, "The Unloved, Part Fourteen: 'Joe Vs. the Volcano'," rogerebert.com, February 3, 2015.

225 "Shanley can tear you a new asshole": Carol Troy, "It's a Cool Gig," *American Film*, April 1990.

225 "That's the most glamorous thing": Cal Fussman, "Confessions of an Average Man," *Esquire*, June 2006.

225 "I didn't know it was Meg": Ibid.

226 "He's just a nut for water": Anthony D'Alessandro, "Working with Hanks," *Daily Variety*, June 12, 2002.

Radio Flyer

228 metaphor for suicide: Stephen Greenfield, "What's the Message?"
     posted by David Mickey Evans as "What Happened to Bobby?..."
     on davidmickeyevansblog.blogspot.com, April 6, 2011.

228 production history: Gregg Kilday, "Making 'Radio Flyer,'"
     Entertainment Weekly, February 28, 1992.

A League of Their Own

229 "She literally got fucked": Penny Marshall, *My Mother Was Nuts,*
     Houghton Mifflin Harcourt, 2012.

230 "Tom had done a handful": Ibid.

231 "I specifically wanted": Amy Wallace, "Average Joe Versus the
     Icons," *Los Angeles Times,* November 7, 1999.

231 "The script described": Kurt Andersen, "The Tom Hanks
     Phenomenon," *The New Yorker,* December 7–14, 1998.

231 "So I tried him in glasses": Marshall.

231 "I didn't have my skinny little wrists": Joe Rhodes, "Back from
     the Bonfire," *Los Angeles Times,* July 5, 1992.

231 "I would say, kill him in 1962": Ibid.

Sleepless in Seattle

234 "I thought it was the bravest thing": Erin Carlson, *I'll Have What
     She's Having,* Hachette Book Group, 2017.

Philadelphia

235 "So, Tom, you have played homosexual before in movies?":
     Jennet Conant, "Tom Hanks Wipes That Grin off His Face,"
     Esquire, December 1993.

235 "Well, Antonio": Ibid.

236 "The greatest acting lessons": *Inside the Actors Studio,* episode
     72, Bravo, December 12, 1999.

Forrest Gump

237 "We didn't know if people would care": Lee Pfeiffer and Michael Lewis, *The Films of Tom Hanks,* Citadel Press, 1996.

238 "It was like creating an alien": Mark Morrison, "Tom Hanks: The US Interview," *US,* August 1994.

239 "You have to stay stock-still": Dolores Barclay, "Tom Hanks: From Forrest to Apollo 13, an Everyman for All Seasons," *Entertainment Today,* June 29, 1995.

Apollo 13

240 "What has Jim Lovell": Joe Leydon, "Aboard the Star Ship," *Los Angeles Times,* June 27, 1995.

240 "Tom was at least 50 percent": Jerry Roberts, "Actor's next film will be a really far-out trip," *Variety,* March 9, 1995.

241 "I don't want to boss you around": Devan Coggan, "Tom Hanks Recounts What He Learned from Kevin Bacon During *Apollo 13*," ew.com, April 22, 2016.

Toy Story

242 "We thought we were making a goofy cartoon!": *Inside the Actors Studio,* episode 185, Bravo, May 14, 2006.

That Thing You Do!

243 "It's a show business story": Scott and Barbara Siegel, "Tom Hanks Does That Directing Thing in *That Thing You Do!*", *Drama-Logue,* October 3–9, 1996.

245 "We don't have a movie": Ibid.

Saving Private Ryan

245 "What is the great national consciousness?": Kurt Andersen, "The Tom Hanks Phenomenon," *The New Yorker,* December 7–14, 1998.

247 "Actors—who are like dry sponges," Steven Spielberg and David James, *Saving Private Ryan,* Newmarket Press, 1998.

You've Got Mail

249 "to do it in the next five minutes": Edward Guthmann, "Ephron Puts Her Stamp on 'Mail'," *San Francisco Chronicle,* December 13, 198.

249 "The thing I liked": Erin Carlson, *I'll Have What She's Having,* Hachette Book Group, 2017.

251 "In the Park": Tom Hanks and Meg Ryan, "We've Got Their Mail," *Time,* December 21, 1998.

251 "I knew just what he was doing": Richard Corliss and Cathy Booth, "Tom Terrific," *Time,* December 21, 1998.

Toy Story 2

252 "It kinda blew me outta my hut": Chris Connelly, "Hollywood Survivor," *Talk,* November 2000.

252 "Nothing wrong with that": Ibid.

253 "The astronaut's not that smart": Peter Travers, "Tom Hanks," *Rolling Stone* 1039, November 15, 2007.

The Green Mile

254 "There's a great dichotomy": Lisa Henricksson, "Men of the Year: Tom Hanks," *GQ,* December 1999.

Cast Away

256 "It's almost like making a silent movie": James Poniewozik, "Saving Tom Hanks," *Time,* May 15, 2000.

257 "a big chunk": Martyn Palmer, "A Year of Living Dangerously," *The Times* (London), January 11, 2001.

Road to Perdition

258 "We respected each other's territory": Jess Cagle, "Two for the Road," *Time,* July 8, 2002.

258 "If he wants to call me 'kid'": Ibid.

258 "I called him": Author interview with Peter Scolari.

Catch Me If You Can

261 "Not a lot of costume changes": "Tom Hanks as Carl Hanratty," *Catch Me If You Can* DVD, Dreamworks Video, 2003.

The Ladykillers

262 "I had this vision": Shawn Levy, "The British Are Going to Crucify Us," *The Guardian* (UK), May 10, 2004.

262 "We called it": Ibid.

262 "There's no formula": Ibid.

262 "Mr. Hanks": Joe McGovern, "Tom Hanks: Read His Full Speech from MoMA Tribute," ew.com, November 16, 2016.

The Terminal

263 "I wanted to do another movie": "The Total Film Interview," *Total Film,* September 2004, as archived at gamesradar.com

The Polar Express

266 "I was rail thin": Anwar Brett, "Tom Hanks: The Polar Express," bbc.com, December 3, 2004.

Elvis Has Left the Building

267 "That type of visibility": Jerry Roberts, "A Superstar Talks Business," *Variety,* March 9, 1995.

267 "He said that's the only time": commentary track on *Elvis Has Left the Building* DVD, Lions Gate, 2005.

The Da Vinci Code

268 "I loved the media reaction": Marshall Sella, "Introducing the Next Tom Hanks," *GQ*, December 2007.

Charlie Wilson's War

271 "You don't know the consequences": "'Charlie Wilson's War' Was Unlikely, But True," *Morning Edition*, NPR, December 20, 2007.

The Great Buck Howard

272 "I've taken a lot of meetings": Author interview with Sean McGinly.

Toy Story 3

275 "We found out": Crystal Bell, "21 Surprising Things You Never Knew About 'Toy Story'," mtv.com, October 16, 2015.

Larry Crowne

275 "You have to be infected": Paul Devine, "Larry Crowne—Tom Hanks Interview," thepeoplesmovies.com, November 25, 2011.

276 "Larry Crowne can maybe look back": Ibid.

277 "we constantly quote *Larry Crowne*": Truman Hanks, "I am the youngest child of Tom Hanks. Would anyone be interested in an AMA?", AMA ("Ask me anything") on reddit.com, 2012.

277 Terry Gross: "Tom Hanks Says That Self-Doubt Is 'A High-Wire Act That We All Walk,'" (transcript of *Fresh Air* interview), April 26, 2016, npr.org.

277 "Hey, kiddo, come on in": "Fun on Set," *Larry Crowne* DVD, Universal Pictures Home Entertainment, 2011.

277 "That is the funniest thing": Ibid.

Extremely Loud & Incredibly Close

278 "kitsch": Nick Pinkerton, "Extremely Loud and Incredibly Close to Schmaltz," *Dallas Observer*, January 19, 2012.

278 "colossally misguided": Rene Rodriguez, "Extremely Loud and Incredibly Close," *The Miami Herald,* January 18, 2012.

278 "extremely loud and incredibly manipulative": David Edelstein, "'Extremely Loud' and Incredibly Manipulative," *Fresh Air,* NPR, January 6, 2012.

279 "September 9": Ken Lombardi, "Tom Hanks talks role as 9/11 victim in 'Extremely Loud and Incredibly Close,'" cbsnews.com, December 22, 2011.

Cloud Atlas

280 "And then once he said": Tasha Robinson, "The Wachowskis explain how *Cloud Atlas* unplugs people from the Matrix," avclub.com, October 25, 2012.

281 "How often do you get": Julie Hinds, "Interview with Tom Hanks about *Cloud Atlas*," phoenixfilmfestival.com, October 25, 2012.

Captain Phillips

282 "Welcome to the movie": "Full Ahead," *Captain Phillips* DVD (Sony, 2014).

282 "I thought we were going to keep this tense": Ibid.

282 "Yeah, I guess so": Ibid.

283 "I understood what the scene was about": Rodrigo Perez, "Interview: Tom Hanks & Paul Greengrass Talk 'Captain Phillips' and the Raw Acting Ability of Barkhad Abdi," indiewire.com, January 9, 2014.

283 "Hey, Doc": Mike Hixenbaugh, "Change puts Navy woman Face-to-Face with Tom Hanks," *The Virginian-Pilot,* October 11, 2013.

284 "Tom's blood pressure": Geoff Edgers, "The Evolution of Tom Hanks," *The Washington Post,* December 1, 2014.

Saving Mr. Banks

285 "I don't look too much like him": Christina Radish, "Emma Thompson and Tom Hanks Talk Saving Mr. Banks, Bringing the Essence of Their Characters to the Screen, and How P. L. Travers Would Have Reacted," collider.com, December 9, 2013.

285 "You can't just go in": Steve "Frosty" Weintraub, "Tom Hanks Talks Saving Mr. Banks, His Reluctance to Play Walt Disney, Working with Paul Greengrass on Captain Phillips, Cloud Atlas, and More," collider.com, November 20, 2013.

286 "Honey, you're gonna make": Ibid.

Bridge of Spies

286 "When you play somebody real": Meredith Alloway, "Steven Spielberg and Tom Hanks Talk 'Bridge of Spies,' James Donovan, and More," collider.com, October 15, 2015.

288 "The car had to park": Author interview with Scott Shepherd.

A Hologram for the King

291 "It was printed all over the pages": Charles McGrath, "'A Hologram for the King' Finds Tom Hanks in the Desert, Desperate to Sell Phantoms," *The New York Times,* April 15, 2016.

291 "It's not going to convince me": Brendan Lemon, "Tom Hanks," *Interview,* December 1993.

292 "Not everybody looks like": "Tom Hanks on *A Hologram for the King*, the Challenges of Age and the Rise of Donald Trump," *Radio Times,* May 20, 2016.

Sully

294 "The pleasure of working": Rebecca Keegan, "Eastwood and Hanks talk 'Sully,' their film about the 'humble, smiling hero' who landed on the Hudson River," *Los Angeles Times, September* 1, 2016.

294 "I spent a lot of time": Ibid.

Inferno

295 "I'm always running in these movies": Lou Gaul, "Look Out for 'Inferno' on Home Video," *The Times* (Beaver, PA), January 22, 2017.

The David S. Pumpkins Halloween Special

297 "Fellas, I don't breakdance": Jesse David Fox, "An Oral History of 'David Pumpkins,'" vulture.com, November 23, 2017.

297 "I don't know why": Ibid.

299 "I don't quite know": Ibid.

299 "That is how much he loved it": Ibid.

299 "It's this weird alchemy": Ibid.

300 "The first movie": Ibid.

300 "Just making the world go": Ibid.

The Post

301 "I was going to find some other way": "Transcript: Steven Spielberg, Meryl Streep, Tom Hanks talk new movie at *The Washington Post*," washingtonpost.com, December 14, 2017.

301 "I was drawn toward the guys who didn't look like movie stars": Duane Byrge, "Actor's Dialogue," *The Hollywood Reporter*, March 8, 1995.

301 "he confessed to recording those monologues": Tom Hanks, "I Owe It All to Community College," *The New York Times*, January 14, 2015.